Early Childhood Development in Humanitarian Crises

This book provides an analysis of Early Childhood Development (ECD) in South Sudanese refugee camps in Uganda, making the case for the design and implementation of programmes for ECD in emergency situations.

Illustrating the current place of ECD in the humanitarian landscape and the environment in which South Sudanese refugees in Uganda currently live, this book combines child and human development perspectives to underpin the importance of ECD in emergencies. Developing an ECD tool specific to the cultural context and emergency situation, the author examines the outcomes of an ECD programme focused on refugee children and provides evidence for increased investment into ECD in emergencies.

Contributing to the evidence base for Early Childhood Development, this book will be of interest to students, scholars and practitioners who conduct research on ECD, education or humanitarianism in developing countries.

Sweta Shah received her PhD from The Institute of Education, University College London, UK, in 2016. She is currently Global Lead, Early Childhood Development at the Aga Khan Foundation (AKF), Washington, DC, USA.

I0894929

Routledge Research on African Education
Series Editor: Moses Okech

Early Childhood Development in Humanitarian Crises
South Sudanese Refugees in Uganda
Sweta Shah

Early Childhood Development in Humanitarian Crises

South Sudanese Refugees in Uganda

Sweta Shah

Routledge
Taylor & Francis Group
LONDON AND NEW YORK

First published 2020 by Routledge

2 Park Square, Milton Park, Abingdon, Oxon, OX14 4RN
605 Third Avenue, New York, NY 10017

Routledge is an imprint of the Taylor & Francis Group, an informa business

First issued in paperback 2020

British Library Cataloguing-in-Publication Data
A catalogue record for this book is available from the British Library

Library of Congress Cataloging-in-Publication Data
A catalog record has been requested for this book

ISBN: 978-0-367-22857-6 (hbk)
ISBN: 978-0-367-77759-3 (pbk)

Typeset in Bembo
by codeMantra

To Kalpana and Priya who made me a mother and teach me every day the critical importance of Early Childhood Development. You ignite my passion for this work and make it personal.

To Michael, my best friend, rock and toughest critique. I wouldn't be able to do what I do and be who I am without your constant support and partnership.

Contents

Illustrations

Figures

Tables

Foreword

A call for action to support young children and families in crises

Dr. Kofi Marfo and Dr. Joan Lombardi

Humanitarian crises bring new threats every day to children around the world. The faces of young children and families torn apart by war and continuous conflict appear mundanely in front-page stories across all forms of media, with images of destruction all around. On the African continent, the refugee crisis has become increasingly more intractable as solutions to political instability have become even more elusive. The detrimental impacts of displacement are profound, considering especially that most of these children already face risks to their development from other endemic conditions of adversity.

Never before have we had such clear evidence of the importance of the early years and the impact of toxic stress on the developing brain. The research continues to grow, documenting the fact that what happens in the early years has a profound impact on long-term health, behaviour and learning. We know that the stress of conflict adversely affects parents' capacity to respond to their children's needs and that stress adds to the damaging effects of conflict on the developing child.

Landmark reports by experts across multiple disciplines, as well as international organisations, including the World Health Organization and others, reinforce the importance of nurturing care. Young children need to be assured of good health, adequate nutrition, safety and security, early learning experiences and responsive caregiving. These essential ingredients to child development cannot grow in communities consumed by conflict. This work by Dr Sweta Shah contributes to the growing evidence that we can, and we must, address the needs of young children in times of crises; we must find ways to support families, and we must seek solutions that prevent the violence from occurring in the first place.

In this book, Dr Shah describes how she adopted and modified for her own field study of Plan International's community-based ECD model—known as Community-Led Action for Children (CLAC)—based on the attractiveness of its features and its history of use in several other Eastern and Southern African countries. She then shares with her readers her remarkable experiential journey into implementing and assessing the adapted model in ECD settings serving the needs of South Sudanese refugees in Uganda. The reporting is vividly frank; there is no sugar-coating of what was difficult to execute or what did not work as expected! Thus, the reader interested in understanding the challenges of trying out wonderful ideas in uncertain terrain gets a sense of what is realistic. Her lessons and recommendations—directed at development practitioners, policy makers, ECD specialists and donor agency professionals alike—are offered not just on the basis of data from the case studies she reports in the book but they are also drawn, in part, from her many years of professional experience as a humanitarian practitioner.

We end our prefatory remarks with the fervent hope that our quest for the best intervention models to produce the best outcomes for children will be pursued simultaneously with a quest for a "global order" that prioritises a world in which whole populations are never exposed to marginalisation and avoidable adversity.

Acknowledgements

There are many people who contributed to my learning on this subject and the development of this book.

I would first like to thank my husband Michael Shipler who encouraged me to conduct the research and write this book. He helped me think through the content, structure, reviewed multiple drafts and provided critical feedback.

Other family members were also critical as I wrote this book. My parents, Kishor and Kumkum Shah, always encouraged and supported me. My father and mother-in-law, David and Debby Shipler, read my thesis and provided some suggestions for improving the structure of this book. My daughters, Kalpana and Priya, are the inspiration for my work in this area and have helped me gain insight into the Early Childhood Development field, which allowed me to deeply and critically think about issues presented in this book.

I would also like to thank Plan International, Plan Uganda and Plan South Sudan for allowing me to study this crisis and their programmes. At Plan International Dr Unni Krishnan and Roger Yates who provided me space, time and financial support to travel to Uganda and South Sudan and do this work while I was a full-time employee. At Plan Uganda, I would like to thank Hadijah Nandyose, Rosemary Alweny, Judith Aceng, Denis Oketa and Denis Okulluogang. They helped me think through sampling, how to access the refugee communities, provided logistical support and helped me recruit and train refugees to be research assistants. They were my partners in this research. I would also like to thank Plan South Sudan and especially Alfred Taban for support to visit South Sudanese communities in Lakes district where I began to understand the definition of child development from the South Sudanese cultural perspective and for giving me insight into the dynamics of the crisis.

My PhD supervisor, Dr Moses Oketch, supported me throughout the whole research process, gave me critical feedback and helped me think through the research methodology and sampling. He was the one who first encouraged me to convert my PhD thesis into a book.

Ms Mercedes Maddox, the former Director of Kids' Corner Day Care Center in Washington, DC, helped me understand different child development assessment tools and in particular gave me a better understanding of the

ASQ-3, which I used in this research. I also learned a lot about child development from her.

Dr Kofi Marfo and Dr Joan Lombardi reviewed the manuscript, provided feedback and wrote a foreword for this book. They have always been and continue to be amazing mentors.

Last and most importantly, I would like to recognise and thank the many South Sudanese and Ugandans who opened up their lives to me. They allowed me to learn about their experiences and help me bring their voices and perspectives into this book. Without them, I would not have been able to highlight the important issues of Early Childhood Development in humanitarian contexts.

Introduction

It was a bright morning in Ayillo 2 refugee camp in northern Uganda outside of the town of Adjumani. Over a hundred South Sudanese refugee children between three and five years were standing outside in a circle starting their daily routines. The day started with the morning circle where children came for a half day of play-based learning activities. Halima and two other South Sudanese refugee caregivers led the children in songs and games in Dinka, their mother tongue, and English. While supporting children's language development, the songs and games taught the children about preventive health, hygiene and topics that promoted literacy and numeracy. Next came the game "news news." A little boy went to the centre of the circle to announce the day's news. Everyone clapped to applaud his efforts.

The children then went to one of the three tents—for three-, four- and five-year olds. These tents were used in the morning for Early Childhood Development (ECD) activities and in the afternoon for adolescents and youth. In each tent children were working in small groups led by a caregiver. Some were using chalk and a slate to practice writing. Others were playing a letter-sound game, while a few were sorting leaves, sticks and rocks into different piles.

Some of these children's parents participated in a weekly peer to peer parent support group where they learned about child development, the nutritional value of local foods, good hygiene practices and how to support their children's learning through every day play activities. Some parents stayed for the whole half day to volunteer their time because they enjoyed learning about ways to support their children's development.

This scene, which simultaneously supports children and families, stands in stark contrast to most humanitarian situations where there are no safe spaces such as these for children to learn through play. As paediatrician and researcher Dr Dimitri Christakis said during his TedTalk, "If we change the beginning of the story, we change the whole story" (Christakis, 2011). However, millions of children's stories are not starting off well enough to help them survive and thrive. In many refugee situations across the globe, young children are idle, not being engaged, played with or talked to. This is not uncommon. Young children from birth to five years are regularly left out of humanitarian services, and in particular early learning and stimulation activities. Humanitarian donors often prioritise the delivery of food, water, shelter and treatment of injury or illnesses. These services are critical and may help children survive in the immediate aftermath of an emergency, but not necessarily to thrive in the future.

Why is this a problem?

A generation not reaching its developmental potential

The number of humanitarian crises are increasing, they are lasting longer and more children are being displaced (UNOCHA, 2017). *The Lancet*, one of the oldest and most prestigious peer-reviewed medical journals, published a new series focused on ECD in 2016. In it, authors estimated that 250 million children (43%) younger than five years in low- and middle-income countries around the world are at risk of not reaching their developmental potential (Chan, Lake and Hansen, 2016). In sub-Saharan Africa, the statistics are bleaker—with an estimated 66% of children in 2010 at risk of not reaching their developmental potential (Black et al., 2016). Emergencies add to children's existing adversities, making it even more difficult to flourish. Prior to the war in 2011, Syria's adult literacy rate was high (97% for men and 95% for women) and in 2016, the adult literacy rate has decreased (92% for males, 81% for women) (UNESCO, 2016). These numbers do not include the millions of children who have no access to education (ibid.). A cost-benefit analysis of the economic loss of children dropping out of education in Syria, as of 2012, is estimated to be 17.6% of Syria's pre-crisis GDP (Mizunoya, 2015). This estimate does not include the economic loss of refugee children's future economic activities, which if calculated would increase the overall percentage (ibid.).

Doing nothing to solve humanitarian crises will diminish people's individual potential and a country's economic potential. A whole generation of children not developing to their full potential will be the future workforce of a country and some could be future leaders. They will not only influence and shepherd the generation after it, but they will also be part of the broader world. In the increasingly inter-connected world, stable countries with an educated and skilled population can make the difference between war and peace and economic prosperity and poverty. War and conflict are not often confined to national borders. They can have wide ranging effects at regional and global levels. It is in the interest of the world to ensure all children develop well and can be the leaders of tomorrow that champion peace and lead positive economic development.

Missing out on the unique period of brain development

If you looked inside the brain of an average small child, you would see more than 1,000,000 neurons firing away as the child explores, talks and plays (Center on the Developing Child, 2009). This is because early childhood is the most critical time for developing neural connections in the brain and establishing the foundation for one's life. Approximately 90% of the brain's growth in size occurs within the first five years of life and about 80% of the brain's growth occurs within the first two years of life (Brown and Jernigan, 2012). While the brain continues to grow and mature through early to middle adulthood, the growth process slows down (Brown and Jernigan, 2012; Center on the Developing Child, 2009). During adulthood, the brain prunes unused neural connections and strengthens ones that continue to be used (Center on the Developing Child, 2009). Research indicates that children who are not talked to or interacted with have smaller brains and fewer neural connections (ibid.). These fewer neural connections create the foundation for future growth. A bridge with a weak foundation will not be able to hold vehicles and will collapse. Just like a bridge, if the base structure of a brain is weak, it will not be able to hold as much future learning.

The development of the brain is the most critical part of a human's overall survival and development. Humanitarians talk about survival, but not of the survival and development of brain. The brain survives and grows with both cognitive stimulation and good nutrition. However, in a majority of cases, humanitarian donors fund food, but not cognitive stimulation. Research shows that food alone is not enough for a brain—it craves stimulation and interaction through play-based activities to build neural connections (Conticini and Quere, 2011; Gardner et al., 1999; Grantham-McGregor et al., 1991; Hurley et al., 2016). Studies in Jamaica, Pakistan, Ethiopia and others confirmed more additive benefits of the early stimulation and nutrition supplementation together over nutrition support alone (Conticini and Quere, 2011; Gowani et al., 2014; Grantham-McGregor et al., 1991; Hurley et al., 2016; Yousafzai et al., 2014).

Higher risk of toxic stress and permanent damage

Everyone experiences stress and it is not always bad. However, when it is prolonged and severe and there are few protective factors such as a relationship with a caregiver, it can become toxic (Bryce et al., 2008; Shonkoff and Bales, 2011; Victora et al., 2008). Children in emergencies are at a higher risk of experiencing toxic stress as they may be facing the loss of parents, friends, may be injured, may have lost their homes and daily routines. The destabilising effect of emergencies can greatly decrease a child's ability to fight against the accumulating effects of stress. Research indicates that a significant increase in toxic stress, even when temporary, can negatively influence brain development that can lead to permanent damage for multiple generations (Bryce et al., 2008; Shonkoff and Bales, 2011; Victora et al., 2008).

Financing not giving the best bang for its buck

Evidence from a myriad of studies has indicated that children not reaching their developmental potential can lead to an average reduction of 19.8% in adult annual income (Black et al., 2016). Longitudinal studies from Jamaica,

Turkey, United States and other countries have revealed ECD to have both immediate and longer term positive benefits to developmental outcomes. Some of these studies indicate that the impact has continued into adulthood (Black et al., 2016; Britto et al., 2016). Cost-benefit and cost-effectiveness studies have shown that investments in early childhood to not only have the greatest impact on brain development but also provide the greatest return on investment (Carneiro and Heckman, 2003; Heckman, 2006). Research conducted by Nobel Prize-winning Economist James Heckman and others has shown up to $13 of benefits and savings for every $1 invested (Garcia et al., 2017). This means that governments that invest early and reap the benefits would spend less on remedial classes, class repetition and tutoring when children are older. Longitudinal studies that have followed children over 20–40 years have found that those who participated in an early childhood intervention were more likely to have a job, be earning higher wages and be in better health. They were also less likely to commit crimes and be imprisoned (Black et al., 2016; Britto et al., 2016). Evidence also indicates that the most vulnerable and disadvantaged children benefit more from such programmes as they would likely be missing out on learning and support from families at home (Heckman, 2006). Despite evidence that investing early has a greater bang for the buck, ECD is still not prioritised in non-emergencies and even less so in emergencies.

But there's hope: children are resilient

Children are resilient and science tells us that a child's experience can shift the scale from negative outcomes to positive ones (Center on the Developing Child, 2015). ECD in emergency programmes can support children's resilience and tip that balance when they include nurturing care from a supportive, loving adult (ibid.). Nurturing care includes health, nutrition, safety and security, which are prioritised in humanitarian settings, and responsive caregiving and early learning, which are not prioritised (*The Lancet*, 2016).

Momentum, but challenges remain

Donors supporting the South Sudan refugee crisis and other humanitarian situations are starting to understand the importance of investing in ECD for young children. The Syria Regional Response Plan mentions early learning support, one of the few emergency plans to explicitly do so. The 2016 Lancet ECD series includes new evidence and data. Language around ECD is now a part of the Sustainable Development Goals. Education Cannot Wait, a new global funding mechanism for Education in emergencies, recognises the importance of early learning. Momentum has started to build for aspects of ECD in emergencies.

While these are all positive trends, challenges in the humanitarian sector remain. There is still *insufficient funding for ECD in emergencies* owing to the funding structure. Humanitarian donors and policy makers focus their investments heavily on sectors such as food and water distribution, shelter and the treatment of illnesses. When faced with the choice of what to fund, humanitarian donors are still overwhelmingly de-prioritising the responsive caregiving and early learning aspects of ECD and often all aspects of what young children need to not only survive but also thrive (Their World, 2016). These same donors also fund sectors separately causing gaps in critical services for young children. For example, humanitarian donors might fund immunisations and food for young children, but not care and learning opportunities. What has yet to follow global discussions and promises are the financing and holistic programming to support young children. Even if funding continues to flow through sectors, there needs to be a strategy that includes all aspects of children's developments so that critical gaps from one or two sectors do not remain. Education and learning in emergencies, which is often the sector through which ECD programming is supported, is the worst funded sector in humanitarian response along with child protection. In 2016, 1.4% of all humanitarian funds went to education (which often includes early learning and parenting support) (UNOCHA, 2016). There is currently no data available on what percentage of the 1.4% of education funding or other sectors' funding goes towards the various aspects of ECD.

ECD is cross-sectoral and should be integrated into all major sectors. However, the humanitarian system operates in silos. The humanitarian architecture, formed by the Inter-Agency Standing Committee (IASC) sector clusters and mostly led by various United Nations agencies (i.e. UNICEF, WHO, UNHCR), separates education, health, nutrition, protection—critical services for all emergency affected populations. Agencies that lead multiple sectors in the same country often do not collaborate. This often results in people receiving some, but not all the support they need. Coordination for ECD is also a challenge—which sector should host it? Can it be a stand-alone sector? There is no IASC group for ECD so it could sit under education, which it often does, under child protection or health. However, rarely are all aspects of nurturing care supported by one sector. Additionally, needs assessment often does not include all key questions related to young children and if some questions are included, they are often through one sector. A multi-sectoral needs assessment for young children can ensure key data are collected.

Lastly, even when health and nutrition receive more funding than education many projects do not focus on young children. There is no mechanism where implementing agencies and donors are pushed to consider the needs of young children. In July 2017, the humanitarian system launched the Gender and Age Marker (GAM), which should assess project proposals based on how well issues of gender and age are integrated into the project design. While this is a good step, the age part does not specify that proposals should integrate early childhood. Further, it is a new mechanism which is, at this point, not broadly used when assessing humanitarian proposals.

Roadmap of book

Over the last 18 years, I have worked in the humanitarian, development and ECD spaces. I have seen a wide gap between people working in these different areas. The nexus between ECD and emergencies is now a burgeoning area of work. Practitioners and policy makers are starting to think about the connection between the two. However, gaps remain in the humanitarian space on what is ECD, why is it important and how to implement ECD in emergency programmes. Part of this is due to the dearth of rigorous research and few evidence-based programming models. The purpose of this book is therefore to contribute to filling these gaps. Through analysis of existing literature, collecting quantitative and qualitative data from South Sudanese refugee camps in Uganda and my own experience working in the humanitarian space for over a decade, the book is divided into three parts: (1) Background and Context (Chapters 1–5), (2) ECD in Emergency Programming (Chapter 6) and (3) Evidence for ECD in Emergencies (Chapters 7–9). The book then concludes with a Way Forward for ECD in emergencies, outlining areas where more research is needed and recommendations for key stakeholders.

Chapter 1 starts with the global trends in ECD and why it is important. In Chapter 2, it is highlighted why ECD in emergencies is even more critical for children's survival and well-being. Chapter 3 illustrates the humanitarian landscape, the current situation around the world, the humanitarian architecture, funding mechanisms and opportunities for increasing ECD in emergency financing. Chapter 4 paints a picture of the decades long conflict in South Sudan, the conflict in Uganda and the environment in which South Sudanese refugees in Uganda currently live. Chapter 5 provides another lens for considering child development in humanitarian contexts. It reviews the literature around child and human development and in particular Vygotsky's Socio-cultural theory and Sen's Capability Approach, bringing them together for the first time to provide a stronger theoretical underpinning for ECD in emergencies.

Chapter 6 investigates existing programming frameworks and models for ECD and looks at the adaptation of one model for refugee contexts. Through evidence collected in non-emergency and emergency locations in Uganda, the book suggests one evidence-based ECD in emergency model. It illuminates, for programme staff, policy makers and donors, what may need to be changed for evidence-based ECD models to work well in humanitarian contexts. The chapter concludes with guidance on future ECD in emergency programme design and implementation.

The final part of this book contributes to the evidence base for ECD in emergency programmes. Chapter 7 lays out the methodology used for the research, including the challenges and obstacles of conducting research in a refugee context. Before collecting data from South Sudanese refugee children and parents in Uganda, in Chapter 8, I illustrate the process for adapting an existing child development tool for the South Sudanese cultural context and emergency situation. With qualitative methods, I uncovered the definition of child development and expectations that South Sudanese parents have for their children. The tool developed and the process followed during this research can be used and duplicated for the South Sudan crisis and other humanitarian situations. Lastly, Chapter 9 shows evidence for ECD in emergency programmes. By comparing two groups of children from two refugee camps in northern Uganda, a programme and wait-list control group, the research provides evidence for the differences in children's development when they have access to ECD programmes and when they do not. This chapter also investigates the critical role of parents and caregivers in children's development and tests this literature in the emergency context to see if a correlation exists between parents with higher knowledge and skills and their children's development. The research results show support for providing ECD and in particular early learning services for children three to five years in emergency contexts. Refugee children who received early learning services had higher child development outcomes that were statistically significant, compared with those that did not receive services. A relationship between parents' knowledge, attitudes and practice and children's development outcomes was also analysed. This, however, showed no positive or negative relationship.

Various audiences can use this book. For humanitarian and ECD practitioners and United Nations staff that design and implement programmes, this book shows how effective ECD programmes can be designed, adapted and implemented in emergency contexts. It also provides evidence that these groups can use for advocacy. For policy makers, donors and governments, this book provides evidence and makes the case for why they should invest in ECD in emergency programming. Lastly, for academics and students, this book provides a new theoretical underpinning for ECD in emergencies, the potential obstacles and steps for conducting research in refugee situations and how to adapt data collection tools for different cultural contexts.

References

Beginning of Life Film, www.youtube.com/watch?v=LHqUMqvL1RQ

Black, M. et al. (2016). "Early childhood development coming of age: Science through the life course", *The Lancet*, Series: Advancing Early Childhood Development: From Science to Scale, 389: 77–90, London.

Britto, P. et al. (2016). "Nurturing care: Promoting early childhood development", *The Lancet*, Series: Advancing Early Childhood Development: From Science to Scale, 389: 91–102, London.

Brown, T. and Jernigan, T. (2012). "Brain development during the preschool years", *Neuropsychology Review*, 22(4), 313–333.

Bryce J. et al. (2008). "Maternal and child under nutrition: Effective action at national level", *The Lancet*, 371, 510–526, London.

Carneiro, P. and Heckman, J. (2003). *Human Capital Policy*, NBER working paper 9495, National Bureau of Economic Research, Cambridge, MA.

Center on the Developing Child (2009). *Five Numbers to Remember about Early Childhood Development* (Brief), www.developingchild.harvard.edu.

Center on the Developing Child (2015). *The Science of Resilience*. The In Brief Series. USA: Harvard University.

Chan, M., Lake, A. and Hansen, K. (2016). "The early years: Silent emergency or unique opportunity?", *The Lancet*, Series: Advancing Early Childhood Development: From Science to Scale, 389, 11–13, London.

Christakis, D. (2011). *Media and Children* [video], TedTalks, www.youtube.com/watch?v=BoT7qH_uVNo, last accessed 21 May 2019.

Conticini, A. and Quere V. (2011). "Emotional stimulation for acutely and severely malnourished children in SNNPR", *Field Exchange*, 40, 84–85.

Garcia, J. et al. (2017). "Quantifying the life-cycle benefits of a prototypical early childhood program", https://heckmanequation.org/www/assets/2017/12/abc_comprehensivecba_JPE-SUBMISSION_2017-05-26a_sjs_sjs.pdf, last accessed on 7 April 2019.

Gardner, J., Grantham-McGregor, S.M., Himes, J. and Chang, S. (1999). "Behaviour and development of stunted and non-stunted Jamaican children", *Journal of Child Psychology and Psychiatry*, 40(5), 819–827.

Gowani, S., Yousafzai, A. K., Armstrong, R. and Bhutta, Z.A. (2014). "Cost effectiveness of responsive stimulation and nutrition interventions on early childhood development outcomes in Pakistan", *Annals of NY Academy of Science*, 1308, 149–161.

Grantham-McGregor, S.M. et al. (1991). "Nutritional supplementation, psychosocial stimulation, and mental development of stunted children: The Jamaican study", *The Lancet*, 338(8758), 1–5.

Heckman, J. (2006). *Return on Investments: Cost vs. Benefits.* University of Chicago, www.childandfamilypolicy.duke.edu/pdfs/10yranniversary_Heckmanhandout.pdf

Hurley, K., Yousafzai, A. and Lopez-Boo, F. (2016). "Early child development and nutrition: A review of the benefits and challenges of implementing integrated interventions", *American Society for Nutrition. Advances in Nutrition*, 7, 357–363.

Mizunoya, S. (2015). *Economic Loss from School Dropout due to the Syria Crisis: A Cost-Benefit Analysis of the Impact of the Syria Crisis on the Education Sector.* UNICEF: Amman.

Shonkoff, J. and Bales, S.N. (2011). "Science does not speak for itself: Translating child development research for the public and its policymakers", *Child Development*, 82(1), 17–32.

The Lancet (2016). Advancing Early Childhood Development: From Science to Scale, Vol 389, London.

Their World (2016). *Safe Spaces: The Urgent Need for Early Childhood Development in Emergencies and Disasters.*

UNESCO (2016). *Evaluation of UNCESCO's Role in Education in Emergencies and Protracted Crisis.* UNESCO: Paris.

UNOCHA Financial Tracking Service (2016). https://fts.unocha.org/, last accessed 22 July 2018.

UNOCHA (2017). World Humanitarian Data and Trends 2017, UN, http://interactive.unocha.org/publication/datatrends2017/resources/WHDT2017_Final_Singles.pdf, last accessed 8 August 2018.

Victora, C. et al. (2008). "Maternal and child under-nutrition: Consequences for adult health and human capital", *The Lancet*, 371(9609), 340–357.

Yousafzai, A. K. et al. (2014). "Effect of integrated responsive stimulation and nutrition interventions in the Lady Health Worker Programme in Pakistan on child development, growth and health outcomes: A cluster-randomised factorial effectiveness trial", *The Lancet*, 384(9950), 1282–1293, London.

Part I

Background and context

The first part, which includes Chapters 1–5, lays the foundational background and context for this book. I start with tracing generally the unfolding global trends and evidence for Early Childhood Development (ECD). ECD is a long-standing field that regularly encounters new evidence and approaches to programming. Understanding the latest evidence and the state of the field will illustrate the gaps in knowledge in the humanitarian context. Chapter 2 answers the question of why ECD is particularly important during emergencies, delving deeper into the particular risks and adversities children and families experience during crisis contexts, and the existing obstacles faced when the ECD and humanitarian sectors come together. Chapter 3 provides an overview of the humanitarian landscape, in particular the current state of emergency situations around the world, the increase in professionalisation over the years and the humanitarian aid structure and financing mechanisms. Chapter 4 illustrates the decades-long struggle faced by South Sudan, from the time it was part of Sudan to today's uncertainty. Chapter 5 analyses the nexus of child and human development and how theoretical perspectives from each area provide a lens for understanding ECD in emergency programming for South Sudanese refugees in Uganda.

1 Global trends in Early Childhood Development

ECD focuses on the development of a person from conception to his/her eighth year of life (The Consultative Group on Early Childhood Care and Development, ND; UNICEF, ND; World Bank, ND). ECD encompasses more than just childcare: it is a multi-sectoral, programmatic approach that helps children develop physically, cognitively, socio-emotionally and linguistically. It therefore provides the support for young children in the following sectors: health, nutrition, early education and stimulation, recreational and psychosocial support activities and opportunities to learn one or more languages (ibid.).

The earliest traces of work focused on ECD can be found in sources from the seventeenth and eighteenth centuries (Bruer, 1999; Gray and Mac Blain, 2015; Thomas, 2005). Over the years, it has become more professionalised, through the use of research, theories, programming models and workforce development programmes. The evolution of this field continues with new learning. This chapter reviews the global trends and understanding of this field as it stands today.

The most recent framing of ECD is illustrated in Figure 1.1 (the Nurturing Care Framework). This framework highlights young children's multiple needs: good health (health sector), adequate nutrition (nutrition sector), opportunities for early learning (education sector), security and safety (child-protection sector) and responsive caregiving (*The Lancet*, 2016; WHO, UNICEF and World Bank, 2018). Responsive caregiving does not neatly fit into one sector and can be integral to any of the aforementioned sectors. While the elements included in the Nurturing Care Framework are not new to scholars of ECD, this is the first time that responsive caregiving has been highlighted as a distinct element: this assertion is based on the growing evidence and momentum of the critical role that parents and primary caregivers play in establishing secure attachments and relationships with adults in order to help children thrive (ibid., Center on the Developing Child at Harvard University, NDa, NDb).

Programmatically, ECD includes activities from all aspects of the Nurturing Care Framework. For example, the element of opportunities for early learning includes activities such as early childcare, pre-school education,

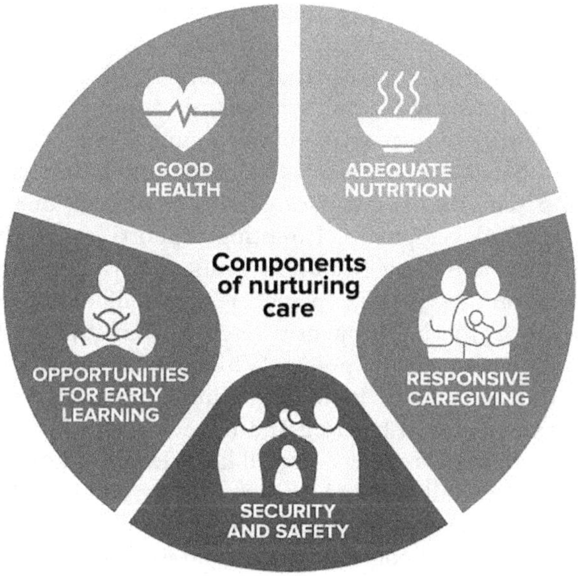

Figure 1.1 Nurturing Care Framework.

transition to primary school and neighbourhood play groups. In emergencies, these activities might be conducted in tents, under trees, in temporary shelters or through mobile visits by caregivers who lead the activities.

Elements of good health and adequate nutrition include health check-ups for children, pre- and post-natal care for women, play corners in community health centres, home visits by community health workers, pregnant women's group discussions, adolescent mother and baby parenting and playgroups, infant and young child feeding, support for breastfeeding, sessions on how to use local produce to prepare nutritious foods for children at different ages and more. UNICEF and WHO have developed the Care for Child Development training package which targets health workers (UNICEF and WHO, 2012). This package has been adapted and used in many countries around the world to strengthen the capacity of health workers to support young children and families. In humanitarian contexts, many of these approaches related to good health and adequate nutrition can be adapted, including the Care for Child Development training package. Whereas in non-humanitarian contexts, community health centres could be used, if these do not exist during an emergency situation, mobile health clinics and support could be used.

The security and safety element includes birth registration, providing support to parents in instilling positive discipline and dealing with violence in the family as a way to prevent abuse, exploitation and neglect of children, establishing referral mechanisms for child victims of abuse, neglect and exploitation, and psychosocial support for children and families. All of these activities can be adapted and implemented in emergency situations. The location and duration may differ; there might be a stronger focus on psychosocial support and the need to provide assistance for parents to manage stress. As separation happens during humanitarian situations, child-protection actors may focus on tracing family members and reunification.

As mentioned previously, responsive caregiving is one element that does not fit within a particular sector; critical activities include strengthening the capacity of parents and primary caregivers to protect, nurture and support their children's development. Parenting support can be through small group sessions, 1:1 counselling (via home visits or during health check-ups), mass communication messages (i.e. parenting apps, billboards, radio spots, or WhatsApp groups). Parenting happens wherever parents are—village-savings loan groups, supermarkets, water points. While conducting parenting sessions focused on child development, some programmes also include education on savings and loans, vocational training and literacy activities. By strengthening parents' and primary caregivers' overall knowledge and capabilities, these programmes can potentially extend support to their children (Center on the Developing Child at Harvard University, NDa, NDb). By providing opportunities for parents to come together to talk and exchange ideas about childcare, learning and development, they not only learn from each other but can also support each other psychologically and emotionally (Britto et al., 2016). It can help families communicate better within themselves, and help communities understand and respect their differences. Therefore, ECD can also contribute to social cohesion, peace and economic prosperity. In addition, these programmes support the establishment of government policies for young children (ibid.). Parenting support programmes can easily be integrated into emergency programmes once the content, duration of the sessions and approach are adapted to meet the needs and realities of a humanitarian context.

Ideally, programmes will include all aspects of nurturing care. However, in reality, and especially in emergency contexts, this can be difficult, especially when funding mechanisms work in siloes.

Why Early Childhood Development (ECD)?

There are six key reasons why ECD is critical. This section delves more deeply into the science and evidence behind these reasons. These six key reasons are that ECD:

1. is critical for brain development;
2. can help tackle poverty and gender inequality;
3. can help promote peace, disaster risk reduction (DRR) and environmental protection;
4. is cost effective;
5. can be crucial for children with disabilities; and
6. is recognised as a human right.

Critical window of opportunity for brain development

The first eight years of a child's life are the most formative, with the greatest rapid cognitive, physical, social and emotional developments (Fox et al., 2010). Some of the earliest neuroscientific research found that on average 700 new neural connections are made in a child's brain every second (Conel, 1959). Harvard University's Center on the Developing Child has now updated this figure to indicate that there can be up to 1,000,000 neural connections made in the child's brain per second (Center on the Developing Child at Harvard University, 2009). The rapid growth of neurons peaks during the period of early childhood; those that are not used consistently disappear, thereby decreasing the overall neural connections in the brain as we age (Conel, 1959). Babies are therefore the best learning machines in the world. Through exploration and play, they are the world's best innovators.

Early childhood is the time when the brain is most flexible, and when external inputs can have positive or negative effects on children's development and influence their life's trajectory (Fox et al., 2010). The brain's architecture is built from conception through to adulthood, but there are certain "sensitive periods" where brain development is accelerated. Early childhood is one of the key "sensitive periods" that builds the foundation for future growth and development. The brain builds on itself, so the foundation needs to be strong (Bruer, 1999; Fox et al., 2010). A strong foundation during a child's earliest years increases the likelihood of positive outcomes and development, while a weak foundation increases the probability of future physical, mental and other difficulties (National Scientific Council on the Developing Child, 2007). Figure 1.2,

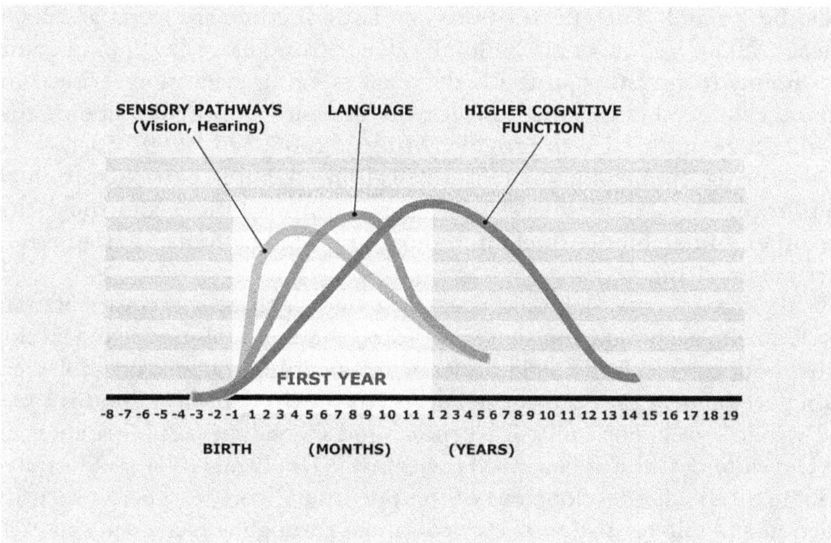

Figure 1.2 Human brain development: neural connections over time.

from the Center on the Developing Child, illustrates how the brain develops over the span of a lifetime, and how the first five years have the greatest growth.

The growth of the neural connections in the brain depends on a few key things, including sufficient nutrition in the first 1,000 days after conception, and the stimulation of the brain through human interaction, known as "serve and return" (National Scientific Council on the Developing Child, 2007). When any child interacts with the world, and especially with his/her parents and family members, he/she learns a lot about how humans act, behave and communicate. He/she begins to understand how to be a social being in his/her cultural context. A child feels safe, loved and important when his/her parents and family members interact with him/her by talking, smiling, hugging, kissing and through eye contact. It is during this time that a child develops attachment with primary caregivers, which is an important part of his/her development (Bowlby, 1988; Gordon et al., 2011; Masten, 2014). Hormones such as oxytocin are released during early attachment between parents and their babies (Gordon et al., 2011). This feeling of safety, love and lack of anxiety is what propels a child to explore the world around him/her, which allows for even greater neural connections (Bowlby, 1988; Gordon et al., 2011; Masten, 2014). In contrast, children's nervous systems can be negatively impacted when they do not have regular, secure and loving relationships and an attachment with parents or other caregivers, or when there is neglect or exposure to violence and severe stress (Teicher, 2000). This can, in turn, affect the child's ability to trust, bond and relate with others, and his/her interest in exploring the world around (ibid.). Without these critical inputs, and the chance for the child to explore his/her world, the child's brain development and physical growth could be stunted. The effects of this can last a lifetime (Bryce et al., 2008; Teicher, 2000; Victora et al., 2008). Evidence from many developing countries points to investing in the early years as being even more critical for the most vulnerable children, as such investment can provide support that families may not be able to provide (Mingat, 2006; Sen, 1999). Early-years support brings tremendous benefits to all children, but in particular to those from lower socio-economic classes, those with disabilities and those that face other vulnerabilities (including those impacted by humanitarian crises) (Hertzman, 2010).

While there is overwhelming scientific evidence that the majority of brain development occurs during the early years, the brain continues to develop throughout a person's life. Additional neuroscientific evidence on adolescent brain development over the last ten years has shown that this period is a second window of opportunity (Blakemore and Choudhury, 2006; Center on the Developing Child at Harvard University, NDb; Dahl, 2004) as illustrated in Figure 1.3. The development of the pre-frontal cortex, where executive function and self-regulation occur, continues through adolescence and early adulthood (ibid.). Executive function, which includes higher-order thinking

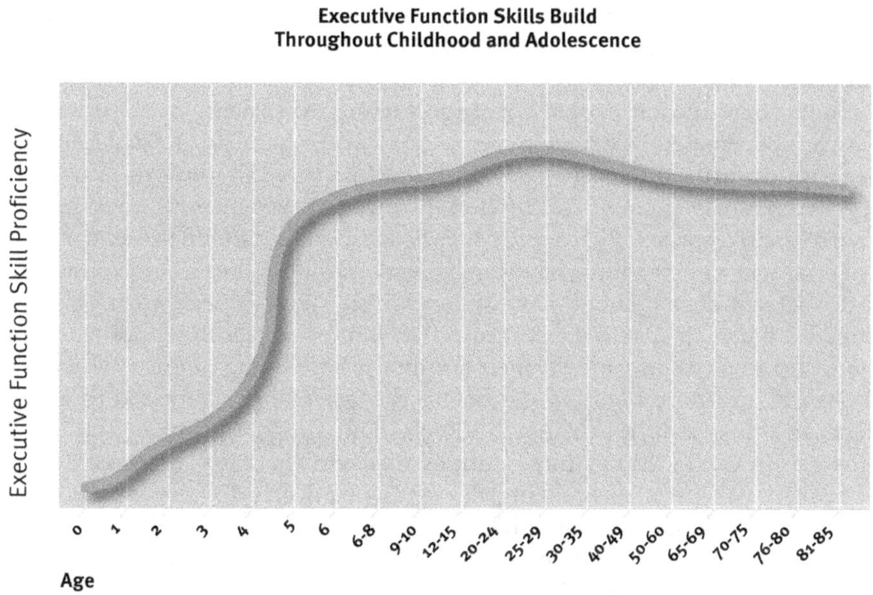

A range of tests measuring different forms of executive function skills indicate that they begin to develop shortly after birth, with ages 3 to 5 providing a window of opportunity for dramatic growth in these skills. Growth continues throughout adolescence and early adulthood; proficiency begins to decline in later life.

Source: Weintraub et al. (In Press).99

Figure 1.3 Development of executive function over a lifetime.

such as planning, decision-making, goal-setting, multi-tasking, reflection, emotional control and metacognition, is seen as critical to success in adulthood (Center on the Developing Child at Harvard University, NDb; Diamond, 2006). Based on this evidence, The Center on the Developing Child at Harvard University is now promoting a two-generation approach to ECD, which focuses on supporting children and their parents, especially those who are adolescents or young adults up to late twenties, in order to take advantage of the second sensitive period in brain development (Center on the Developing Child at Harvard University, NDb).

Tackle poverty and gender inequality

The early years are also the critical time for forming identities and stereotypes, so services for children and families can help tackle socio-economic and gender inequalities (Irwin et al., 2007). There is evidence that ECD services can be a great equaliser, helping the most vulnerable children (i.e. those from low-income families, ethnic or religious minorities, children affected by conflict and emergencies) get to similar levels of development and well-being, academic achievement, and income parity as more well-off children (ibid.).

Today, 836 million people live on less than US$1.25 per day, a situation which is considered "extreme poverty" (MDG Report, 2015). Children experience poverty differently from adults. While an adult may fall into poverty temporarily, a small child who falls into poverty may be stuck in the lowest socio-economic group for life, because even short periods without essential services or appropriate care in early childhood can be detrimental to long-term development. Young people often feel the effects of poverty directly, when they may be forced to go hungry or leave school early to work and generate income for their families. Those living in poverty around the world are more likely to die before the age of five compared to those from wealthier families (Mingat, 2006; Grantham-McGregor et al., 2007; Houweling et al., 2005). Interventions made in the early years have also been seen as critical to breaking the cycle of poverty for the most socio-economically disadvantaged children as they can catch up with their more advantaged peers and become ready for formal learning starting at the same level (Mingat, 2006; Sen, 1999; Grantham-McGregor et al., 2007). A 20-year follow-up study in Jamaica, which looked at the impact of a health and education intervention during children's early years, found that children who received both health and education inputs during early childhood were able to increase their earnings by 25% as adults (Gertler et al., 2013). This evidence points to ECD support increasing the likelihood of helping children break the cycle of poverty. Additional evidence indicates that children from higher socio-economic groups have larger vocabularies compared to children living in poverty, as it is more likely that their parents communicate with them using a larger vocabulary, and regularly read to them (Hackman and Farah, 2009; Hoff, 2013; Suskind et al., 2015). Landmark longitudinal research conducted by Betty Hart and Todd Risley in 1995 found that at the age of four, children from high socio-economic status (SES) families had been exposed to almost 45 million words. In contrast, Hart and Risley found that children from low SES families heard only about 13 million words. This showed a gap of approximately 30 million words, which has now been coined "the 30-million-word gap" (Suskind et al., 2015). The children who heard more words were therefore better-prepared for school. These same children when re-assessed in third grade had larger vocabularies, were more fluent readers and got higher test scores (Hart and Risley, 1995; Suskind et al., 2015). The difference in vocabulary size between socio-economic groups can be seen as early as at 18 months (Fernald et al., 2013), which illustrates that children who are prepared at home prior to starting schooling are given an advantage that poorer children do not have. ECD, and in particular pre-school education, can level the playing field for all children, no matter their socio-economic background (Irwin et al., 2007).

Girls are often particularly at risk when the underlying cultural preference and priority is given to boys. Research has shown that family poverty has more impact on the survival of young girls than it has on boys. A fall of 1% in GDP increases infant mortality by 1.5 deaths per 1,000 births for boys, and by 7.4 deaths per 1,000 births for girls (Stavropoulou and Jones, 2013). In families facing economic constraints, girls and women eat last and eat less as well (ibid.). There is a clear link between stunting in early childhood and impaired cognitive development and poor school achievement, with implications for the rest of the life-course (ibid.).

Poverty is also particularly likely to impact negatively on girls' right to early childhood education, with girls from the poorest quintile of households making up 43% of out of school children (UNESCO and UNICEF, 2012). The challenge for girls in accessing ECD services continues throughout their lives. Economic downturns also have a disproportionate impact on primary school completion rates for girls, which are estimated to decline by 29%—compared to 22% for boys (World Bank, 2010). Boys' education is often prioritised if low-economic families are forced to choose where to invest their limited resources. Lack of employment opportunities for girls once they complete their education can mean that parents in the lowest socio-economic group struggle to see the long-term benefit of educating their daughters. This then increases girls' vulnerability to child marriage and other types of abuse and discrimination (UNFPA, 2012). Other barriers, including the burden of unpaid care and domestic work, and discriminatory social norms deny girls and young women access to training and to decent jobs, and this can be compounded by other factors such as ethnicity, disability, religion, caste and sexual orientation, thus perpetuating cycles of poverty that often start in early childhood.

In humanitarian situations, the situation for girls can be worse. Humanitarian agencies often do not sufficiently address girls' needs and therefore specific support for them is missing from project planning (UNICEF, 2012). The London School of Economics analysed emergencies in 141 countries and found that boys received preferential treatment over girls in rescue efforts and more access to basic services (Neumayer and Plumper, 2007). During the 1991 cyclone near Bangladesh's coastal areas, a father who was unable to stop both his son and daughter from being swept away by a tidal surge let go of his daughter and held on to his son as he believed his son would carry on the family line (WHO, 2002).

The development of a gender identity, gendered attitudes, expectations and behaviours are influenced by both biological factors (the influence of sex hormones on the brain before birth) and gender socialisation (Honig, 1983; UNICEF, 2011). Cumulative disparities that can start prenatally and in the first years of life result in lifetime consequences (Walker et al., 2011). Gender socialisation, a process that starts before birth, is how children learn about the social expectations, attitudes and behaviours associated with one's gender (Honig, 1983; UNICEF, 2011). It is in the first years of life that children are gender socialised through the influence of their external environment: their parents, caregivers, teachers, other children and media, religion and cultural traditions. They become gender aware and quickly assimilate a wide range of culturally-determined stereotypical beliefs about gender and learn about society's expectations and norms for them—as boys and girls—with respect to their behaviours, roles and status. In this way, gender stereotypes and discrimination are transmitted from one generation to the next. By the age of three, children have a sense of gender identity (i.e. an understanding of whether they are a boy or a girl), and by the age of six to seven years, they understand that gender is (relatively) permanent (i.e. a boy becomes a man, a girl is still a girl even if she wears boy's clothes). Once they understand their own gender identity, they begin to pay much more attention to "models" of the same sex and to evaluate their own gender group more favourably than the other gender group. They also begin to learn, and rigidly stick to, gender stereotypes.

Some of the multiple actors that are involved in this process of gender socialisation are given below:

- *Parents/primary caregivers:* who (1) "model" different roles and behaviours inside and outside the home in ways that may stereotype based on gender; (2) may show more preference for one sex over the other (i.e. preference for the male child) and therefore treat them differently in terms of care, services and support offered; (3) encourage gender-stereotyped toys/play activities (i.e. cars for boys and dolls for girls); and (4) communicate to children their understandings of gender such as telling boys that they should not cry or wear pink (Honig, 1983; UNICEF, 2011; Witt, 1997).
- *Teachers/ECD facilitators:* influence gender development when they use curricula/reading materials that reinforce gender stereotypes and promote specific toys and play activities for girls vs. boys; interact and teach in ways that reflect their different expectations about the way boys and girls learn and what each sex will learn better; and allow gender-segregated play as the norm rather than the exception (Cahill and Adams, 1997; Honig, 1983; UNICEF, 2011)
- *Children:* influence other children's gender development. Children prefer to play with peers who are of the same gender. From the age of about three, a process of "gender segregation" occurs: boys and girls will choose to spend more time playing with same sex peers and much less with the other sex. As children spend time with their peers, they become more alike; they begin to develop the same interests, learn the same skills and learn the same gendered behaviour and prejudices. They influence each other, model roles, create norms and encourage or discourage certain behaviours. In the process, they do not learn to the same extent to understand, respect and appreciate the other sex, nor how to interact

with them. Thus, gender stereotypical beliefs, attitudes and biases about and towards the other sex strengthen among children (Honig, 1983; UNICEF, 2011)

- *Government policies:* are gender blind and do not consider the societal-level biases against women and the specific requirements they need to address in order to be on equal footing with their men can perpetuate gender inequality from generation to generation (UNICEF, 2011)

There are also other factors in a child's environment that shape this gender identity. ECD programmes can help children understand that girls and boys have equal rights, the same potential in life, and that they can do similar things. As the child grows, this will help in the long run to tackle gender inequality that is present in many societies.

While there have been some longitudinal studies looking at ECD and poverty alleviation, there have been virtually no longitudinal studies looking at ECD and gender equality and very few rigorous research studies of ECD in humanitarian crises. ECD in emergencies research has mostly included a few qualitative evaluations, policy papers and anecdotal evidence presented in unpublished documents and programme reports (Shah, 2013).

Promote peace, disaster risk reduction and environmental protection

As young children's brains are shaped during the years of early childhood (0–8 years), there is tremendous opportunity to teach children about peace, preparing for future disasters and protecting the environment. Integrating activities that promote peace, disaster risk reduction and environmental protection into existing early childhood programmes can help children develop critical skills thought to be important for the 21st century including, but not limited to, empathy, tolerance, respect for diversity, non-violent ways to solve problems, cooperation, and critical thinking.

While the role of ECD in promoting peace is an emerging area of research, it has been slowly documented over the last decade (Ang and Oliver, 2015; Leckman et al., 2014; Smith, 2015; Sunar et al., 2013; UNICEF, 2015). New research from Yale University and other institutions globally is illuminating the role of ECD in promoting peace. The Dutch government's investment in 2012 into education and peace building, which included pre-school education, increased the empirical knowledge based on implemented programmes (UNICEF, 2015; Ang and Oliver, 2015). UNICEF launched an Early Childhood Peace Consortium in 2013, which brought together key stakeholders from the United Nations (UN), international NGOs, national NGOs, business sector, foundations, etc. (UNICEF, ND). This group is working towards a common goal of identifying and analysing the links between ECD and peace building through supporting and disseminating scientific research and advocating for better policies that support the way for achieving sustainable peace (ibid.).

Johan Galtung first coined the term "peacebuilding" in 1976 when he discussed three approaches to peace: peacekeeping, peacemaking and peace building (Galtung, 1976). John Paul Lederach, a key scholar in the area of peace studies, took this initial concept and developed it further. Lederach defined peace building as a "...comprehensive concept that encompasses, generates, and sustains the full area of processes, approaches, and stages needed to transform conflict toward more sustainable, peaceful relationships" (Lederach, 1997, 20). UNICEF adds to this definition by stating that peace building cuts across all sectors and should occur at local and national levels, and with the participation of governments, civil society, the UN system, international and national actors, communities and children themselves (UNICEF, ND). It addresses both the causes and consequences of conflict, and aims to change negative approaches to dealing with conflict into positive ones (ibid.). Lederach further adds that peace building is a social construct, meaning that it can be shaped (Lederach, 1997).

Many contemporary theories acknowledge that childhood itself is also socially constructed, and children are not only active agents in shaping their own lives but also in the social world around them (Ang and Oliver, 2015). Ang and Oliver (2015) in their systematic review of ECD and peace building programmes put together a new conceptual framework that looks at the connection between ECD and peace building. Like Bronfenbrenner's ecological systems theory and Vygotsky's socio-cultural theory (see Chapter 5 for more details), they see the child at the centre that is surrounded by the family, community, civil society, and the society's culture, history, social, political and economic situations (Ang and Oliver, 2015). Ang and Oliver place the child at the centre of policy because children are active agents in constructing their own lives and worlds (ibid.). The macro level is where ECD policy, social sector education policy and peace building policy can interact with each other (if they are separate policies). The child's world, which is represented through the various concentric circles, interacts with conflict on the one hand and sustainable peace on the other (ibid.). The framework highlights the complexities of moving from conflict to peace (ibid.).

ECD programmes can promote peace at individual, community and societal levels. At the individual level, these programmes help children develop skills such as cooperation, managing conflict, regulating emotions, showing appreciation for diversity and being empathetic and understanding others' perspectives (UNICEF, 2015). Well designed programmes help improve children's interaction level and willingness to play with others (including those from different cultural, socio-economic and ethnic backgrounds), ability to understand how being excluded makes one feel and ability to recognise instances of exclusion without prompting (ibid.). At the community level, ECD programmes that bring parents and community members together through parenting groups and neighbourhood play groups and can promote understanding others' perspectives and cultures, thereby promoting social cohesion. Furthermore, parenting groups can help strengthen relationships between couples within a family. At the societal level, ECD programmes influence global-level policies that promote peace and social cohesion. While there is growing evidence linking ECD and peace building and an increasing recognition of the complexity and links between these two areas, it is still not clear exactly which ECD activities are key factors that influence a person to be tolerant, empathetic and use nonviolent ways to solve problems (Ang and Oliver, 2015). There is still no clear evidence whether peaceful behaviours are more innate and biologically motivated or whether they are more learned than others (ibid.).

UNICEF supported ECD services in rural areas of Uganda that have little access to social services as part of the four-year peace building project (UNICEF, 2015). The project was implemented near the border with eastern Democratic Republic of Congo where Congolese people crossed the border into Uganda for safety in refugee camps. The emphasis for the project was on Ugandan and Congolese pre-school children aged three to five years who received support for community-based ECD activities. The project supported children and parents/caregivers in 424 ECD centres. While there were activities for children, the centres also provided the platform for parents and family members to interact with others. Some key changes that this programme achieved include keeping inter-ethnic lines of communication open and re-starting inter-ethnic dialogue, promoting tolerance and respect between the groups which prevented the triggering of additional conflict, protecting children when conflict broke out in 2014, an increasing sense of security and the establishment of a dedicated community management committee that provided a platform for community peace building (ibid.).

A longitudinal study conducted over ten years in Turkey known as the Turkish Early Enrichment Project (TEEP) also showed some links between ECD interventions and peace building (Leckman et al., 2014). TEEP included two elements: centre-based pre-school activities and home-based training for mothers. During the first follow-up on children and mothers, there were positive benefits seen in terms of children's cognitive abilities, school adjustment and performance, social acceptance and decrease in aggressive behaviour (ibid.). Secondary benefits seen during the first follow-up indicated that mothers and families saw improved family relations and increasing intra-family status of women (ibid.). The same families were followed up again. Benefits for children in terms of cognitive skills were sustained. In addition, the interaction between parents helped in creating social bonds across ethnic, cultural and religious boundaries (ibid.). There are a few other pieces of research and, in particular, case studies that looked at ECD and peace building issues (Connolly et al., 2007). Moreover, there are few longitudinal studies such as this one. Additional empirical evidence will strengthen this point.

In addition to peace, support during the early years can also be critical in developing interest and skills to care for the environment, develop the skills to preserve it, and prepare for different types of potential emergencies (DRR) (Shah, 2013; UNESCO, 2007; UNICEF, 2011). A report released by UNICEF in December 2017 highlights the impact of climate change and in particular air pollution on young children's brain development (Rees, 2017). The report highlights some critical ways that air pollution can negatively affect young children's brain. Due to their smaller bodies, children take in more air per unit of body weight than adults, thereby inhaling more toxic air. This can negatively affect their growing lungs, immune system and brain. Particles in polluted air can easily enter the blood stream and swell or destroy the barrier protecting the brain from toxic substances. Pollutants formed from burning fossil fuels reduce the white matter and neural connections in the brain which are critical for different parts of the brain to communicate with each other and for the brain to learn and develop. UNICEF refers to research that has shown a link between exposure to air pollution and decreases in IQ and memory and increases in anxiety, depression and attention disorders. Pollutants inhaled by pregnant women can cross into the placenta, thereby affecting a baby's birth weight and brain development (ibid.).

Research focused on young children's role in caring for the environment and preparing for future calamities can similarly be integrated into early-years work and has shown positive results (UNESCO, 2007; UNICEF, 2011). Such programmes emphasise the role played by children themselves in developing practical, context-specific plans to keep schools and other important places safe from natural hazards, and support efforts that promote environmental preservation (ibid.). It is widely believed that young children cannot understand the risks of different types of hazards, the need for environmental protection and hence would not be able to lead the change. However, Boyden and Mann (2005) maintain that children possess inner resources which, when combined with positive interpersonal relationships, help increase their resilience. Furthermore, child development theorist Lev Vygotsky believed that children are active agents in their own environment and can help shape it (Vygotsky, 1981). Research indicates that children from about the age of three can play a key role in building their own resilience and that of their peers (Cairns, 1996; Kamel, 2006; UNICEF, 2011). They can be agents of change when given the opportunity to learn about the environment, the risks of various types of hazards and the chance to solve their own problems with others (Wisner et al., 2004). Just as parents may explain, even to very young children, the risks around sharp objects, hot stoves, electricity sockets, etc., teaching children about DRR and environmental conservation can also have similar effects (UNICEF, 2011). Integrating DRR and environmental awareness into early childhood programmes can have many advantages starting from increased knowledge and skills for children. This knowledge and skills learned at a young age will likely be sustained throughout their lives and can be passed on to the next generation (ibid.).

A number of such projects, especially in Asia, have shown positive results (UNESCO, 2007; UNICEF, 2011). Plan International Bangladesh after floods in 2012 engaged pre-school children, aged three to five years, in learning about hazards, risks and DRR in their communities and how to deal with them (Shah, 2013). These activities were facilitated through play and allowed children and their parents to think about ways to prepare for future calamities. Often in early childhood programmes, parents participate so that the learning easily extends to them (ibid.). Based on this experience of integrating DRR into ECD in emergencies programmes, DRR-related activities are now integrated into longer-term ECD programmes that include a wider community group, including local government officials (ibid.). Smaller children, along with the older ones in primary schools, were supported to be change agents in their communities by raising awareness among other family and community members (ibid.). Children created drawings, comic books, magazines and household discussions. In addition, community-based organisations with children of mixed ages were formed which worked together to develop community DRR and contingency plans (ibid.). After this project, one hundred children's organisations were able to actively contribute to DRR and environmental awareness in the Barguna district of Bangladesh (ibid.).

Another successful project that integrates ECD with DRR is in the Philippines. Philippines is at high risk for natural hazard and conflict emergencies. For more than five years, Plan International has been working with the Philippines' Department of Education (DepEd) on DRR and environmental awareness; one way of doing this has been through early childhood programmes (Shah, 2013). Plan International, in collaboration with DepEd, developed a film series and puppetry activity known as "Tales of Disaster." Tales of Disaster introduced key concepts of DRR, climate change adaptation, environmental awareness and conflict resolution for the various types of risks that the country faces, including typhoons, landslides, earthquakes, floods, tsunamis and conflict (ibid.).

As young children's brains are shaped during the years of early childhood (0–8 years), there is tremendous opportunity to teach children about tolerance, peace, diversity, problem solving and gender equality, and prepare them for future disasters and environmental protection. While no longitudinal studies exist looking at the long-term impact of ECD and DRR and more rigorous research is needed to strengthen this point, research done thus far has shown promising results.

Cost effective

The importance of early intervention has been documented in many research studies (Shonkoff, 2009). Research and, in particular, cost-benefit

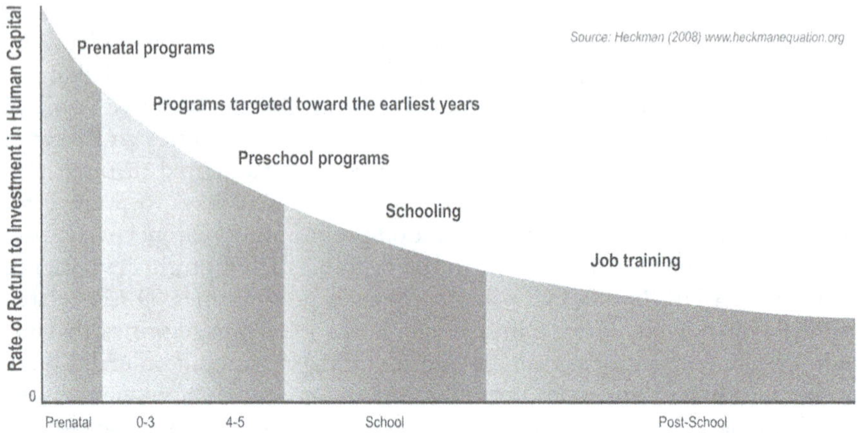

Figure 1.4 Rates of returns by age.

analyses have shown high returns on investment (Carneiro and Heckman, 2003; Heckman, 2006, 2008). These studies have also found that later interventions are likely to be less successful and in some cases to be ineffective (Carneiro and Heckman, 2003; Heckman, 2008; Shonkoff, 2009). Nobel Prize winning economist Dr James Heckman found in his research that the greatest returns on investment were found with pre-school programmes over primary and secondary schools and remedial programmes for older children (Heckman, 2006, 2008). Further, he and other researchers found returns on investment in savings and benefits up to US$13 for every US$1 invested, with the greatest returns to the most disadvantaged children (Garcia et al., 2017). Figure 1.4 illustrates Dr James Heckman's myriad cost-benefit research studies. His work shows that the highest returns are during the prenatal period, while the lowest returns are after a child completes his/her schooling.

Another major longitudinal ECD study that focused on disadvantaged African American children in the United States was the High Scope Perry study which showed significant positive results of the programme. The High Scope Perry study after 40 years showed a return on investment up to 13:1. This means that for every US$1 invested for ECD programming, there has been US$13 worth of savings and benefits to society (Belfield et al., 2006). Cost-benefit analyses have further shown that the benefits of ECD programmes have been greatest among the most disadvantaged groups (ibid.). Multi-sectoral services that integrate education, health, nutrition and child protection can be more efficient and support more domains of children's development (ibid.). Some studies have included cost-effectiveness of education interventions as well as parenting education as a particular variable. However, these issues have not been investigated in humanitarian situations. The argument of ECD as cost effective is widely accepted, but there have been studies that showed lower rates of return and a fade-out effect where the benefits lasted up to early primary years, but not beyond (Barnett, 1995; Lee and Loeb, 1994).

Early interventions can help children with disabilities

WHO and the World Bank estimate that there are more than a billion people (15% of total world population) in the world with some type of disability (WHO and UNICEF, 2012). Within this 15%, between 110 million people (2.2%) and 190 million adults (3.8%) have significant disabilities that severely affect their normal functioning (ibid.). Statistics for disabilities tend to be approximate because many people do not report family members with disabilities. Approximately 80% of these people live in low-income countries in Africa and Asia (Lata, 2015). Most of these people are not able to gain access to the critical support they need to help them improve their functioning and ability to contribute to society because of discrimination prevalent in the culture and lack of knowledge about how to help people with disabilities (Lata, 2015; WHO and UNICEF, 2012). Out of an estimated 1.6 million children with disabilities in Ethiopia, only 2.1% are supported by special schools. This pattern is also seen with similar levels of access to educational opportunities in Nicaragua (2.4%), El Salvador (less than 1%) and other countries (Lata, 2015). An estimation of the cost of disability in Bangladesh is 1.7% of the GDP or US$1.2 billion annually (WHO, 2011). This estimated loss to the country's GDP is due to lack of schooling for people with disabilities from childhood and their subsequent inability to contribute to the labour market (ibid.).

The early years, however, are a vital time to assist children with disabilities access crucial interventions that can help them reach their full potential in life. The Convention on the Rights of Persons with Disabilities (CRPD) defines disability as having long-term physical, mental, intellectual or sensory impairments which in interaction with other barriers can inhibit a person's ability to fully participate in society on an equal basis (Lata, 2015; WHO and, UNICEF, 2012). Persons with disabilities can have delays in their development in relation to age mates or an impairment that restricts their functioning (Vargas-Baron et al., 2009). Disability is neither purely biological nor only social, but it occurs during the interaction of the two (Lata, 2015; WHO and UNICEF, 2012). A child can be born with some genetic disposition that delays his/her development or functioning in comparison with other children of a similar age, and this is where ECD interventions are critical (Lata, 2015). Inequalities that affect the likelihood of a child having a disability can also begin prenatally before a child is born (Walker et al., 2011).

Walker and colleagues (Walker and Unterhalter, 2007; Walker et al., 2011) narrowed down key risk factors that influence child development outcomes in resource-poor locations (Walker and Unterhalter, 2007; Walker et al.,

2011). These include stunting (due to chronic malnutrition), micronutrient deficiencies, especially iodine and iron, and insufficient cognitive stimulation (ibid.). These ailments affect about 20–25% of young children in developing countries (ibid.). These conditions are worsened by low birth weight (due to mothers' malnutrition or lack of micronutrients), infectious diseases, environmental toxins and exposure to violence and other humanitarian conditions (ibid.). There are many preventable maternal risks, including poor nutrition, infections during pregnancy, exposure to drugs and alcohol; all of these have been found to be associated with intrauterine growth restriction (which can cause low birth weight in babies), birth defects, low IQ, learning difficulties and increased risks of developmental difficulties (Klebanov and Brooks-Gunn, 2006; Noland et al., 2003; Tofail et al., 2008).

Research has also found a bi-directional link between humanitarian situations and disability (WHO and UNICEF, 2012). While all children are vulnerable during an emergency, those with disabilities face additional adversities. The heightened stress, injury or death of parents, and/or primary caregivers in an emergency situation can further affect the parent-child interaction and therefore a disabled child's ability to progress along a positive development path. In certain situations such as earthquakes, children may experience additional disabilities like losing limbs, etc. (ibid.). There may be fewer services catering to disabled children's needs due to a combination of discrimination and lack of awareness, lack of knowledge of how to help such children and limited resources to be able to support disabled children in the way they need.

However, there is also evidence that early intervention can make a real difference—both from prenatal support of pregnant women to early support for infants and toddlers (Lata, 2015). Interventions such as maternal education, exclusive breastfeeding along with responsive and stimulating care have seen positive cognitive and non-cognitive gains in children at risk of developmental delay (Walker and Unterhalter, 2007). Iron supplementation to tackle anaemia has been found to have the greatest benefit on children's IQ when addressed within the first six months of life (ibid.). Research on deaf and hard of hearing infants found that these children had significantly better language development if the problem was addressed before the age of six months (Yoshinaga-Itano et al., 2010). This is because babies absorb a lot of sounds and language during this time, and if they can hear, they can better develop language skills. Furthermore, Yoshinaga-Itano et al. (2010) found that children who received cochlear implants before 24 months could achieve similar language abilities as their normal hearing peers (ibid.). In contrast, children who received cochlear implants after seven years showed poorer language abilities than their normally developing peers because the critical window when the greatest auditory development occurs has passed (Sharma et al., 2005). Dawson (2008) further found that when social engagement through parent-child interactions was enhanced before the full expression of autistic symptoms, this could affect genetic expression, brain development and behavioural manifestation of autism.

Recognised as a human right

The importance of children's earliest years is included as a child's right in the Convention on the Rights of the Child (CRC) and through Articles 6, 7, 19, 24, 28 and General Comment 7. General Comment 7 emphasises that early childhood is a critical period for the realisation of the rights mentioned in the UN CRC articles. General Comment 7 clarifies that every child's right to education begins at birth. It is closely tied to the right to development. Moreover, it supports a vision for comprehensive community services through early and middle childhood, both for children and for parents as their key educators and caregivers. General Comment 7 also acknowledges that activities in the family and home settings provide the foundation for children's development, well-being and progression into primary education. Clause 36 in particular highlights the additional support young children require during emergency situations.

Global developments in Early Childhood Development

While there is still a long way to go for the ECD field, there has been tremendous progress over the last decade. In this section, I describe three global developments in the ECD field: (1) increase in evidence base, (2) more national ECD policies and (3) recognition through Sustainable Development Goals (SDGs).

Greater efforts to strengthen the evidence base

Over the last decade, there have been efforts to increase the evidence base in ECD. More donors are financing research, more implementing organisations are commissioning research, there is greater work on widely disseminating the latest evidence, and more work is going into translating the science of ECD into policy and practice recommendations. Harvard University's Center on the Developing Child has been leading the field with cutting-edge research, policy and practice recommendations that have provided greater visibility to this area of work.

The *Lancet* journal, a prestigious medical journal, has published three series on ECD—in 2007, 2011 and 2016. These series brought forward the most up-to-date and rigorous evidence on ECD and began to attract international attention. *The Annals of the New York Academy of Sciences* published special issues on ECD in 2014 and 2018. Bernard Van Leer Foundation publishes a journal known as *Early Childhood Matters* every year with the latest research, evidence and practice about ECD.

The National Academies of Science's boards on Global Health and Children, Youth and Families came together in 2014 to establish the Forum on Investing in Young Children globally (iYCG). This collaboration aimed to integrate knowledge with action in regions around the world to inform evidence-based, strategic investments in young children. iYCG included experts working to ensure that investments in the world's children are informed by integrative science and are a top priority on the policy agenda, both globally and nationally. As part of this initiative, nine workshops were held in different cities around the world between 2014 and 2016. Bringing experts and researchers at events like this also helped turn the global attention to ECD.

In November 2017, the Institute for Human Development (IHD) at the Aga Khan University held its second global ECD conference. This conference, which was held in Tanzania, showcased some of the latest research and practice, particularly from the African continent. By being in Tanzania, it raised the profile of ECD to government officials of the country.

The Aga Khan Development Network, Red River College and the University of Toronto designed the Science of Early Childhood Development (SECD) online and a face-to-face course that aims to make current ECD research accessible to anyone interested in learning more about the impact of early experience on lifelong health and well-being. The SECD course has recently been adapted and translated for use in the Middle East, East Africa and other places—over 43 countries (AKDN, ND).

While ECD in non-humanitarian contexts has received significantly more attention than a decade ago, a strong evidence base for ECD in emergencies context is still weak (Britto et al., 2016; Yusra and Shiffman, 2016). Much of the evidence currently around ECD in emergencies is anecdotal or only with the use of qualitative methods (ibid.). The Education in Emergencies (EiE) sector has seen some progress in investment in research through a new funding from Dubai Cares known as E-cubed or Evidence for Education in Emergencies (INEE, ND). Thus far, no research focused on ECD in emergencies has been funded through this mechanism. The Inter-agency Network for Education in Emergencies (INEE) also has a journal known as the *Journal for Education in Emergencies*, but to date, no article focused on ECD in emergencies has been published. INEE also created an Early Childhood Care and Development in Emergency Situations Annotated Bibliography which includes a summary of 274 entries related broadly to this topic (Hayden et al., 2010). This bibliography includes peer-reviewed academic articles and non-peer-reviewed organisation reports and guides (ibid.). While the bibliography has some articles relevant and useful for this research, much of it encompasses articles and papers beyond the global definition of ECD. Due to this, there is also a weak theoretical framework that underpins this work. Developing stronger evidence and a theoretical framework for ECD in emergencies work might result in higher outcomes for children and families that are cost effective and can help countries meet the SDGs.

More governments establishing national ECD policies

According to UNICEF's 2009 data, more than 30 governments around the world have established national early childhood policies and 70 countries have some type of national mechanism for the various sectoral ministries to coordinate (Shonkoff, 2010). Despite these positive trends, ECD is still not getting sufficient attention in international and national policies. While the 2000 Education for All Dakar Declaration calls for "expanding and improving comprehensive early childhood care and education," it is the only goal without a quantifiable indicator or target (UNESCO, 2000). There is no agreed-upon measurement to track the progress of this statement. More than half of the countries in the world have no policy on ECD or a mechanism through which the various departments related to early childhood (i.e. education, health, social services/protection) can coordinate to provide holistic services for young children. Where such policies or mechanisms exist, they remain statements of intent rather than enforceable or implementable plans with a government budget (Shonkoff, 2010). Recent information gathered from the Global Education Monitoring (GEM) Report state that only Kenya considers ECD as their first priority among other education issues while Australia is the only other country who has even prioritised ECD (GEM, 2016). ECD in emergencies is even less likely prioritised as few countries have specific policies, plans and budgets in place to respond to emergencies (UNESCO, 2006). The newly established Global Early Childhood Development Action Network (ECDAN), the Global Partnership for Education and others are making efforts to support more governments to establish policies for multi-sectoral ECD, including ECD in emergencies. However, the processes are slow as there needs to be political will and then a budget to establish and roll out policies.

Recognised by the sustainable development goals

Another positive trend that is raising the profile of ECD globally is its inclusion into the SDGs. UN Secretary General Ban Ki-moon stated, "The SDGs recognise that ECD can help drive the transformation we hope to achieve over the next 15 years" (Richter et al., 2016). The SDGs have recognised the importance of various contexts, including emergencies, and have set goals related to ECD through education, maternal and child health and nutrition, protection and other sectors. Other goals that do not explicitly integrate ECD need it in order to achieve their targets. A summary of these goals and targets are given below (Britto, 2015; Richter et al., 2016). Furthermore, several major actors, including the UN Secretary General and UNICEF, have acknowledged that holistic ECD programming represents one of the most cost-effective approaches for achieving commitments that are at the heart of the SDGs, while ensuring that no one is left behind.

Goals that integrate aspects of ECD

Goal 2: Zero Hunger: End hunger, achieve food security and improve nutrition and promote sustainable agriculture.

Goal 2 refers to maternal and child nutrition and focuses on pregnancy to five years, a core aspect of ECD. Target 2.1 and Target 2.2 have a goal of ending hunger, malnutrition and stunting and wasting in children below 5 years of age and ensuring pregnant and lactating women's nutritional needs are met.

Children who receive early stimulation with nutrition supplements have better outcomes than children who only receive nutrition supplements, thereby amplifying the impact of nutrition (Conticini and Quere, 2011; Gardner et al., 1999; Grantham-McGregor et al., 1991; Hurley et al., 2016). Furthermore, ECD interventions buffer the negative effect of stress, thereby improving absorption of nutritional intake.

Goal 3: Good Health and Well-being: Ensure healthy lives and promote well-being for all at all ages.

Goal 3 refers to Maternal Nutrition and Child Heath (MNCH) and infectious diseases that are major killers of under-fives and another critical aspect of ECD. ECD interventions early in life set a trajectory for good lifelong health. It can lead to lower incidence of cardiovascular and non-communicable diseases and can increase well-being. With ECD, not only do children survive, they thrive.

Target 3.1: By 2030, reduce the global maternal mortality rate to fewer than 70 per 100,000 live births.

Target 3.2: By 2030, end preventable deaths of newborns and children below 5 years of age, with all countries aiming to reduce neonatal mortality rate to at least as low as 12 per 1,000 live births and under-5 mortality rate to at least as low as 25 per 1,000 live births.

Target 3.3: By 2030, end the epidemics of AIDS, tuberculosis, malaria and neglected tropical diseases and combat hepatitis, water-borne diseases and other communicable diseases.

Target 3.9: By 2030, substantially reduce the number of deaths and illnesses from hazardous chemicals and air, water and soil pollution and contamination.

Goal 4: Quality Education: Ensure inclusive and quality education for all and promote lifelong learning.

This goal is focused on education and lifelong learning, but frames a commitment to ECD. Learning begins at birth. ECD interventions have proved to be the foundation for later learning, academic success and productivity. A study on increasing pre-school enrolment in 73 countries found higher future wages of US$6 to US$17 per dollar invested, which indicates potential long-term benefits ranging from US$11 to US$34 billion (Heckman, 2008).

Target 4.2. By 2030, ensure that all girls and boys have access to quality ECD, care and pre-primary education so that they are ready for primary education.

Goal 16: Peace, Justice and Strong Institutions

Target 16.2. End abuse, exploitation, trafficking and all forms of violence against and torture of children.

This is a critical element of ECD as children need to be physically safe from violence.

In addition, early childhood interventions have the potential to instil values and behaviours that can create empathy, celebrate diversity, reduce violence and promote peace. ECD interventions have been shown to lead to lower rates of violence in the home and greater social cohesion in communities.

Goals for which ECD is needed to achieve the SDGs

Goal 1: No Poverty: End poverty in all its forms everywhere.

This goal does not explicitly mention ECD; however, positive outcomes of children in the early years are critical to achieving this goal. ECD has been documented to be one of the most cost-effective strategies for poverty alleviation as it can help level the playing field for more and less advantaged children. Early in life, when the brain has the maximum capacity to develop in the fullness of its complexity, children learn the skills that will help them flourish in the twenty-first-century economy. As they learn skills needed for the twenty-first century, they will increase adult productivity and income, and reduce inequities.

Goal 5: Gender Equality: Achieve gender equality and empower all women and girls.

The nexus between ECD and women's economic empowerment is clear. Greater investment in high-quality and affordable childcare is linked to greater opportunities for women's economic advancement and empowerment. ECD interventions improve opportunities and motivation for learning, particularly for girls, so that boys and girls can benefit equally from schooling and enter the job market. ECD is also the time when gender norms and values are established. Young children start understanding that they are girls or boys and what society expects from them. ECD programmes can help children navigate the social pressures so they are not boxed into doing things that are only considered for boys or for girls.

Goal 8: Decent Work and Economic Growth: Promote inclusive and sustainable economic growth, employment and decent work for all.

Adequate childcare is a critical element of the decent work agenda. Investments in professionalisation of the early childhood workforce contribute to full and productive employment, especially for women.

Goal 10: Reduced Inequalities: Reduce inequality within and among countries.

Inequality often begins before birth. ECD is a powerful equaliser. The first few years of a child's life offer a window of opportunity to provide interventions that can close the inequality gap between children born into disadvantage and those born with many advantages. Disadvantaged children who receive ECD services earn up to 25% more as adults compared with children who did not receive the services and almost catch up in earnings to their non-disadvantaged peers. Early childhood stimulation and food supplementation interventions enable children with low birth weight or stunting or living in extreme poverty to attain developmental outcomes similar to their peers.

Goal 12: Responsible Consumption and Production: Ensure sustainable consumption and production patterns.

ECD programmes set in place patterns of consumption, attitudes towards conservation and behavioural practices that will preserve the environment. What children learn early lasts a lifetime.

Goal 17: Partnerships for the Goals: Revitalise the global partnership for sustainable development.

Measurement of ECD at global, regional and national levels can serve as a powerful tool to revitalise global partnerships. UNICEF's Multiple Indicator Cluster Survey (MICS) provides population-level data that are suitable to measure Target 4.2 of the SDGs. ECD interventions have the potential to strengthen coordination across sectors for common health, social and economic goals, and to bring together international, governmental and civil society partners.

There is evidence from research that investments in ECD are fiscally smart, given the multiplier effect of ECD across several SDGs and sectors. Achieving the SDGs will be the next global challenge, and it is inextricably linked to humanitarian and ECD in emergency work. Despite the myriad efforts and advances in the ECD field, from the SDGs including language around ECD, to strengthening the evidence base, to more governments establishing policies on ECD, the field of ECD and especially ECD in emergencies have a long way to go. Financing for large-scale ECD work, from country government budgets and international donor governments, is still minimal, at best. While financing for ECD through foundations is growing, there has been little movement with large government bilateral and multi-lateral donors, developing country donors who could prioritise ECD through their own government financing and the private sector. ECD programmes have scaled in only a few countries such as Chile and Cuba. In the next chapter, I delve deeper into the rationale for why ECD is critical in humanitarian contexts.

References

Aga Khan Development Network (ND). *The Science of Early Child Development Building Knowledge about the Importance of Early Child Development*, www.aku.edu/ihd/projects/Documents/AKDN%20SECD%20Global%20Brief.pdf

Ang, L. and Oliver, S. (2015). *A Systematic Policy Review of Early Childhood Development and Peacebuilding in Fourteen Conflict-affected and Post-conflict Countries*. London: UNICEF and UCL Institute of Education.

Barnett, S. (1995). *The Future of Children Long Term Outcomes of Early Childhood Programs*, Vol. 5, No. 3, Winter. Princeton: Princeton University.

Belfield, C.R., Nores, M. Barnett W.S. and Schweinhart, I. (2006). "The High Scope Perry Pre-school Program: Cost-benefit analysis using data from the age 40 follow up", *Journal of Human Resources*, 41(1), 162–190.

Blakemore, S.J. and Choudhury, S. (2006). "Development of the adolescent brain: Implications for executive function and social cognition", *Journal of Child Psychology and Psychiatry*, 47(3/4), 296–312.

Bowlby, J. (1988). *A Secure Base: Parent-Child Attachment and Healthy Human Development*, Routledge: Great Britain, www.abebe.org.br/wp-content/uploads/John-Bowlby-A-Secure-Base-Parent-Child-Attachment-and-Healthy-Human-Development-1990.pdf

Boyden, J. and Mann, G. (2005). "Children's risk, resilience, and coping in extreme situations", In Unger, M. (Ed.) *Pathways to Resilience*. Thousand Oaks: Sage Publications.

Britto, P. (2015). "Why early childhood development is the foundation for sustainable development", UNICEF, https://blogs.unicef.org/blog/why-early-childhood-development-is-the-foundation-for-sustainable-development/

Britto, P. et al. (2016). "Nurturing care: Promoting early childhood development", *The Lancet*. Series: Advancing Early Childhood Development: From Science to Scale, 389(10064), 91–102, London.

Bruer, J. (1999). *The Myth of the First Three Years: A New Understanding of Early Brain Development and Lifelong Learning*. New York: The Free Press.

Bryce, J. et al. (2008). "Maternal and child under-nutrition: Effective action at national level", *The Lancet*, 371, 510–526.

Cahill, B. and Adams, E. (1997). "An exploratory study of early childhood teachers' attitudes toward gender roles", *Sex Roles*, 36(7), 517–529.

Cairns, E. (1996). *Children and Political Violence*. Oxford: Blackwell Publishers.

Carneiro, P. and Heckman, J. (2003). *Human Capital Policy*, NBER Working Paper 9495, National Bureau of Economic Research, Cambridge, MA.

Center on the Developing Child at Harvard University (NDa). *Building Adult Capabilities to Improve Child Outcomes: A Theory of Change*, https://developingchild.harvard.edu/resources/building-adult-capabilities-to-improve-child-outcomes-a-theory-of-change/, last accessed 22 July 2018.

Center on the Developing Child at Harvard University (NDb). *Using Brain Science to Build 2 Generation Programs*, http://developingchild.harvard.edu/resources/using-brain-science-build-new-2gen-intervention/), last accessed 22 July 2018.

Center on the Developing Child at Harvard University (2009). *Five Numbers to Remember About Early Childhood Development (Brief)*. www.developingchild.harvard.edu

Conel, J.L. (1959). *The Postnatal Development of the Human Cereal Cortex*. Cambridge, MA: Harvard University Press.

Connolly, P., Hayden, J. and Levin, D. (2007). *From Conflict to Peace building: The Power of Early Child Initiatives, Lessons from Around the World*. North Ryde: Institute of Early Childhood, Macquarie University.

The Consultative Group on Early Childhood Care and Development (ND). www.ecdgroup.com/about-eccd-2/, last accessed 12 June 2016.

Conticini, A. and Quere, V. (2011). "Emotional stimulation for acutely and severely malnourished children in SNNPR", *Field Exchange*, 40, 84–85.

Dahl, R. (2004). "Adolescent brain development: A period of vulnerabilities and opportunities. Keynote address", *Annals of the New York Academy of Sciences*, 1021(1), 1–27.

Dawson, G. (2008). "Early behavioral intervention, brain plasticity, and the prevention of autism spectrum disorder", *Development and Psychopathology*, 20, 775–803.

Diamond, A. (2006). "The development of executive functions", In Bialystock, E. and Craik, F. (Eds.) *Lifespan Cognition*. Oxford: Oxford University Press.

Fernald, A., Marchman, N. and Weisleder, A. (2013). "SES differences in language processing skill and vocabulary are evident at 18 months", *Developmental Science*, 16(2), 234–248.

Fox, S., Levitt, P. and Nelson, C. (2010, Jan/Feb). "How the timing and quality of early experiences influence the development of brain architecture", *Child Development*, 81(1), 28–40.

Galtung, J. (1976). "Three approaches to peace: Peacekeeping, peacemaking, and peacebuilding", In *Peace, War and Defense: Essays in Peace Research*, Vol. II. Christian Ejlers: Copenhagen.

Garcia, J. et al. (2017). "Quantifying the life-cycle benefits of a prototypical early childhood program", https://heckmanequation.org/www/assets/2017/12/abc_comprehensivecba_JPE-SUBMISSION_2017-05-26a_sjs_sjs.pdf, last accessed 7 April 2019.

Gardner, J. et al. (1999). "Behaviour and development of stunted and nonstunted Jamaican children", *Journal of Child Psychology and Psychiatry*, 40(5), 819–827.

GEM (2016). *Education for People and Planet: Creating Sustainable Futures for All*, https://en.unesco.org/gem-report/report/2016/education-people-and-planet-creating-sustainable-futures-all#sthash.S9B9DFCm.dpuf, last accessed 7 April 2019.

Gertler, P. et al. (2013). *Labor Market Returns to Early Childhood Stimulation: A 20-Year Followup to an Experimental Intervention in Jamaica*, The National Bureau of Economic Research Working Paper No. 19185, Massachusetts.

Gordon, I. et al. (2011). "Oxytocin and Social Motivation", *Developmental Cognitive Neuroscience*, 1(4), 471–493.

Grantham-McGregor, S., Powell, C.A., Walker, S.P. and Himes, J.H. (1991). "Nutritional supplementation, psychosocial stimulation, and mental development in stunted children: The Jamaican Study", *The Lancet*, 338, 1–5.

Grantham-McGregor, S. et al. (2007). "Developmental potential in the first 5 years for children in developing countries", *The Lancet*, 369, 60–70.

Gray, C. and Mac Blain, S. (2015). *Learning Theories in Childhood*. London: Sage Publications Ltd.

Hackman, D. and Farah, M. (2009). "Socioeconomic status and the developing brain", *Trends in Cognitive Sciences*, 13(2), 65–73.

Hart, B. and Risley, T. R. (1995). *Meaningful differences in the everyday experience of young American children*. Baltimore, MD: Paul H Brookes Publishing.

Hayden, J., Dunn, R. and Cologon, K. (2010). *Early Childhood Care and Development in Emergency Situations: Annotated Bibliography*. New York: Inter-agency Network for Education in Emergencies (INEE).

Heckman, J. (2006). *Return on Investments: Cost vs. Benefits*. Chicago: University of Chicago.

Heckman, J. (2008). "Schools, Skills and Synapses", *Economic Inquiry*, 46(3), 289–324.

Hertzman, C. (2010). "Framework for the social determinants of early child development", In Tramblay, R.E., Boivin, M. and Peters, R.D. (Eds.), *Encyclopedia on Early Childhood Development* [online], Centre of Excellence for Early Childhood Development and Strategic Knowledge Cluster on Early Child Development: Montreal, Quebec.

Hoff, E. (2013). "Interpreting the early language trajectories of children from low-SES and language minority homes: Implications for closing achievement gaps", *Developmental Psychology*, 49(1), 4–14.

Honig, A. (1983). "Sex role socialization in early childhood", *Young Children*, 38(6), 57–70. National Association for the Education of Young Children.

Houweling, T., Kunst, A., Looman, C. and Machenbach, J. (2005), "Determinant of under-5 mortality among the poor and the rich: a cross-national analysis of 43 developing countries", *International Journal of Epidemiology*, 34(6), 1257–1265.

Hurley, K., Yousafzai, A. and Lopez-Boo, F. (2016). "Early child development and nutrition: A review of the benefits and challenges of implementing integrated interventions", *American Society for Nutrition. Advances in Nutrition*, 7, 357–363.

INEE (ND), www.ineesite.org/en/research/e-cubed

Irwin, L., Siddiqui, A. and Hertzman, C. (2007). *Early Childhood Development: A Powerful Equalizer.* Geneva: World Health Organization.

Kamel, H. (2006). *Early Childhood Care and Education in Emergency Situations: Background Paper Prepared for the Education for All Global Monitoring Report 2007, Strong Foundations: Early Childhood Care and Education*, Paris: UNESCO.

Klebanov, P. and Brooks-Gunn, J. (2006). "Cumulative human capital and psychological risk in the context of early intervention links with IQ at ages 3, 5 and 6". *Annals of NY Academy of Science*, 1094, 63–82.

Lata, D. (2015). "Reducing disparities, enhancing capabilities, embracing diversity: harnessing the power of early childhood care and education to advance disability rights", Ch. 7, In Marope, P.T.M. and Kaga, Y. (Eds.) *Investing against Evidence: The Global State of Early Childhood Care and Education.* Paris: UNESCO.

Lancet (2016). *Advancing Early Childhood Development: From Science to Scale.*

Leckman, J., Panter-Brick, C. and Salah, R. (2014). "Peace is a lifelong process". In Leckman, J., Panter-Brick, C. and Salah, R. (Eds.) *Pathways to Peace: The Transformative Power of Children and Families.* Strongman Forum Report, volume 15, Cambridge: MIT Press, 3–17.

Lederach, J. P. (1997). *Building Peace: Sustainable Reconciliation in Divided Societies.* Washington, DC: United States Institute of Peace Press, 87–97.

Lee, V. and Loeb, S. (1994). *Where Do Head Start Attendees End Up?: One Reason Why Preschool Effects Fade Out.* Ann Arbor: University of Michigan.

Masten, A.S. (2014). "Promoting the capacity for peace in early childhood", In Beckman, J.F., Panter-Brick, C. and Salah, R. (Eds.) *Pathways to Peace: The Transformative Power of Children and Families.* Strungmann Forum Reports. Cambridge: MIT Press.

MDG Report (2015). *United Nations*, www.un.org/milleniumgoals/2015_MDG Report/pdf/MDG%202015%20rev%20(July%201).pdf

Mingat, A. (2006). *Early Childhood Care and Education in Sub-Saharan Africa: Towards Expansion of Coverage and Targeting of Efficient Services.* Working Draft Document, Association for the Development of Education in Africa, Biennale on Education in Africa, Libreville, Gabon.

National Scientific Council on the Developing Child (2007). *The Timing and Quality of Early Experiences Combine to Shape Brain Architecture,* Working Paper #5, Harvard University.

Neumayer, E. and Plumper, T. (2007). "The gendered nature of natural disasters: The impact of catastrophic events on the gender gap in life expectancy, 1981–2002", *Annals of the Association of American Geographers*, 97(3), 551–566.

Noland, J. S., Singer, L.T. and Arendt, R.E. (2003). "Executive functioning in preschool-aged children prenatally exposed to alcohol, cocaine, and marijuana", *Alcoholism: Clinical and Experimental Research*, 27(4), 647–656.

Rees, N. (2017). *Danger in the Air: How Air Pollution Can Effect Brain Development in Young Children*. New York: UNICEF.

Richter, L. et al. (2016). "Investing in the foundation of sustainable development: Pathways to scale up for early childhood development". *The Lancet*, Special issue: Advancing Early Childhood Development From Science to Scale, 389(10064), 103–118, London.

Sen, A. (1999). "Investing in early childhood: Its role in development", Conference on Breaking the Poverty Cycle. Investing in Early Childhood, Inter-American Development Bank: Washington, DC.

Shah, S. (2013). *Investing in the Youngest: Early Childhood Care and Development in Emergencies.* Woking, UK: Plan International.

Sharma, A., Dorman, M.F. and Kral, A. (2005). "The influence of a sensitive period on central auditory development in children with unilateral and bilateral cochlear implants", *Hearing Research*, 203, 134–143.

Shonkoff, J. (2009). "Investment in early childhood development lays the foundation for a prosperous and sustainable society", In Tremblay, R.E., Boivin, M., Peters, RDev (Eds.). *Encyclopedia on Early Childhood Development* [online]. Montreal, Quebec: Centre of Excellence for Early Childhood Development and strategic Knowledge Cluster on Early Child Development. www.child-encyclopedia.com/documents/ShonkoffANGxp.pdf [16 June 2016]

Shonkoff, J. (2010). "Building a New Biodevelopmental Framework to Guide the Future of Early Childhood Policy", *Child Development*, 81(1), 357–367.

Smith, W.G. (2015). *Early Childhood Education and Peacebuilding in Areas of Ongoing Conflict and Refugee Settlements in Western Uganda: Achievements, Challenges and Lessons Learned.* Nairobi: UNICEF.

Stavropoulou, M. and Jones, N. (2013). *Off the Balance Sheet: The Impact of the Economic Crisis on Girls and Young Women: A Review of the Evidence.* London: Plan International and ODI.

Sunar, D. et al. (2013). "Is early childhood relevant to peacebuilding?", *Journal of Peacebuilding and Development*, 8(3), 81–85.

Suskind, D., Suskind, B. and Lewinter-Suskind, L. (2015). *Thirty Million Words: Building a Child's Brain: Tune In, Talk More, Take Turns.* New York: Penguin Random House.

Teicher, M. (2000). "Wounds that time won't heal: The neurobiology of child abuse", *Cerebrum*, 2(4), 50–67.

Thomas, M. (2005). *Comparing Theories of Child Development* (6th Edition). Belmont, CA: Thomson Learning Inc. and Wadsworth.

Tofail, F. et al. (2008). "Effects of prenatal food and micronutrient supplementation on infant development: A randomized trial from the Maternal and Infant

Nutrition Interventions, Matlab study", *American Journal of Clinical Nutrition*, 87, 704–711.

UNESCO (2000). *The Dakar Framework for Action, Education for All: Meeting Our Collective Commitments.* Dakar: World Education Forum.

UNESCO (2006). *Education for All Global Monitoring Report, 2007: Strong foundations: Early Childhood Care and Education.* Paris: UNESCO.

UNESCO (2007). *Progress for Children: A World Fit for Children, Statistical Review.* Geneva: UNICEF.

UNESCO and UNICEF (2012). *Asia-Pacific End of Decade Notes on Education for All: Early Childhood Care and Education.* Bangkok: UNESCO and UNICEF.

UNFPA (2012). *Marrying Too Young: End Child Marriage.*

UNICEF (ND). www.unicef.org/earlychildhood/index_70959.html

UNICEF (2011). *Promoting Gender Equality through UNICEF-Supported Programming in Young Child Survival and Development.* New York: UNICEF.

UNICEF (2012). *Girls more Vulnerable to Climate Disasters.* New York: UNICEF.

UNICEF (2015). *Evaluation of UNICEF's Peacebuilding, Education, and Advocacy Programme.* New York: UNICEF.

UNICEF and WHO (2012). *Care for Child Development Package*, www.unicef.org/earlychildhood/index_68195.html, last accessed 8 August 2018.

United Nations (ND). UN Sustainable Development Goals, https://sustainabledevelopment.un.org/?menu=1300

Vargas-Baron, E., Janson, U. and Mufel, N. (2009). *Early Childhood Interventions, Special Education and Inclusion: A Focus on Belarus.* Geneva: UNICEF Regional Office for CEE/CIS.

Victora, C. et al. (2008). "Maternal and child under-nutrition: Consequences for adult health and human capital", *The Lancet*, 371(9609), 340–357.

Vygotsky, L. (1981). *Thought and Language.* Cambridge: MIT Press.

Walker, S. et al. (2011). "Inequality in early childhood: Risk and protective factors for early childhood development", *The Lancet*, Child Development 1 series, 378, 1325–1338, London.

Walker, S. and Unterhalter, E. (2007). "The Capability Approach: It's Potential for Work in Education", In Walker, M. and Unterhalter, E. (Eds.) *Amartya Sen's Capability Approach and Social Justice in Education.* New York: Palgrave Macmillan.

WHO (2002). *Gender and Health in Disasters.* Geneva: WHO.

WHO (2011). *World Report on Disability.* Geneva: WHO.

WHO and UNICEF (2012). *Early Childhood: Development and Disability, A discussion paper.* Geneva: WHO.

WHO, UNICEF and World Bank (2018). *Nurturing Care for Early Childhood Development: A Framework for Helping Children Survive and Thrive to Transform Health and Human Potential.* Geneva: WHO.

Witt, S. (1997). "Parental influence on children's socialization to gender roles", *Adolescence*, 32(126), 253–259.

Wisner, B. et al. (2004). *At Risk: Natural Hazards, People's Vulnerability and Disasters.* London and New York: Routledge.

World Bank (ND). www.worldbank.org/en/topic/earlychildhooddevelopment, last accessed 12 June 2016.

World Bank (2010). *Global Monitoring Report 2010: The MDGs after the Crisis.* Washington, DC: World Bank.

Yoshinaga-Itano, C. et al. (2010, October). "Describing the trajectory of language development on the presence of severe profound hearing loss: A closer look at children with cochlear implants versus hearing aids", *Otology and Neurotology*, 31(8), 1266–1274.

Yusra, R. and Shiffman, J. (2016). "Generation of global political priority for early childhood development: the challenges of framing and governance", *The Lancet*, Series Advancing Early Childhood Development: From Science to Scale, 389, 119–124, London.

2 Why Early Childhood Development in emergencies?

There are many additional adversities children and families face when there are humanitarian situations such as increased stress, weakened protective environments, even fewer stimulation and learning opportunities during a critical period of brain development, and fewer nutrition and health services. While children and families face additional challenges in crisis contexts, the Early Childhood Development (ECD) and humanitarian sectors have five key challenges that make raising funds for programming even more difficult. This chapter outlines the specific impacts of emergencies on children and the critical obstacles to financing and scaling such programmes.

Why ECD in emergencies: impact of emergencies on young children

Emergencies, whether they are due to natural hazards (i.e. earthquakes, typhoons) or due to conflict, pose the greatest risks to the youngest—those between 0 and 8 years. This age group, considered the period of early childhood, is the most vulnerable as children depend on a strong protective environment—namely their parents, extended family and community—to ensure their safety, development and well-being. During emergencies, the protective environment or the layers of the child's ecology that support and influence children's development can be weakened and unbalanced, thereby affecting a child's life trajectory. In these situations, children could become separated from their families, injured or displaced from their homes. The risk of death can be 20 times higher than in normal situations (Their World, 2016). Parents may not be able to care for their children in the same way as they may be injured, distressed or too busy searching for food or a safe place to live (Bryce et al., 2008; Victora et al., 2008; Williams et al., 2005). Without this layer of protection that parents and other caregivers (older siblings, step parents, grandparents) provide, young children can face risks to their physical safety and security. They could experience the most dangerous type of stress—toxic stress—and a weak immune system, which can affect the body's ability to ward off disease. They could lose out on proper nutrition, immunisations and regular health check-ups. All of this could increase the chance of death from preventable illness and long-term psychological difficulties (Bryce et al., 2008; Victora et al., 2008). Young children could additionally lose out on the safety of their daily routines, early cognitive stimulation and learning which could impair their brain circuitry and abilities to succeed in school and life (ibid.). Neuroscience research indicates that about 90% of brain growth occurs in the first five years of life and 80% in the first three years of life (Conel, 1959). After the period of early childhood, the brain continues to develop and mature, especially by pruning unused neural connections, but it never grows at the speed it did during early childhood. Without key services, children who may have already been in a vulnerable position prior to an emergency face increasing risks when a disaster strikes (Williams et al., 2005). Developmental damage that can occur without support during emergencies may never be fully reversed (Bryce et al., 2008; Victora et al., 2008).

This chapter explains four key impacts of emergencies on young children: (1) increase in toxic stress, (2) weakened protective and caring environment, (3) missing the critical time for brain development and (4) losing important nutrition and health support.

Increase in toxic stress

Stress, which is often elevated during emergencies, has been found to have significant impacts on young children's brain architecture, chemical makeup and overall development over a lifetime (Shonkoff et al., 2012). This, in turn, increases the chance of death from preventable illnesses and long-term psychological difficulties as well as impaired abilities to succeed in school and later life. Stress includes the internal or external influences that disrupt a person's normal state of well-being by causing emotional distress and physiological changes (Middlebrooks and Audage, 2008). Physiological changes that occur when a person is stressed include increased heart rate, increased blood pressure and a dramatic rise in hormone levels, especially the hormone cortisol (ibid.). Some symptoms of severe distress among children (including those affected by emergencies) include thumb sucking, bed-wetting, clinging to parents, sleep disturbances, loss of appetite, fear of the dark, withdrawal from friends and routines, and regression in behaviour (ISSA, 2010).

One major risk during emergencies is when severe stress becomes "toxic stress" which can cause physiological and chemical changes in the body that may never be fully reversed (Bryce et al., 2008; Victora et al., 2008). There are three types of stress a person can experience: positive, tolerable and toxic (Shonkoff et al., 2012). A protective environment is key to helping children, especially the youngest, bounce back from stressful situations and be resilient. For infants and young children, parents and/or other caretakers are central to a strong protective environment.

Positive stress

Positive stress is brief and mild to moderate in magnitude (ibid.). A person's heart rate and stress hormone (cortisol) levels increase briefly. The presence of a caring and responsive adult provides the protection for children to deal with the challenge and quickly overcome it with no damage to the actual brain (ibid.). Positive stress can also help a child learn and grow if it occurs in a stable and supportive environment.

Tolerable stress

Tolerable stress occurs when a child experiences a situation which is not normal such as a death in the family, serious illness or injury, divorce of his/her parents or an emergency situation. A person's heart rate and cortisol (stress hormone) levels increase to a greater degree. Tolerable stress can be dangerous and could turn toxic. The key to tolerable stress is that it does not occur often and that the child has a strong protective environment of parents and/or caretakers to help him/her return to normal physiological and mental state. If a child has these supports, tolerable stress will not turn toxic.

Toxic stress

When a person experiences severe stress that is prolonged or frequent (such as separation from a family member, death of a family member, displacement and annual floods), has multiple adversities (poverty, abuse, neglect, single-parent household) and does not have a supportive and caring parent or primary caregiver, normal stress can become toxic. The Center on the Developing Child's research indicates that a significant increase in toxic stress, which often happens in humanitarian situations, *even when temporary*, has shown to negatively influence children's brain development, learning and well-being by altering the hormones and chemical makeup in the body (National Scientific Council on the Developing Child, 2007). Toxic stress increases blood pressure, heart rate and hormones such as cortisol (stress hormone) that can turn off the body's normal ability to manage difficult situations. For example, each person has the ability to respond to a threat known as the "fight or flight" ability. In most people, hormone levels may increase when there is severe stress, but they return to normal levels once the person is safe. Toxic stress erodes a person's ability to return their hormones, heart rate and blood pressure to normal levels once there is safety.

Children, in particular, are extremely vulnerable because they depend on parents and/or primary caregivers to help shield the threat. In humanitarian situations, there can be separation, death or injury of primary caregivers, so children's normal shield is absent, weakening their ability to fight off the negative effects of severe stress. When stress becomes toxic, especially during sensitive periods of development, such as early childhood, it can affect brain circuitry and organ and metabolic functioning (Shonkoff et al., 2012). Such disruptions increase the likelihood of developmental delays and health problems such as alcoholism, depression, heart disease and diabetes (National Scientific Council on the Developing Child, 2007, 2010; Shonkoff et al.,

2012). Further, it can impair all aspects of a child's development: cognitive (i.e. learning, executive function, working memory, decision-making), linguistic, socio-emotional (i.e. behaviour, impulse control, mood and self-regulation problems) and physical (i.e. physical and mental illness) (ibid.). In addition to short-term changes in observable behaviour, the chemicals that toxic stress produces can lead to permanent changes in brain structure and function and even be passed on from one generation to the next (Shonkoff et al., 2012).

Some risk factors found in the Adverse Childhood Experiences Study capable of causing toxic stress include child abuse, neglect, parental substance abuse and maternal depression (Felitti et al., 1998). Harvard University's Center on the Developing Child adds poverty, exposure to violence and mental illness to the possible risk factors (National Scientific Council on the Developing Child, 2007).

In humanitarian situations, the difficult circumstances mentioned in the adverse childhood experiences study and those mentioned by Harvard University do not go away, but are compounded by additional risks that can cause more stress. During emergencies, the likelihood of children being separated from their parents, being displaced from their homes, not having enough food to eat, being injured or falling ill is higher, thereby increasing a child's likelihood of experiencing toxic stress (National Scientific Council on the Developing Child, 2010; UNICEF, 2014). Research shows that the more risk factors a child has in his/her life, the more likely he/she is to experience toxic stress (Shonkoff and Bales, 2011; Shonkoff et al., 2012).

The loss of a parent in particular has been highlighted as one of the most stressful events for children. This stress has been linked with future psychiatric disorders such as depression (Boyden and Mann, 2005). Studies from the National Scientific Council on the Developing Child have found that young children who have secure, trusting relationships with parents and other caregivers and their constant support experienced minimal stress hormone activation when scared by a strange or abnormal event and are better able to fight against the damaging effects of stress (Shonkoff, 2009). Contrastingly, young children who did not have secure relationships with parents or other caregivers and inconsistent support had greater activation of the stress response system (Shonkoff, 2009). Myriad scientific research concludes that by helping young children develop strong, supportive and constant relationships with parents or other caregivers as early in life as possible, we can prevent or reverse the negative effects of toxic stress (ibid.). The attachment with a caregiver helps children form resiliency.

Resilience

Science tells us that children are ***resilient*** and support can help them shift the scale from negative outcomes to more positive ones (Center on the Developing Child, 2015). ECD in emergency programmes can support children's resilience and tip that balance when they have a combination of the following types of inputs (which are not exhaustive): a stable, responsive and nurturing caregiver, access to early learning and stimulation through play, availability of nutritious food and immunisations. The more positive inputs a child receives, especially in emergencies, the higher the likelihood that he/she will follow a positive development trajectory. Figure 2.1 illustrates how positive and negative aspects in a child's environment can shift the balance.

Some characteristics of resilient children include bonded/attached to a parent or primary caregiver, requests help when needed, independent, interacts with children and adults, curious, adapts to change, explores and plays actively (Donahue-Colletta, 1992; Duncan and Arnston, 2004). Further, when parental stress levels are not elevated, this can help children keep their stress levels in balance (ibid.). Therefore, supporting parents manage their stress is critical for children's development.

Stress and malnutrition were major factors in children's survival rates in the study mentioned previously in Ethiopia during the 2008 food crisis. The programme taught parents how to provide early stimulation for their young children. This helped parents reduce their own stress, but with the outcomes of increased weight and higher survival rates, it seems to have reduced young children's stress as well (Conticini and Quere, 2011).

Research from humanitarian situations indicates that in most emergencies a majority of children are resilient to the effects of stress and not in need of traditional mental health and psychiatric services (IASC, 2007; Pine et al., 2005). In most circumstances, the incidence of children that might need traditional mental health and psychiatric services is usually around 1–3% (ibid.). A study of the Syrian refugee children revealed an anomaly, indicating that this crisis has significantly increased children's stress levels, more than other humanitarian situations (Their World, 2016). The research found that among Syrian refugee children, 45% of them were found with symptoms of post-traumatic stress disorder (PTSD), which is ten times higher than children surveyed in other humanitarian situations (ibid.). In the Syria crisis context, children have fewer buffers (i.e. parents and primary caregivers to support them). This is mostly because many parents and primary caregivers themselves are suffering from severe stress and struggle to care for their children as they did prior to

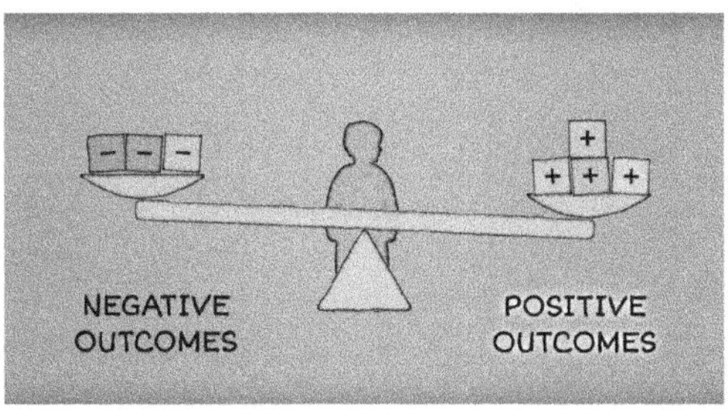

Figure 2.1 The balance of resilience.

the conflict (ibid.). These elements are tipping the scales towards negative outcomes. The Inter-Agency Standing Committee (IASC) in their global Guidelines on Mental Health and Psychosocial Support in Emergency highlight the psychosocial intervention pyramid to help humanitarian staff implement programmes (ibid.). Figure 2.2 shows the intervention pyramid.

At the bottom, which would be relevant to virtually the whole displaced population, are basic services and security which includes the (re)establishment of security and services to address basic physical needs (i.e. food, shelter, water, basic health care). For young children, these services would not just focus on them, but also basic services for their families. Services considered as essential for initial survival such as food distribution, non-food item kits and tents for temporary housing would be included here. The second level of interventions, which would be important for a large group of the displaced population, but a slightly smaller group than those included in the most bottom level, includes community and family support activities. For ECD in emergencies, this could include establishing child friendly spaces, play and recreation activities for children and support services for parents. This level can also include family tracing and reunification (which is especially critical for young children), parenting programmes, formal and non-formal education

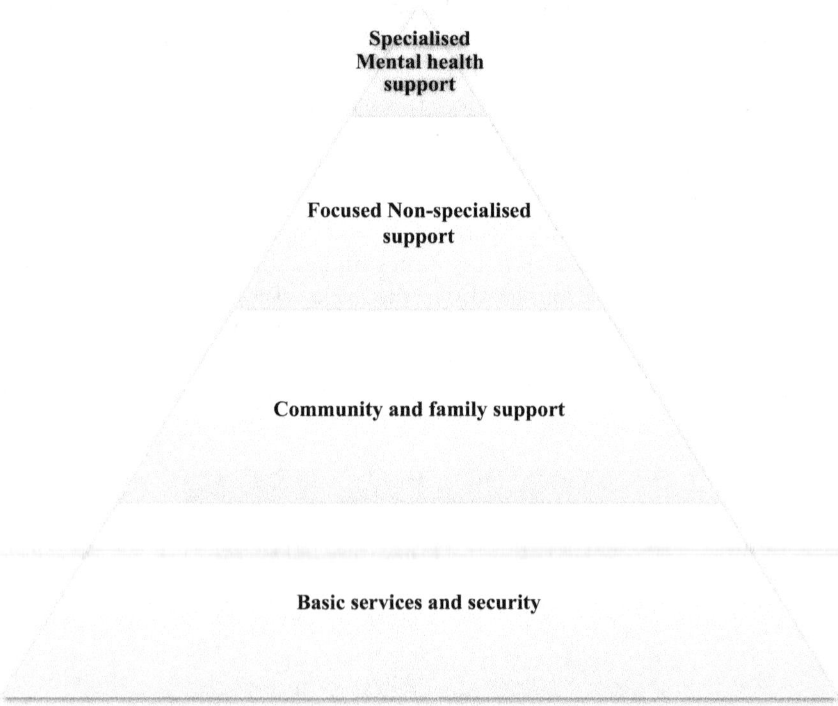

Figure 2.2 Psychosocial pyramid.
Source: Based on Inter-agency Standing Committee (IASC), 2007.

activities, mourning and communal healing ceremonies, livelihoods activities and the activation of social networks (i.e. women's groups, youth clubs). These two bottom layers are able to help the majority of people during a humanitarian crisis. About 10% of the affected population may need focused, non-specialised support, which is the third layer up from the bottom. This includes focused individual, family or group interventions by trained and supervised workers. These workers would not be psychologists or psychiatrists and would not have had the myriad years of training to treat mental illness. Activities in this level would include psychological first aid which is a person to person conversation that helps people express their feelings and emotions with a person who can listen and support them through the healing process. It could be targeted small group support for children that require additional support, but do not need professional mental health services. Approximately 1–3% of most affected populations in a humanitarian crisis would need mental health services that can only be provided by a psychologist or a psychiatrist. This is not the type of work that any agency can do as it requires people with the right professional license and expertise (ibid.).

Normal reactions to stress among children during emergencies

As mentioned previously, everyone experiences stress and some of it is healthy for positive development. The psychosocial intervention pyramid from the IASC provides general guidance for the types of supports that can be given to an affected population. Most emergency affected children would only need level 1 or level 2 support as indicated on the bottom two levels of the psychosocial intervention pyramid. Each child reacts differently to stressors in his/her life in humanitarian situations. This all depends on the child's past experiences and adversities such as poverty, abuse, exploitation, family violence, neglect, etc. (Donahue-Colletta, 1992; Duncan and Arnston, 2004; Save the Children, 1995, 2013). Children who have experienced long-term stress may also react and express themselves differently than children who have been in safe and nurturing environments (ibid.). Many children will temporarily regress in their own development (ibid.). A summary of normal reactions of children of different ages to stress is given below (ibid.).

1 *Babies and Toddlers: 0 to 2 years*

   Babies and toddlers depend on their family and parents for a sense of safety and security (Donahue-Colletta, 1992; Duncan and Arnston, 2004; Save the Children, 1995, 2013). They need emotional nurturing, through loving and reassuring interactions, and help with coping in an ongoing and consistent way; this is how babies and toddlers develop and grow. During their early months and years, children are very sensitive and are easily affected by stress affecting their parents or main caregivers. Separation from their parents or caregiver, sharp noise, parental distress or lack of routine can cause distress in a young child. Routine helps young children feel safe and secure.

Some common normal reactions of babies and toddlers (0 to 2 years) to stress may include:

- Increased clinginess to parents and/or primary caregivers and unusually high levels of distress when separated from their parents or primary caregiver.
- Changes in sleep patterns.
- Cry more or are more irritable.
- Afraid of things that did not frighten them before.
- Poor concentration or hyperactivity.
- Avoid eye contact.
- Loss of playful and engaging smiles and "cooing" behaviour.
- Loss of appetite or desire to eat.
- Regression in gross motor skills such as sitting, crawling or walking.
- Reduced exploration and play.
- More sensitive to how others react.

2 *Children: two to five years*

Between two and five years, children can speak, but they may not yet be able to use words to fully describe how they feel. Their distress will show through changes in behaviour and functioning. Pre-school age children still need the assistance of parents and caregivers to feel safe, understand the experience and recover. A child's response to a distressing or frightening experience will depend on their age, stage of development and personality, as well as the impact of the crisis on their parents, primary caregivers or significant others. A child may react based on his/her parents' reactions. Children may not react in the way caregivers/parents expect.

Children's responses to high stress can vary, but could include the following:

- New or increased clingy behaviour such as following the parent around the house.
- Regression with basic skills like sleeping, eating, going to the toilet, bed-wetting or paying attention.
- Mood changes—the child might not seem to enjoy daily routines or activities they used to like or may seem more inactive and withdrawn.
- Changed behaviour—some children might be more aggressive to parents or playmates.
- Increased fear—for example, the child may be more agitated or startle easily, develop new fears, have more nightmares, talk about the frightening event more or have it in their play or drawings.
- More physical complaints for which no cause can be found such as stomach ache or headache, being tired and other problems.
- Blaming themselves—small children are likely to misunderstand the events of the trauma and somehow think it was their fault.

3 *Children: five and eight years*

Children in this age group begin to understand what has happened in an emergency better and may be able to describe their emotions better, but will still follow the lead of their parents. If the parents are calm, the child will behave accordingly. Children still need the safety and security of their parents and families.

- Physical reactions—children could bite their nails, be aggressive with other children or caregivers, regress in their behaviour, seek attention, be clingy to their caregiver or bully other children. Some children change their eating habits, have headaches or stomach aches.
- Sleep problems—children may not want to go to bed at night or have difficulties falling asleep, staying asleep. Some children might experience nightmares.
- Fear of being separated from their parents or caregivers, changes in their relationships with siblings such as becoming more competitive or aggressive.
- Needing to express their experience through drawing, acting out some of what they experienced through pretend play.
- Behavioural problems at school, not wanting to go, or drop in academic performance.
- Withdrawal—for example, the child may not want to discuss their thoughts or feelings in case it upsets their parents or caregivers. They may not want to play with other children.
- Unable to concentrate.

While each child will react differently to stress they experience during an emergency situation, a key buffer to help them through their experience is a strong protective and caring environment.

Weakening of a caring and protective environment

Emergencies, whether they are due to natural hazards such as earthquakes, floods, landslides, or due to conflict, can weaken or break down children's protective environment through separation or death of family and friends, severe injury, short or prolonged displacement, loss of income or psychological distress (Attanayake et al., 2009; Barbarin et al., 2001). Parents or primary caregivers may not be able to care for their children in the same way as before the emergency as they may themselves be injured, distressed or too busy searching for food or a safe place to live (Evans, 2006). The impact of emergencies on parents can expose children to emotional neglect, violence of conflict within the home (Barbarin et al., 2001; Betancourt, 2015). Young children could therefore lose out on the safety and security of their daily routines, early stimulation and nurturing care, learning, nutrition, immunisations and other supports that are essential for their healthy development and well-being.

There is evidence that even in utero, maternal stress and depression can affect how a child develops (Thabet et al., 2009). Stress that pregnant women may experience has been associated with childhood under-nutrition, stunting, cognitive and socio-emotional development (Feldman et al., 2013; Thabet et al., 2009). It is unclear how maternal stress affects a child's development while he/she is still in the womb. However, there is some evidence pointing to a mother's elevated levels of stress hormones (cortisol) crossing the placenta to the baby and causing similar effects as tolerable or toxic stress (Van den Bergh et al., 2005). Further, there are also links between post-natal stress and anxiety of mothers and their abilities to provide appropriate care for their children and the ability of the child to form a secure attachment (Field, 2010; McMahon et al., 2006). Research also points to exposure to violence affecting marital tension, discipline styles being harsher than normal which, in turn, can affect a child's own anxiety and behaviours in a negative manner (Betancourt, 2015; Dybdahl, 2001). Without a caring and protective environment with stable parents/caregivers, children who may have already been in a vulnerable position prior to an emergency face increasing risks when a disaster strikes (Williams et al., 2005).

Strong parents and primary caregivers with the knowledge and capabilities of protecting, caring for and ensuring their children's optimal development are key to establishing a strong protective and caring environment. This idea is underpinned by Bronfenbrenner's ecological systems theory and Vygotsky's belief of a strong influence from the external environment on children's development (Bronfenbrenner, 1979; Vygotsky, 1978). Parents can physically protect and care for children and provide the nurturing and emotional support children need to survive and grow (Masten and Monn, 2015; Shonkoff, 2009, Shonkoff and Levitt, 2010; Shonkoff et al., 2012). Child protection is defined as the "prevention of and response to abuse, neglect, exploitation and violence against children" (Child Protection Working Group, 2012). According to "UN Convention on the Child's Right," children need special protection until they have reached a level of physical, mental and emotional maturity to take on the duties and responsibilities of an adult (UN CRC). Care of a child goes beyond simply protecting them from harm and exploitation. Care is an interactive process between the child and the parent/caregiver. This interaction determines the quality of the care the child receives and the ways in which a child can take in the stimulation it receives; this all ultimately affects a child's development (Evans, 2006). When children receive appropriate care from an adult, with whom they have a safe and secure attachment, children can make remarkable gains in physical and motor, social and emotional, linguistic and cognitive development (Bowlby, 1988; Evans, 2006). Having at least one strong relationship or attachment to a caring adult is critical to his/her survival, growth and development (Evans, 2006). Harvard University has developed a theory of change which focuses on strengthening adult capabilities to improve children's outcomes (Harvard University, 2013). The theory of change looks at ways to strengthen the capabilities of parents and other adult community members because if these are strong, they can support the healthy and optimal development of children (ibid.).

Parenting programmes are defined as interventions or services aimed at improving parents' knowledge, attitudes, behaviours and practices so they can more positively interact with their children and promote their optimal development (Britto et al., 2016). These programmes can be implemented through group-based sessions where 20–30 people come together or through individual home visits or short counselling sessions at health facilities (ibid.). Evidence from Bangladesh and Brazil points to a combination of group sessions and individual home visits or support to have the best results on children and parents (ibid.). However, group programmes in Bangladesh and Uganda have revealed improved maternal health and increased children's cognitive and linguistic capabilities (ibid.).

Parenting education in numerous evaluations in developing countries, including Uganda, Bangladesh and Pakistan, has shown positive results on parents' knowledge and skills and children's development outcomes in fragile contexts (Aboud, 2007; Britto et al., 2016; Singla et al., 2015; Yousafzai et al., 2014). A randomised control trial of institutionalised Romanian children who remained in institutions when compared with those who were moved to responsive and caring foster care before age 2 revealed how early interventions were able to reverse the negative effects of extreme neglect and lack of a safe and secure protective environment and early stimulation (Black et al., 2016; Nelson et al., 2007). At a 54-month follow-up assessment, the children in foster care were more likely to form safe and secure attachments to their foster families, had greater protection from stressors in their environment, and had greater cognitive stimulation. This, in turn, led to more children having increased IQs and brain activities in comparison to children who remained in institutional care (ibid.).

One of the most thoroughly researched parent programmes is the Nurse-Family Partnership (NFP) in the United States. This programme began in 1977 at three sites and included 2,000 families. An experimental design was used with a control and treatment group. The programme included parenting education and support prior to their baby's birth and during its first year of life. Longitudinal follow-ups of the participating mothers and children showed 56% fewer arrests and 81% fewer convictions among the children and families who participated in the programme than among the control group (Evans, 2006).

Care and protection of young children are often thought of as a mother's job. However, fathers and other caregivers are equally critical in their children's protection, care and development. While more research investigating the impact of fathers' active involvement in children's care and development is needed, especially in emergencies, a number of studies point to positive outcomes on children's development and mothers' stress levels (Britto et al., 2016). A study of fathers in South Africa estimated that over 50% of fathers did not have daily contact with their children (Evans, 2006). This trend is common in many countries; however, there is also research that the active involvement of fathers is important for their child's development (Spielberger et al., 2015). One study found that fathers' active involvement reduced mothers' stress levels which, in turn, created a more positive family environment where children can better flourish (Nomaguchi et al., 2012). Parents who are unable to care for their children due to various stressors in their lives also need support from extended family members, community and government (Evans, 2006). Therefore, in addition to parents, other relatives, older siblings and community members are also important for children's protective environment, especially as in many cultures the concept of family extends beyond biological parents and includes multi-generational and multi-family households.

Large research gaps, especially in humanitarian contexts, remain around parenting programmes and ECD activities aimed to strengthen children's protective environment. For large-scale refugee crises where funding is likely to be limited, the right combination of approach (home visits, group sessions, counselling at health centres), number of sessions (10, 15, 20) and timing of sessions (weekly, fortnightly, monthly) is critical to understand. Furthermore, these same issues need to be better understood in non-emergency contexts as well so that countries can affordably take programmes to scale. The current evidence points to services focused on strengthening children's protective environment and particularly parents' capabilities as critical elements for children, especially in humanitarian situations.

Lose early stimulation and learning opportunities

As mentioned previously, early childhood is a critical "sensitive" period for brain development. It is the period where the brain grows the most and when the foundation for future learning and development is established. The lack of early stimulation and learning can have tremendous influence on a brain's initial development and architecture, more so than insufficient food as revealed in multiple studies (Grantham-McGregor et al., 1991; Yousafzai et al., 2014). Early stimulation refers to cognitive stimulation through exploration and play and the "extent that the environment provides physical stimulation through sensory input (e.g. visual, auditory, tactile), as well as emotional stimulation provided through an affectionate caregiver-child bond" (WHO, 2016). The environment in which a child grows shapes his/her brain and creates the foundation for future learning and capacities. Deficiencies in early stimulation and learning during the earliest years of a child's life can delay their cognitive, linguistic, socio-emotional and physical development (Heckman, 2006). These delays can affect returns on financial investment (ibid.).

Perry and Pollard (1997), in their landmark research of children with severe sensory deprivation and neglect, showed significant differences in their brains at age 3 with those normally developing at the same age (Perry and Pollard, 1997). When compared, the children that experienced severe sensory deprivation and neglect such as lack of linguistic stimulation, physical contact and interaction with others had smaller brains in terms of size, but also lower brain density, indicating fewer neural connections (ibid.).

Humanitarian situations can mirror this type of neglect and deprivation as parents may not be able to or may not understand the importance of talking to their child, hugging, playing, looking and smiling at them. They may also be distressed or injured and unable to support their children. Emergencies increase the likelihood of this type of brain development if support is not provided. These are the ways children begin learning about the world (Arnold, 2004).

Additionally, a randomised trial conducted in Bangladesh that looked at the impact of psychosocial stimulation and food supplementation of severely malnourished children showed greater effects of psychosocial stimulation (Nahar et al., 2012). Children that received psychosocial stimulation had higher cognitive skills and higher weight for age scores in comparison to those that received food supplementation, but no stimulation (ibid.).

Lose important nutrition and health services

Malnutrition and preventable diseases are major threats to young children's lives during disaster situations when they can be displaced, live in unsanitary conditions and not able to access healthy food regularly. The mortality rate for children below the age of five in humanitarian situations is considerably higher than for other age groups. Proper nutrition and health support the development of a child's brain. Studies in emergency and non-emergency contexts have found that malnutrition in the first five years of life has significant long-lasting negative effects on cognitive, physical, social and emotional development. Malnourished children, when compared with well-nourished ones, were more likely to start school late, concentrate less in school and have lower academic outcomes (Sanchez, 2009). A study conducted by the University of Sussex in Zimbabwe explored the impacts of pre-school malnutrition on subsequent human capital formation in Zimbabwe. The study found that even temporary malnutrition and lack of health services during drought and conflict times resulted in lower development indicators including lower height and weight and fewer years of schooling. The researchers estimated a loss of lifetime earnings of around 14%. Results from the longitudinal data of the multi-country Young Lives survey, led by the University of Oxford, showed a strong positive association between stunted height during the first two years of life and cognitive achievement four years later (Sanchez, 2009). Another study from the *Lancet* provides evidence from multiple countries of the effects of maternal and child under-nutrition on adult health and reduced economic productivity (Victora et al., 2008).

While nutrition and health support for young children can have significant benefits, this in combination with early stimulation can have an even greater effect. A landmark study of Jamaican stunted malnourished children found evidence to support the combination of early stimulation and nutritional supplementation (Grantham-McGregor et al., 1991). In this study, the researchers had five groups of children they followed over time. Two groups of children did not receive any intervention as they were either healthy, normally developing children or assigned to a control group. One intervention group received nutritional supplements only, another received early stimulation only and a third received both early stimulation and nutritional supplements. The healthy children had the best child development outcomes, but after them were the children who had both the early stimulation and nutritional supplements, followed by the children who had only early stimulation. The children with the lowest development scores were those with nutritional supplementation only and those that received no support (the control group). This indicates a few things: first, ECD interventions need to start before a child is born so that they can develop normally. For malnourished and stunted children, a combination of early stimulation and nutritional supplements is important to help them get close to a normal development trajectory. However, this research found that no interventions helped children reach the same development level as those that were never stunted and malnourished in the first place (ibid.). Evidence from Ethiopia during the 2008 food crisis shows that children's weight and survival rates increased when nutrition and health services were provided with early stimulation and parenting education (Conticini and Quere, 2011). They found that the combination helped children recover faster from acute malnutrition than nutrition support alone (ibid.). Additional research from Bangladesh, Pakistan and other countries has also found that children who receive nutritional supplements along with early stimulation and learning that promotes brain development have higher survival rates, healed faster and returned to a more normal development trajectory compared with those who did not receive nutritional supplements (ibid., Gowani et al, 2014; Hamdani et al., 2006; Nahar et al., 2009, 2012; Yousafzai et al., 2014).

Quality programming on ECD in emergencies can address challenges young children face and positively influence communities' resilience to future calamities. However, it is often not prioritised. The next section explores the five key obstacles and challenges for ECD.

ECD not prioritised: obstacles and challenges

The field of ECD has made tremendous leaps through rigorous research, an increase in actors interested in this area of work at country and global levels and an increase in financial resources. During an interview, Anthony Lake, UNICEF's former Executive Director said "…reaching the children affected by emergencies—and providing them with the opportunity to learn—serves both humanitarian needs and development goals. In fact, it is an area where humanitarian and development interests are almost perfectly aligned" (Lake, 2015). He along with other senior officials of large humanitarian and development agencies are beginning to champion the cause of education and ECD in emergencies. However, there remains some key obstacles and challenges for this field to get to the next level of global attention and commitment, especially in humanitarian contexts (Black et al., 2016; Britto et al., 2016; Yusra and Shiffman, 2016). These obstacles and challenges are (1) varying definitions of ECD, (2) gaps in knowledge, especially around the effectiveness of ECD in emergencies, (3) the acceptance of Maslow's Hierarchy of Needs by the humanitarian community, (4) few evidence-based ECD in emergency programmatic models, and (5) few humanitarian response plans that include ECD and (6) governance challenges (ibid.).

Varying definitions

One of the key obstacles and challenges to the field of ECD is the lack of understanding and varying definitions of what it is, especially among humanitarians. Many people see ECD as part of education and therefore not a priority, especially in humanitarian situations. However, as mentioned earlier, ECD is multi-sectoral support for children from conception to eight years. While the general types of activities for ECD in emergencies are similar to non-emergency situations, the objectives and manner of implementation may be different. Where objectives of working in non-emergency contexts focus on longer term government systems change, policies and support, ECD in emergency programming focuses on the immediate and unique needs of children in disaster situations. Sometimes this can last three to six months if it is a small-scale landslide, flooding, earthquake or last over a generation in the case of chronic crisis and war. Short-term ECD in emergency programmes' objectives may focus on saving lives through nutritious food, water, health care and shelter, creating an environment where children can feel a sense of normality, where they can start reducing their levels of distress and where they can continue normal development and learning. So the knowledge about ECD is critical to understanding how it can be implemented in a short-term or long-term emergency context. Even when the focus is on short-term goals, ECD in emergencies can begin to tackle longer term aspects of children's development that will help them reach their full potential.

In practice, programming for young children is not always labelled "ECD in Emergencies" and sometimes goes under different names such as early childhood education (ECE), pre-school education, Early Childhood Care and Development (ECCD), child friendly spaces, and health and nutrition for young children (Kamel, 2006). ECD in emergencies activities can be implemented in temporary classrooms, child friendly spaces, community buildings, under a tree, in nutrition centres, at a health post, while a mother is waiting in line for food distribution or in a child's home or shelter—in fact in any safe space where services are provided. Various sectors and government departments can implement these activities. During the initial stages of a disaster, it may not be practical to implement all aspects of support young children need. Instead, various sectors can implement different aspects of what is a comprehensive approach for young children in emergencies over a period of time.

Gaps in understanding the science of ECD in emergencies

A second key obstacle for ECD in emergencies is the gap among humanitarian donors and decision makers about the science and evidence for ECD. Empirical evidence of the benefits of ECD in humanitarian situations is virtually non-existent; however, the evidence from non-humanitarian contexts of extreme poverty and multiple adversities provides a strong understanding of the science behind the importance of investing in children's early years. Evidence now points to the critical importance of nutrition and cognitive stimulation, learning opportunities through play and supporting parents and primary caregivers.

In emergencies, where ECD interventions exist, they tend to be confined to a particular sector such as education (i.e. pre-school education), health and nutrition (child survival, malnutrition, maternal health) or child protection/ social services (abuse, exploitation, neglect) rather than working synergistically to obtain the best outcomes for children (ibid.). Science now provides evidence for the inter-relatedness of the various sectors and greater positive outcomes of programmes that have a multi-sectoral lens rather than through one sector (Shonkoff and Levitt, 2010). Humanitarian actors and donors, for example, do not know that adding parent and early stimulation support to an emergency health programme can increase the likelihood a baby will not only survive but also thrive in these circumstances. Further, these activities are relatively inexpensive. By understanding the science and making small modifications in programmes designed and funded in emergencies, the outcomes for children and families could be greater.

Acceptance of Maslow's Hierarchy of Needs

There is also limited understanding of ECD and ECD in emergencies because of the overwhelming acceptance among humanitarian and development workers, including donor agencies, of Abraham Maslow's Hierarchy of Needs (Maslow, 1943). In fact, there is an acceptance of Maslow's theory in other sectors as well (Pearson and Podeschi, 1997; Wahba and Bridwell, 1976). Maslow's Hierarchy of Needs has underpinned humanitarian work and other sectors for decades (Maslow, 1943; Sinclair, 2002; Williamson and Robinson, 2006). Maslow identified a pyramid (re-drawn in Figure 2.3) that outlines five important aspects of a person's life, broadly divided into basic and growth needs. Basic needs include the bottom two levels of Maslow's pyramid: physiological and safety/security. Physiological needs include the need for food and water, health care for survival, whereas safety and security needs include shelter, basic clothing, a safe and nonthreatening environment free from violence, abuse, neglect (Henniger, 2009). Only once these

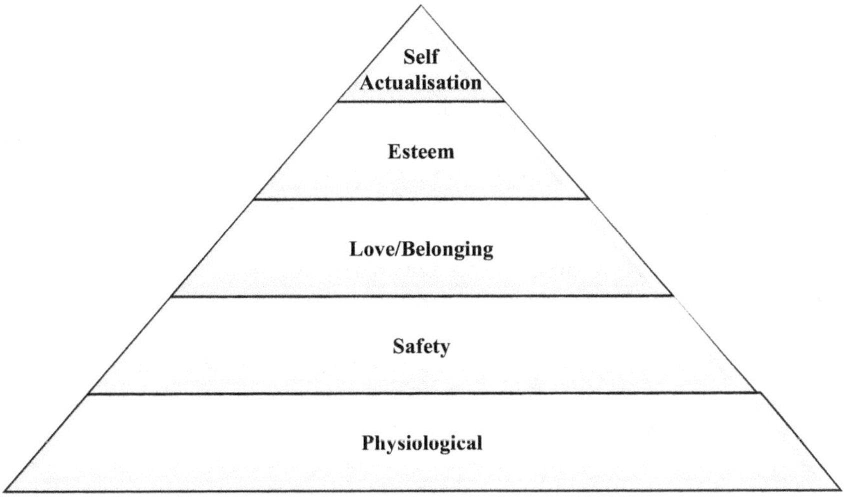

Figure 2.3 Maslow's Hierarchy of Needs.
Source: Based on Maslow, A. H., 1954.

needs are met, Maslow believed a person would require growth needs that include love and belonging (feeling loved, having friends, being part of a group), self-esteem and finally self-actualisation. A person that reaches self-actualisation would be able to reach his/her potential (ibid.).

While Maslow does not explicitly say that education and early learning are not basic needs, he does say that physiological and safety and security needs must be met first before an individual can meet his/her other needs (Henniger, 2009; Maslow, 1943). Hagerty (1999) places primary, secondary and tertiary education enrolment within the self-actualisation area based on the idea that higher education, in particular, encourages creativity and knowledge-generation. While Hagerty also feels that some aspects of primary education could meet basic needs, it does not fit Maslow's categories. Many humanitarians also do not consider education and early learning as life-saving and part of the bottom parts of Maslow's pyramid of needs. Rather, for many humanitarian workers, education would be one of the last things a person needs and something that can wait.

The whole humanitarian field has been built on the idea of prioritising physical and life-saving needs such as food, health and shelter over what are considered not life-saving such as education (Sinclair, 2002). In 1997, the Sphere humanitarian standards were launched, solidifying this perspective of the importance of physical needs over other needs. Education and early learning were not a part of the Sphere humanitarian standards. The Inter-Agency Network for Education in Emergencies (INEE) was thus set up in 2003 to counteract this approach to humanitarian work and Maslow's Hierarchy of Needs framework.

While the practitioners working on education in emergencies disagreed with Maslow's theory, there were those in other fields who were already critiquing his work (Buchanan and Huczynski, 1985; Davis and Filley, 1963; Dye et al., 2005; Hitt et al., 2005). First, while many fields widely accept the "Hierarchy of Needs," there is the lack of empirical evidence (Wahba and Bridwell, 1976). Wahba and Bridwell reviewed over a dozen research studies and found only partial support for the concept of the need hierarchy (Wahba and Bridwell, 1976). While some researchers and academics agree with categorising human needs, they do not necessarily believe they should be set up in a hierarchy as Maslow indicates in his framework (ibid.).

However, practical experience and recent research capturing voices of affected communities show that people can manage to strive for the higher levels even when their lower level needs are only partly fulfilled (Plan International, 2010; Save the Children, 2015). These affected communities want education and early learning; the majority of these studies found that education was either prioritised above other services or at same level as other services (ibid.). Save the Children listened to 8,749 emergency affected children from 17 different types of humanitarian situations; 99% of them highlighted education as a priority (Save the Children, 2015). Save the Children in South Sudan found that 52% of the respondents for the study thought education should be provided immediately after the onset of an emergency because it provides psychosocial support for children, protects them from recruitment and other dangers during conflict and increases their likelihood of a successful future (Save the Children, 2015). Rather than seeing the various sectors as separate, the majority of families surveyed in South Sudan wanted all services at the same time (Save the Children, 2015). In South Sudan, when affected children and communities were asked to rank the importance of various social services including education, health, water, food, shelter and play, 28% of children and 25% of community members ranked education as their top priority; this was a larger per cent than the other options provided (Save the Children, 2015). Additionally, in South Sudan, an affected man said, "The family is improved when there is everything together—education, health, water, food and the others" (Save the Children, 2015, 5). A displaced father in Mingkaman, Lakes state (who is originally from Jonglei state) said, "The only thing we want is for our children to learn. I am not educated and this makes me vulnerable. We do not want them to be vulnerable like us" (Save the Children, 2015, 24). Further, a 15-year-old displaced South Sudanese girl said, "... education is more important than food. If you are educated, you can get your own food" (Save the Children, 2015, 12).

New research is contradicting the traditional approach to humanitarian work and Maslow's Hierarchy of Needs. Despite all of this, many non-educationalists are still not convinced about the importance of education and early learning immediately following an emergency. The impact of Maslow's Hierarchy of Needs on the humanitarian field is deep rooted and has resulted in significantly less funding going to education and early learning services.

Many humanitarian training programmes and funding decisions are sometimes unconsciously based on Maslow's Hierarchy of Needs, which is one of the main reasons why education receives such little funding in relation to other sectors, such as food, water and sanitation and health, in humanitarian crisis (Williamson and Robinson, 2006). Further, when education is funded, the majority of investment goes to primary education and little to early-years support when evidence indicates greater rates of return (Carneiro and Heckman, 2003; Heckman, 2006) and secondary education (as this is seen as a luxury). Slowly additional funding is coming to education and early learning as indicated earlier with the establishment of the "Education Cannot Wait" global fund for education in emergencies. A similar global platform that encompasses all aspects of ECD and priorities multi-sectoral support for the youngest children is still a huge gap.

Few evidence-based ECD in emergency programmatic models

There are a few evidence-based emergency programmatic models for ECD work in humanitarian contexts. The Global Consultative Group on Early Childhood Care and Development (www.ecdgroup.com) created the Four Cornerstones framework for non-emergency contexts (CG, accessed 22 May 2016). The Four Cornerstones look at four areas: start at the beginning (which looks at pre-natal to age 2 and support for parents), provide new opportunities for discovery and learning (which focuses on pre-school aged children three to five years), make schools ready for children (which focuses on the transition of children from early childhood and pre-school types of activities to formal primary school) and address the development of policies on early childhood (which emphasises change at a national policy level that can support young children) (ibid.). This framework is being used by many agencies in many countries to guide the design and implementation of programmes, but the adaptability of these Four Cornerstones in their entirety has not been tested in a humanitarian context when projects are often short term and have different aims. Agencies such as Plan International, UNICEF, Save the Children, International Rescue Committee and others are implementing ECD in emergency work and testing different models. Some global programming guidance has been published (Plan International, 2013; Plan International and UNICEF, 2016a, 2016b; UNICEF, 2014; UNICEF and WHO, ND). However, these models are still being tested. This book is focused on the adaptation of the Community-Led Action for Children, a model based on the Four Cornerstones. It presents one evidence-based ECD in emergency programmatic model.

Limited financial and political investment in ECD

Another major challenge for ECD, particularly in emergencies, is the limited investment by donors and governments. Education and Child Protection, two sectors that often implement ECD programmes, are two of the least funded in humanitarian situations (Brannelly et al., 2009; Save the Children, 2008; Turrent and Oketch, 2009). UNESCO's Global Education Monitoring (GEM) report for 2017 found that overall aid for education, including for emergencies, peaked at 2010, but has since then stagnated (UNESCO, 2017). Pre-school education is considered part of basic education and support to this area has actually decreased while assistance for secondary education has increased (ibid.).

Limited understanding of the evidence base and lack of sufficient quantitative data in humanitarian contexts have resulted in under-investment by humanitarian and non-humanitarian funding mechanisms, the United Nations (UN) and international non-governmental organisations (NGOs) (Arnold, 2004). Few major international donors prioritise ECD and most allocate less than 2% of their overall development assistance to pre-primary education (ibid). For example, the US Agency for International Development (USAID), one of the largest donors for education globally, has three main goals in its global education strategy (USAID, 2011). The first is about early grade reading. The second is about employment of youth and the third is focused on access to basic primary education in conflict and fragile states (ibid.). Within these three goals, USAID usually does not fund ECD or pre-school education. At times as part of goal 1 of early grade reading, some activities related to emergent literacy that happen between three and five years of age can be included.

The Global Partnership for Education (GPE), another large global fund for education that supports select governments create and implement comprehensive policies for education, includes ECE as part of its overall strategic plan for 2016–2020 (GPE, 2016). However, GPE is struggling to achieve its goals for pre-primary education because it needs more technical guidance and expertise and because many governments they support are not requesting funds for ECD. Further, many of the governments that GPE supports are in conflict-affected fragile contexts where there are refugee situations. However, in these countries as well, GPE is struggling to convince governments to have policies and goals for early learning. In most countries, less than 1% of the total education budget is allocated to ECD. In many African countries, allocation for ECD in Ministry of Education budgets is less than 0.01% (Arnold, 2004).

Education Cannot Wait (ECW), another large fund specifically established to disburse funds for education in emergencies (acute and longer term refugee crises), has language around early learning within its strategic plan. However, ECW also has not funded many early learning in emergency programmes. When I spoke with a member of the ECW board that makes funding decisions, he said that they have not received that many requests for pre-school education from countries experiencing humanitarian crises.

Each crisis has a regional- and/or country-level humanitarian response plan. Humanitarian response plans outline the priority areas for financing, so the inclusion or exclusion of ECD in this can make a critical difference in whether it gets funded by many bi-lateral and multilateral funding agencies (Their World, 2016). The sectors included in most humanitarian response plans are education, protection, shelter, food, health, nutrition, non-food items, water and sanitation, agriculture, economic recovery and infrastructure and coordination (ibid.). The UN Office for the Coordination of Humanitarian Affairs (OCHA) keeps track of humanitarian financing and humanitarian response plans. Out of 38 active response plans identified in 2016 on the OCHA Financial Tracking Services website, only 10 made any mention of ECD, ECE or similar ECD terminology (ibid.), which means that over 60% of active humanitarian response plans did not include comprehensive ECD services or ECE (Their World, 2016). Most of the information with regard to early learning or multi-sectoral ECD was included in education and child protection sector plans, whereas health and nutrition services for children from birth to three years were most often mentioned in health and nutrition sector plans. Two recent humanitarian situations that have ECD mentioned in its humanitarian response plans include the Syria refugee response plan and Ethiopia as part of the South Sudan regional refugee response plan (ibid.). Until there is more demand from country and regional levels for ECD in emergencies, the cycle of less demand, and less disbursement from major donors, is expected to continue.

The result of low investment in the earliest years has been documented in several research studies; however, this has often not reached the ears of donors and governments that make funding decisions. In one study, the World Bank estimated that in West African nations, the funds saved by reducing grade repetition would be sufficient enough to pay for quality parenting education and pre-school programmes for young children in each nation (Jaramillo and Mingat, 2003). Investments in young children can also help older siblings and mothers who may have been caring for children (Lokshin et al., 2000). In many countries while boys are able to continue with their education, girls often drop out due to childcare or household duties, or family's financial situation which necessitates that children work. Young children in ECD programmes can take away one of the barriers girls face in continuing their education as it can change perceptions on the importance of girls' education by providing them access early on in life. It can also ensure that an older girl that may previously had to care for younger siblings can go to school while her younger siblings are cared for in ECD programmes. Likewise, mothers who have a safe and nurturing place for their young children can work and support the economic health of the family (ibid.). Interviews I conducted with refugee mothers from Ivory Coast who crossed the border into Liberia told me that the ECD in emergency programmes allowed them to return to their farms in Ivory Coast to get food for their families and keep their harvest growing.

Governance challenges

Finally, in order to get to scale, whether in a refugee or natural disaster context or at a country level in non-emergencies, there has to be government commitment and policies that support ECD. Even in countries where the other pieces of the ECD puzzle are present, the challenge of governance, which refers to coordination, accountability and ownership, is often the hardest to achieve, especially during emergencies (Black et al., 2016; Richter et al., 2016; Yusra and Shiffman, 2016). Because ECD is multi-sectoral, it leads to many governance challenges (ibid.). The first part of the governance challenge is to create a policy or law that supports the holistic needs of children. Which department should own and coordinate other ministries and departments to create policies and laws? Even in countries and contexts where multiple government ministries and/or departments understand the importance of ECD, they may feel that it does not fall under their specific mandate. Most Education ministries start support for children at the age of five when they begin first grade or kindergarten, while others start support at the age of three. The majority of Education ministries do not extend their mandate to support 0–3 age group or pregnant women, other critical aspects of ECD. Ministries of Health focus solely on health aspects and may include the whole ECD range of conception to eight years, but they would only provide immunisations, check-ups and other health specific services. Some countries have Ministries of Women, Children and Social Protection or something similar that might be willing to lead an effort to develop a policy, but do they have the convening power to bring high-level representatives from other ministries and departments together? Once policies are established, how will these be implemented? What workforce will be used for the implementation of these policies and how will they be financed?

In Cote d'Ivoire, mid-level staff at the Ministry of Planning were initially leading an effort to establish a national ECD policy. They initially established an inter-ministerial committee focused on ECD. During this time, Prime Minister Amadou Gon Coulibaly had spoken at the World Bank and affirmed his commitment to supporting the youngest children, especially as a way to combat stunting (World Bank, 2017). He committed to reducing childhood stunting from its 2012 level of nearly 30% to 20% by 2020 (World Bank, 2017). So while there was some high-level political support, the inter-ministerial ECD committee, led by the Ministry of Planning, was not formally recognised at higher political levels and was not led by decision makers in the government. Bernard Van Leer Foundation, Jacobs Foundation and others supported the Ministry of Planning to strengthen this inter-ministerial coordinating body, but as the members are not decision makers and not recognised at higher political levels, this group has stagnated. It has not been able to get a national-level ECD policy. Due to the Prime Minister's interest in reducing stunting, another possibility was to have a national ECD policy led by the National Nutrition Council (NNC), which was established as a separate government department that is part of and reports directly to the Prime Minister's office. While the NNC's head is interested in leading a national effort for ECD, she does not have the staffing or financial resources. The newly established Global Early Childhood Development Action Network (ECDAN) (www.ecdan.org) has members working with government officials in the Cote d'Ivoire government to find the right home for ECD. There are now discussions for the Ministry of Gender, Women and Social Protection to take the lead in championing ECD and coordinating the Ministry of Health, Ministry of Education, the NNC, the Ministry of Planning, Finance and others. This process has been going on for years and there is still no resolution. The case of Cote d'Ivoire illustrates the myriad complications and politics involved in developing a national ECD policy. A lot of resources and time need to go into a process before something can be set up.

Some countries have made great steps and established national-level ECD policies that address the multi-sectoral needs of young children. In Uganda, the Ministry of Gender, Labour and Social Development is taking the lead and owns the National Integrated ECD policy that was adopted in 2016 (Uganda Government, 2016). They brought together other ministries in Uganda, including Education, Health and Finance, to develop the policy, and coordinate implementation. However, the Ugandan government does not yet have the financing or total buy in from all relevant ministries and is struggling to implement this policy. So, it is stagnating and dependent on outside donors, the UN and international non-governmental organisations (INGOs) to support.

India's National Early Childhood Care and Education (ECCE) policy, which was adopted in 2013, is owned and led by the Ministry of Women and Child Development (India Government, 2013). ECCE is one of the six free services provided through India's 1.4 million Anganwadi centres located across the country under the Integrated Child Development Service (ICDS) scheme of Ministry of Women and Child Development (PTI, 2016). It provides a comprehensive package of services for young children and caregivers—medical check-ups, immunisations, referral services, supplementary feeding, pre-school and health and nutrition education for adolescent girls and mothers (Richter et al., 2016). In 2014, ICDS served 104.5 million people—including 46.7 million children from birth to three years, 38.2 million children from three to six years and 19.6 million pregnant and lactating women (ibid.). While India has a national-level policy and there have been some gains in children's enrolment into pre-school and ICDS, challenges of enrolling more children and issues of drop out remain. The government committed to universalising ICDS for all beneficiaries in 1995, but the political will to reach this goal has only been evident in recent years (ibid.). With the large population of India and decision-making authority at the state level, national-level policies and commitments are taking time to ensure universal access. In India, the governance challenge includes the national, state and local levels—all of whom need to have the political will and financing to implement national-level policies.

Two countries where governments have made tremendous steps in not only promulgating a national multi-sectoral ECD policy but also implementing that policy to scale are the Philippines and Chile. In 2000, the Philippines government passed the ECCD Act of 2000 which is the national

ECCD policy framework of the Philippines (Manual and Gregorio, 2011). The ECCD Act of 2000 mandated the National Council for the Welfare of Children (CWC) to coordinate the act's implementation through a new inter-ministerial group known as the National ECCD Coordinating Council (NECCDCC) initially under the Office of the President, but then shifted to the Department of Social Welfare and Development (DSWD). The coordinating body has representatives from the health, education, social welfare and interior and local government departments. Additionally, the council included NGOs and ECCD experts. The national coordinating council worked with counterparts at the local levels to implement the ECCD Act. In 2009, the President changed the governance structure to streamline it based on experience in implementing the act. The President abolished the CWC and the NECCDCC and established the ECCD Council. This council has five members: Department of Health (DOH), DSWD, Department of Education (DepED), NNC and the Union of Local Authorities of the Philippines (ULAP) (ibid.). The interesting aspect of this model is that it had full support of the President, and it has financing to implement the act.

Similarly, Chile also broke down the barriers of governance and is scaling ECD in the country (Delpiano and Vega, 2011; Richter et al., 2016). This was also due mostly to high-level political interest and political will (ibid.). When ECD champion and President of Chile, Michelle Bachelet, came into power in 2006, she mandated an advisory board consisting of 14 experts with wide-ranging political views to analyse the situation of young children in Chile and propose a series of policies (Delpiano and Vega, 2011). In October 2006, President Bachelet announced the "Chile Crece Contigo" programme (Chile Grows with You), which officially started in 2007. The programme is being coordinated by the Ministry of Planning and has brought together the Ministries of Health, Education, Employment, Justice, Housing and Town Planning, Treasury, the Presidency General Secretary's Office and the Women's National Service (ibid.). This coordination led at the national level extends down to the local levels and reaches all 345 municipalities (Delpiano and Vega, 2011; Richter et al., 2016). The Chile Crece Contigo has created its own branding that all ministries use, has a central information system and has its own website—www.crececontigo.gob.cl/. Additionally, the people selected to be the ministry members that took forward Chile Crece Contigo also have a good understanding of ECD, which made a big difference (Delpiano and Vega, 2011). Ten years on and the Chile Crece Contigo programme has had great results, some of which are mentioned below (Bachelet, 2017):

- 2 million pregnant mothers participated in the parental monitoring schedule.
- 1,600,000 boys and girls were born and protected by the system.
- Exclusive breastfeeding up to the sixth month increased to 56.1% in 2016.

- Catching children with developmental delays early so they can be properly supported—42% of children who were found to be falling behind have now caught up.
- 90% net rate of nursery school attendance for four and five year olds.
- 30% net attendance of children from birth to three years in early childhood centres, up from 16.4% when Chile Crece Contigo started.

In humanitarian contexts, often the cluster system is established or United Nations High Commissioner for Refugees (UNHCR) is coordinating services in collaboration with government counterparts. Similar challenges of where ECD should sit and which sector or department should take the lead in championing ECD become an issue. In an emergency context, Central African Republic (CAR) was successful in creating a formal multi-sectoral government coordination body with the assistance of Plan International and UNICEF (Shah, 2016). While in the other cases mentioned previously, it was high-level politicians who initiated the national ECD efforts, in CAR it was Plan International and UNICEF who started the process, but then handed over ownership to the government of CAR. CAR previously had few ECD services in the country and limited understanding of ECD among government officials (ibid.). The conflict in CAR and influx of humanitarian aid provided the opportunity and additional funding and technical expertise to engage with the government of CAR and jump start a process that the government became excited about and eventually took ownership of. Plan International and UNICEF specifically began by engaging the Ministries of Education and Social Affairs as a way to provide education and protection services to the most marginalised children in the conflict-affected areas of CAR. Together they established a subgroup of the IASC Education Cluster. Meetings of the subgroup began and this provided an opportunity for the government to think strategically about holistic, long-term support for young children and families. The group became an inter-ministerial group that included representation from the Ministries of Education, Social Affairs, Justice, Water and Sanitation, and Health. Over time, the committee became an active member in the support of ECD in CAR, and the government now leads the implementation of ECD, with active involvement from Plan International and UNICEF (ibid.).

ECDAN has identified governance as a challenge it wants to take on and is now in the process of supporting nine countries establish national multi-sectoral ECD committees that would create and implement policies that support young children's holistic needs. While there has been some positive trends and momentum in overcoming the governance challenges for ECD in some countries and in a few humanitarian and fragile contexts, there is still a long way to go if ECD is to be raised higher on the global agenda and there is to be global scale to support young children. Governance remains one of the toughest obstacles.

References

Aboud, F. (2007). "Evaluation of an early childhood parenting programme in rural Bangladesh", *Journal of Health, Population and Nutrition*, 25(1), 3–13.

Arnold, C. (2004). "Positioning ECCD in the 21st century". In Hanssen, E. and Zimanyi, L. (Eds), *Coordinators' Notebook: An International Resource for Early Childhood Development*. No. 28, 1–34. Toronto: The Global Consultative Group on Early Childhood Care and Development, Ryerson University.

Attanayake, V. et al. (2009). "Prevalence of mental disorders among children exposed to war: A systematic review of 7,920 children", *Medicine, Conflict and Survival*, 25(1), 4–19.

Bachelet, M. (2017). "Chile Crece Contigo: 10 Years on", *Early Childhood Matters*, The Hague: Bernard Van Leer Foundation.

Barbarin, O.A., Richter, L. and DeWet, T. (2001). "Exposure to violence, coping resources, and psychological adjustment of South African children", *American Journal of Orthopsychiatry*, 71(1), 16–25.

Betancourt, T.S. (2015). "The inter-generational effect of war", *JAMA Psychiatry*, 72(3), 199–200.

Black, M. et al. (2016). "Early childhood development coming of age: Science through the life course", *The Lancet*, Series: Advancing Early Childhood Development: from Science to Scale, 389, 77–90, London.

Bowlby, J. (1988). *A Secure Base: Parent-Child Attachment and Healthy Human Development*. London: Routledge, www.abebe.org.br/wp-content/uploads/John-Bowlby-A-Secure-Base-Parent-Child-Attachment-and-Healthy-Human-Development-1990.pdf

Boyden, J. and Mann, G. (2005). "Children's Risk, Resilience, and Coping in Extreme Situations". In Unger, M. (Ed.) *Pathways to Resilience*. Thousand Oaks, CA: Sage Publications.

Brannelly, L., Ndaruhtse, S. and Rigaud, C. (2009). *Donors' Engagement: Supporting Education in Fragile and Conflict Affected States*. Paris and London: UNESCO and CfBT Education Trust.

Britto, P. et al. (2016). "Nurturing care: Promoting early childhood development", *The Lancet*, Series: Advancing Early Childhood Development: From Science to Scale, 389, 91–102, London.

Bronfenbrenner, U. (1979). *The Ecology of Human Development: Experiments by Nature and Design*. Cambridge, MA: Harvard University Press.

Bryce, J. et al. (2008). "Maternal and child under nutrition" effective action at national level", *The Lancet*, 371, 510–526, London.

Buchanan, D. A. and Huczynski, A. (1985). *Organizational Behaviour*. London: Prentice Hall.

Carneiro, P. and Heckman, J. (2003). *Human Capital Policy*, NBER working paper 9495, National Bureau of Economic Research, Cambridge, MA.

Center on the Developing Child (2015). *The Science of Resilience*. The In Brief Series. Cambridge, MA: Harvard University.

Child Protection Working Group. (2012). http://cpwg.net

Conel, J.L. (1959). *The Postnatal Development of the Human Cereal Cortex*. Cambridge, MA: Harvard University Press.

Consultative Group for ECCD. www.ecdgroup.com/about-eccd-2/4-corenerstones

Conticini, A. and Quere V. (2011). "Emotional stimulation for acutely and severely malnourished children in SNNPR", *Field Exchange*, 40: 84–85.

Davis, R.C. and Filley, A.C. (1963). *Principles of Management*. New York: Alexander Hamilton Institute.

Delpiano, P. and Vega, M. (2011). "Chile Crece Contigo: Success factors in an integrated early childhood development policy", *Early Childhood Matters*, The Hague: Bernard Van Leer Foundation.

Donahue-Colletta, N. (Ed.) (1992). *Understanding Cross-Cultural Child Development and Designing Programs for Children*. Washington, DC: PACT.

Duncan, J. and Arnston, L. (2004). *Children in Crisis: Good Practices in Evaluating Psychosocial Programming*. London: Save the Children.

Dybdahl, R. (2001). "Children and mothers in war: an outcome study of a psychosocial intervention program". *Child Development*, 72(4), 1214–1230.

Dye, K., Mills, A.J. and Weatherbee, T. (2005). "Maslow: Man interrupted – reading management theory in context", *Management Decision*, 43(10), 1375–1395.

Evans, J. (2006). *Parenting Programmes: An Important ECD Intervention Strategy*. Background paper prepared for the Education for All Global Monitoring Report 2007, Strong foundations: early childhood care and education, Paris: UNESCO.

Feldman, R., Vengrober, A., Eidelman-Rothman, M., Zagoory-Sharon, O. (2013). "Stress reactivity in war-exposed young children with and without posttraumatic stress disorder: Relations to maternal stress hormones, parenting and child emotionality and regulation", *Development and Psychopathology*, 25, 943–955.

Felitti, V. et al. (1998). "Relationship of childhood abuse and household dysfunction to many of the leading causes of death in adults: The adverse childhood experiences (ACE) study", *American Journal of Preventive Medicine*, 14(4), 245–258.

Field, T. (2010). "Postpartum depression effects on early interactions, parenting, and safety practices: A review", *Infant Behavior and Development*, 33(1), 1–6.

Gowani, S., Yousafzai, A.K., Armstrong, R. and Bhutta, Z.A. (2014). "Cost effectiveness of responsive stimulation and nutrition interventions on early child development outcomes in Pakistan", *Annals of NY Academy of Sciences*, 1308:149–161.

GPE (2016). *Education for People and Planet: Creating Sustainable Futures for All*. Paris: UNESCO.

Grantham-McGregor, S., Powell, C.A., Walker, S.P. and Himes, J.H. (1991). "Nutritional supplementation, psychosocial stimulation, and mental development in stunted children: The Jamaican study", *The Lancet*, 338, 1–5.

Hagerty, M. (1999). "Testing Maslow's hierarchy of needs: National quality of life across time", *Social Indicators Research*, 46(3), 249–271.

Hamdani, J.D., Huda, S.N., Khatun, F. and Grantham-McGregor, S.M. (2006). "Psychosocial stimulation improves the development of malnourished children in rural Bangladesh", *Journal of Nutrition*, 136, 2645–2652.

Harvard University (2013). *The Science of Early Childhood Development*. Cambridge, MA: The Center on the Development Child, Harvard University.

Heckman, J. (2006). *Return on Investments: Cost vs. Benefits*. Chicago: University of Chicago, www.childandfamilypolicy.duke.edu/pdfs/10yranniversary_Heckmanhandout.pdf

Henniger, M. (2009). *Teaching Young Children: An Introduction*. London: Pearson.

Hitt, M.A., Black, J.S. and Porter, L.W. (2005). *Management*. Upper Saddle River, NJ: Prentice Hall.

IASC (2007). *IASC Guidelines for Mental Health and Psychosocial Support in Emergency Settings*. Geneva: IASC.

India Government (2013). www.childlineindia.org.in/pdf/The-National-Policy-for-Children-2013.pdf

ISSA (2010). *Early Childhood Development and Education in Emergencies.* Amsterdam.

Jaramillo, A. and Mingat, A. (2003). *Early Childhood Care and Education in Sub-Saharan Africa: What Would it Take to Meet the Millennium Development Goals?* Washington, DC: World Bank.

Kamel, H. (2006). *Early Childhood Care and Education in Emergency Situations.* Background paper prepared for the 2007 Education for All Global Monitoring Report.

Lake, A. (2015). "Education in Emergencies", *The Jordan Times*, www.jordantimes.com/opinion/anthony-lake/education-emergencies, last accessed 17 May 2019.

Lokshin, M., Glinskaya, E. and Garcia, M. (2000). *The Effect of Early Childhood Development Programs on Women's Labor Force Participation and Older Children's Schooling in Kenya*, Working Paper Series #15, Policy Research Report on Gender and Development.

Manual, M. and Gregorio, E. (2011). "Legal frameworks for early childhood governance in the Philippines", *International Journal of Child Care and Education Policy*, 5(1), 65–76.

Maslow, A. H. (1943). "A theory of human motivation", *Psychological Review*, 50(4), 370–396.

Masten, A.S. and Monn, A.R. (2015). "Child and family resilience: A call for integrated science, practice, and professional training", *Family Relations*, 64(1): 5–21.

McMahon, C. A., Barnett, B., Kowalenko, N.M. and Tennant, C.C. (2006). "Maternal attachment state of mind moderates the impact of postnatal depression on infant attachment". *Journal of Child Psychology and Psychiatry*, 47(7): 660–669.

Middlebrooks, J.S. and Audage, N.C. (2008). *The Effects of Childhood Stress on Health across the Lifespan.* Atlanta: Centers for Disease Control and Prevention, National Center for Injury Prevention and Control.

Nahar, B. et al. (2009). "Effects of psychosocial stimulation on growth and development of severely malnourished children in a nutrition unit in Bangladesh", *European Journal of Clinical Nutrition*, 63, 725–731.

Nahar, B. et al. (2012). "Effects of psychosocial stimulation on improving home environment and child-rearing practices: Results from a community-based trial among severely malnourished children in Bangladesh", *BMC Public Health*, 12, 622.

National Scientific Council on the Developing Child. (2007). *The Timing and Quality of Early Experiences Combine to Shape Brain Architecture*, Working Paper #5, Harvard University.

National Scientific Council on the Developing Child. (2010). Persistent fear and anxiety can affect young children's learning and development: Working paper no. 9. Boston, MA: NSCDC.

Nelson, C.A. et al. (2007). "Cognitive recovery in socially deprived young children: The Bucharest early intervention project", *Science*, 318(5858), 1937–1940.

Nomaguchi, K., Brown, S. and Leyman, T. (2012). *Father Involvement and Mothers' Parenting Stress: The Role of Relationship Status*, Fragile Families Working Paper, http://crcw.princeton.edu/workingpapers/wp12-07-ff.pdf, last accessed 12 June 2016.

Pearson, E. and Podeschi, R. (1997). "Humanism and individualism: Maslow and his critics", *Adult Education Research Conference,* Paper 35.

Perry, B.D. and Pollard, D. (1997). *Altered Brain Development Following Global Neglect in Early Childhood.* Society for Neuroscience: Proceedings from Annual Meeting, New Orleans.

Pine, D., Costello, J. and Masten, A. (2005). "Trauma, proximity, and developmental psychopathology: The effects of war and terrorism on children", *Neuropsychopharmacology*, 30, 1781–1792.

Plan International (2010). *Anticipating the Future: Children and Young People's Voices in Haiti's Post Disaster Needs Assessment (PDNA).* Haiti: Plan International.

Plan International (2013). *Early Childhood Care and Development in Emergencies: A Programme Guide.* Woking: Plan International.

Plan International and UNICEF (2016a). *Early Childhood Development, Health and Nutrition in Emergencies.* Woking: Plan International.

Plan International and UNICEF (2016b). *Early Childhood Development, Child Protection in Emergencies.* Woking: Plan International.

PTI (2016). "Govt notifies early childhood care and education policy", *Indian Express,* http://indianexpress.com/article/education/govt-notifies-early-childhood-care-and-education-policy/

Richter, L. et al. (2016). "Investing in the foundation of sustainable development: Pathways to scale up for early childhood development". *The Lancet*, Special issue: Advancing Early Childhood Development from Science to Scale, 389, 103–118, London.

Sanchez, A. (2009). *Early Nutrition and Later Cognitive Achievement in Developing Countries*, Paper commissioned for the EFA Global Monitoring Report 2012, Reaching the Marginalized. Paris: UNESCO.

Save the Children (1995). *Promoting Psychosocial Well-being among Children Affected by Armed Conflict and Displacement: Principles and Approaches.* London: Save the Children.

Save the Children (2008). *Delivering Education for Children in Emergencies: A Key Building Block for the Future.* London: Save the Children.

Save the Children (2013). *Psychological First Aid Training: Manual for Child Practitioners.* Denmark: Save the Children.

Save the Children (2015). *Hear it From the Children: South Sudan, 'We Want to Learn – Even during War'.* South Sudan: Save the Children.

Shah, S. (2016). "Inequity in Central African Republic: ECD in Emergencies as an Entry Point for National Level Policies", Case Study 8 in *Global Report on Equity and Early Childhood*, The Global Consultative Group on ECCD, www.ecdgroup.com/cg2/wp-content/uploads/2016/05/Case-Study-8_round-2.pdf

Shonkoff, J.P. (2009). "Investment in early childhood development lays the foundation for a prosperous and sustainable society". In Tremblay, R.E., Boivin, M. and Peters, RDeV (Eds.) *Encyclopedia on Early Childhood Development* [online]. Montreal: Centre of Excellence for Early Childhood Development and Strategic Knowledge Cluster on Early Child Development, www.child-encyclopedia.com/documents/ShonkoffANGxp.pdf, last accessed 16 June 2016.

Shonkoff, J. and Levitt, P. (2010). "Neuroscience and the future of early childhood policy: Moving from why to what and how", *Neuron*, 67 (5), 689–691.

Shonkoff, J. and Bales, S.N. (2011). "Science does not speak for itself: Translating child development research for the public and its policymakers". *Child Development*, 82(1), 17–32.

Shonkoff, J.P. et al. (2012). "The lifelong effects of early childhood adversity and toxic stress". *Pediatrics*, 129(1): e232–246.

Sinclair, M. (2002). *Planning Education in and After Emergencies.* Paris: UNESCO.

Singla, D., Kumbakumba, E. and Aboud, F. (2015). "Effects of parenting intervention to address maternal psychological wellbeing and child development and growth in rural Uganda: A community-based, cluster-ramdomised tial", *The Lancet*, 3, 458–469.

Spielberger, J., Gouvea, M., Dinata, E. and Fleischman, L. (2015). *Father Involvement in Early Childhood Development: A Brief Report from the Palm Beach County Family Study.* Chicago, IL: Chapin Hall at the University of Chicago.

Thabet, A. A., Ibraheem, A. N., Shivram, R., Winter, E. A. and Vostanis, P. (2009). "Parenting support and PTSD in children of a war zone", *International Journal of Social Psychiatry*, 55(3), 226–237.

Their World. (2016). *Safe Spaces: The Urgent Need for Early Childhood Development in Emergencies and Disasters.* London: Their World.

Turrent, V. and Oketch, M. (2009). "Financing universal primary education: An analysis of official development assistance in fragile states", *International Journal of Educational Development*, 29(4), 357–365.

Uganda Government (2016). www.unicef.org/uganda/FINAL_NIECD_POLICY_FINAL_BOOK_approved_by_Acting_PS__Mpagi.pdf

UNESCO (2017). *Aid to Education Is Stagnating and Not Going to Countries Most in Need.* UNESCO, Global Education Monitoring report: Paris.

UNICEF (2014). *Early Childhood Development in Emergencies Integrated Programme Guide.* New York: UNICEF.

UNICEF and WHO (ND). *Integrating Early Childhood Development (ECD) Activities into Nutrition Programmes in Emergencies. Why, What and How,* www.who.int/mental_health/emergencies/ecd_note.pdf, last accessed 8 August 2018

USAID (2011). *USAID Education Strategy 2011–2015.* Washington, DC: USAID.

Van den Bergh, B.R. et al. (2005). "Antenatal maternal anxiety and stress and the neurobehavioral development of the fetus and child: Links and possible mechanism", *Neuroscience and Biobehavioral Reviews*, 29(2), 237–258, London.

Victora, C. et al. (2008). "Maternal and child under-nutrition: Consequences for adult health and human capital", *The Lancet*, 371(9609), 340–357, London.

Vygotsky, L.V. (1978). *Mind in Society: The Development of Higher Psychological Processes.* Cambridge, MA: Harvard University Press.

Wahba, M. and Bridwell, L. (1976). "Maslow reconsidered: A review of research on the need hierarchy theory", *Organizational Behavior and Human Performance*, 15, 212–240.

WHO (2016). "The early years: Silent emergency or unique opportunity?" www.who.int/mediacentre/commentaries/early-years-opportunity/en/, last accessed 8 August 2018.

Williams, J.R.A. et al. (2005). "Save the Children's experience: ECD in emergencies", *Early Childhood Matters*, 124. The Hague: Bernard Van Leer Foundation.

Williamson, J. and Robinson, M. (2006). "Psychosocial interventions, or integrated programming for well-being?" *Intervention*, 4(1), 4–25.

World Bank (2017). "Countries commit to strong action on human capital to drive economic growth", www.worldbank.org/en/news/feature/2017/10/20/countries-commit-to-strong-action-on-human-capital-to-drive-economic-growth

Yousafzai, A.K. et al. (2014). "Effect of integrated responsive stimulation and nutrition interventions in the Lady Health Worker program in Pakistan on child development, growth and health outcomes: A cluster randomised factorial effectiveness trial", *The Lancet*, 384(9950), 1282–1293, London.

Yusra, R. and Shiffman, J. (2016). "Generation of global political priority for early childhood development: the challenges of framing and governance", *The Lancet*, Series Advancing Early Childhood Development: From Science to Scale, 389, 119–124, London.

3 Overview of the humanitarian landscape

The state of humanitarian situations around the world

Globally, there is growing recognition of the human and financial impacts of humanitarian situations. United Nations Office for the Coordination of Humanitarian Affairs (UNOCHA) found in 2017 that 141 million people were affected by conflict and natural disasters (UNOCHA, 2018a). Of this, 95.1 million people were affected by natural disasters and 68.5 million were forcibly displaced by violence and conflict (ibid.). Of the 68.5 million forcibly displaced, 40 million were internally displaced persons (IDPs) (displaced within their country), 25.4 million were refugees (displaced outside of their country) and 3.1 million were asylum seekers (UNHCR, 2017a; UNOCHA, 2018b). Over half of the 25.4 million refugees were under 18 years (UNHCR, 2017b, 2017c).

In 2017, the top five refugee producing countries were Syria (6.3 million), Afghanistan (2.6 million), South Sudan (2.4 million), Myanmar (1.2 million) and Somalia (0.99 million) (UNOCHA, 2018a, 2018b). This is 53% of the world's refugees (ibid.). These numbers do not include those internally displaced, which increases the overall displaced population numbers, especially for the Syria and South Sudan crises (ibid.). South Sudan remains one of the largest conflicts in the world and is still classified as an L3 emergency, which requires intervention by the international humanitarian sector. Uganda currently hosts the most refugees from South Sudan (1.4 million) and is in the top three countries hosting refugees (UNHCR, 2017a, 2017b). Ethiopia, Sudan, Kenya and the Democratic Republic of Congo also host South Sudanese refugees (ibid.). In addition to South Sudanese refugees, Uganda also hosts refugees from the Democratic Republic of Congo, Burundi, Somalia and Rwanda (UNOCHA, 2018a). The United Nations High Commissioner for Refugees (UNHCR) estimates that 45% of refugees today live in protracted crisis settings (UNHCR, 2017a). UNHCR defines protracted refugee situations as those where at least 25,000 refugees of one nationality have been displaced for at least five consecutive years (ibid.). In these contexts, humanitarian support is beyond immediate life-saving and focuses on finding durable solutions. Unfortunately, durable solutions in these situations are difficult to achieve (ibid.). South Sudanese refugees in Uganda and Ethiopia are considered protracted refugee situations (ibid.). Further, UNHCR has found that 86% of refugees are hosted in developing countries, who themselves struggle to fully support their own population (ibid.).

At any given time, it is estimated that more than 200 million children under the age of five in developing countries are not reaching their developmental potential due to poverty, malnutrition, poor health and lack of early-years support (Engle et al., 2007; Grantham-McGregor et al., 2007). In emergency situations, children face additional adversities that make it even more difficult, especially for the youngest of them below the age of five, to survive and thrive. The former Executive Director of UNICEF, Anthony Lake, said "Children are not responsible for the conflict and carnage created by the adults. But they are the first victims" (Lake, 2017). UNHCR estimated that 51% of all refugees worldwide are under 18 years (Their World, 2016). Among the approximate 655,000 Rohingya Muslims refugees in Bangladesh, Save the Children estimated in August 2017 that about 380,000 are minors and at least 30% of the total refugee population is younger than 5 years (Beech, 2018). In 2015, UNICEF estimated that about 306,000 Syrian babies were born as refugees (Their World, 2016). Given the protracted nature of the conflict in Syria, many have only known life in refugee camps and settlements (ibid.).

The damage that this mass displacement, due to conflict, war, typhoons, earthquakes and other natural hazards, has created is tremendous. Over the last 12 years, disasters have resulted in $1.3 trillion in damage, 2.7 billion people affected and 1.1 million people killed, setting back development and increasing people's likelihood of staying in or falling into poverty (Moensch, 2007). In 2011, there were 11 massive emergencies with loses of over $360 billion (Ferris and Solis, 2013). 2012 fell below a 10-year average with losses of about $160 billion (ibid.). In 2017, UNOCHA estimated the economic cost of conflict at $14.8 trillion, which is equivalent to about 12.4% of the global gross domestic product (UNOCHA, 2018a). The total estimated damage in 2017 due to natural disasters was $340 billion (ibid.).

The number of emergencies due to conflict, impact of climate change, etc. are increasing, lasting longer, becoming more expensive and affecting more children and families (UNOCHA, 2018a). However, the funding to support this has not followed (ibid.). In 2014, the funding requirement for the myriad humanitarian situations around the world was $17.9 billion while a decade earlier in 2004, it was $3 billion (Swithern, 2015). The average humanitarian funding for all sectors in 2014 was 65% of the need, with food and health receiving the largest percentages (ibid.). Over the last few years, education (which is often where Early Childhood Development in emergencies funding comes from) received the smallest percentage of the total humanitarian funding (UNESCO, 2015). In 2014, the food sector received approximately $2.9 billion, health received $1 billion and education received $186 million (ibid.). Over a ten year average, the education sector has received about 2% of all humanitarian funding (Nicolai et al., 2016). In 2016, the small percentage of funding to education in emergencies was despite the fact that about 75 million children had their education disrupted by conflict and natural hazards (ibid.). This 2% does not differentiate how much went to early learning (ECD), primary or secondary education. However, within the education sector, the priority tends to be to increase primary education access. During a meeting with the European Union (EU) in Uganda in November 2017, the representatives specifically mentioned access to primary education and accelerated learning (condensed primary education) as priorities for their emergency funding. Early childhood ends up at the bottom of the priority list even within the main sector (education) that supports it.

Greater professionalisation

In order to respond to the increase to the humanitarian situations and the need for a strong workforce, both development and humanitarian work have become increasingly professionalised over the past few decades (Davey et al., 2013; Willemse, 2010). The conceptual, operational and institutional roots of the modern humanitarian system are in the nineteenth century (Davey et al., 2013). The establishment of the International Committee of the Red Cross (ICRC) in 1863 and then the League of Nations' High Commissioner for Refugees after the First World War created the foundation for many international organisations focused on humanitarian aid (ibid.; Paulmann, 2013). The beginnings of humanitarian action are rooted in colonial practices in the nineteenth century (Davey et al., 2013). For example, in India in the 1880s, the Famine Codes established by Britain defined famine and proposed ways of measuring it, as well as providing guidelines to govern its prevention and response (ibid.). The early to mid-twentieth century saw the establishment of relief agencies such as Save the Children, Oxfam and CARE (Paulmann, 2013). Many more development and aid organisations flourished after the First World War (ibid.). Humanitarian aid continued to rise in the 1960s as missionaries and volunteers from Western countries went to poorer countries to help with little or no compensation for their time and work (Willemse, 2010). In the 1980s, there was a proliferation of international non-governmental organisations (INGOs) that activated humanitarian operations and began to compete with each other for funds (Paulmann, 2013).

Within the broader development and humanitarian sectors, education, including early childhood education, in emergencies is becoming increasingly professionalised as well (Ade, 1982; Kagawa, 2005; Martin, 2006; O'Flaherty and Ulrich, 2010; Rey Marcos, 2010; Slim, 1995; Walker, 2003; Willemse, 2010). This area of work first emerged as education provided for refugees in conflict situations, but has since evolved to include myriad humanitarian contexts including earthquakes, floods, tsunamis and cyclones (Kagawa, 2005; Sinclair, 2002). Emergency education, which includes formal and non-formal education from pre-school through secondary school, takes place when a country's national and community education systems are weakened or destroyed to the point where governments can no longer guarantee children's right to education (Kagawa, 2005; Sinclair, 2002). Thirty years ago, it was not difficult to secure a post doing emergency education in a developing country because there were few people doing this work (Kagawa, 2005). The number of workers was fewer than the overall need for staff. Many people who entered the humanitarian field 20–30 years ago, before there was a recognised education in emergencies profession, said that they did not need any specific credentials such as a Master's degree or a particular number of years of experience to get a job. They just needed a desire to help others and be willing to live in often difficult conditions (ibid.). As the provision of education became increasingly recognised as crucial to humanitarian response, both education in emergency practitioners (including those doing early learning) and those outside of the field started to professionalise this area of work.

During the 1990s, there was an increase in the international activities of humanitarian agencies (Sinclair, 2002). This was particularly the case for the Rwandan genocide in 1994 and the conflict in the Great Lakes region of Africa (ibid.). Unsatisfied with the response which had a catastrophic impact on Rwandans and the region, humanitarian practitioners from various technical sectors including health, water, sanitation and nutrition came together in 1996 to develop a set of minimum standards for emergency response (Gostelow, 2009). This collaboration resulted in the creation of the Sphere handbook that includes the Humanitarian Charter and Minimum Standards in Disaster Response (The Sphere Project, 2011). At this time education was not included as a core life-saving response. Further the specific needs of young children were not explicitly addressed. The 2000 Dakar World Education Forum committed to meeting the education needs of people affected by armed conflict and natural disasters (Anderson and Roberts, 2005). In 2001, the Inter-Agency Network for Education in Emergencies (INEE) was established to address the gap of education in emergencies in the Sphere handbook (www.ineesite.org).

Soon after, the INEE Minimum Standards handbook, which also includes early learning, was developed through a multi-country, inter-agency process. It set up global minimum standards for education in emergencies, programming which are still used today. INEE is now a network of more than 12,000 individual members and 130 partner organisations in 170 countries. INEE members are practitioners working for national and INGOs and United Nations (UN) agencies, ministry of education and other government personnel, donors, students, teachers and researchers (ibid.). This network reinvigorated ECD in emergencies task force (ibid.). Establishing INEE and the minimum standards transformed the humanitarian perspectives on the importance of education in emergencies. It is now recognised as a "fourth pillar" of humanitarian aid that saves and sustains lives alongside food and water, shelter and health care (Kagawa, 2005). The early learning aspect of ECD is carried by momentum around and recognition of INEE and education in emergencies. However, ECD in emergencies, as a multi-sectoral response, is still not fully understood and its profile does not reach as high as other emergency sectors.

Humanitarian structure

Definition of emergency and the disaster cycle

An emergency can be defined in many ways. It can be defined as a sudden, serious, unexpected, often dangerous and overwhelming event that requires immediate action (Burnham, 2008). An emergency can affect all the various levels: the individual, household, community, country or multi-country level or beyond (Burnham, 2008). While this is the general definition of an emergency, in the international development and humanitarian fields, an emergency goes beyond a single individual or family. For the purposes of this book, an emergency, disaster or humanitarian crisis would not include situations such as car accidents, house fires or injury that affects an individual or a family. The term refers to a serious event that affects multiple countries, a whole society or a large part of a population. It can be caused by internal or cross-border armed conflict that results in internal displacement, creating internally displaced persons (IDPs) or external displacement, creating refugees (Burnham, 2008). An emergency can also be caused by a natural hazard (i.e. flooding, typhoon, hurricane, landslides, tsunamis, earthquakes) (ibid.). The term "emergency" is often used alongside "disaster," and "humanitarian crisis." While some agencies define these terms differently, many use them inter-changeably to mean the same thing. In this book, I will inter-changeably use the term "emergency," "disaster" and "humanitarian crisis" to mean the same thing.

An emergency can be a short-term situation lasting a few months or it can last over many years. The entire emergency or disaster cycle (as shown in Figure 3.1) process begins before an actual life-threatening event occurs such as an earthquake, beginning of fighting, etc.

This aspect of the emergency cycle is called preparedness. When something occurs such as escalation of fighting, increased displacement of people, an

Figure 3.1 Disaster risk management cycle.

earthquake or typhoon, we move to the next stage which is called relief. This is immediately after a life-threatening event occurs to affect a large percentage of a country's population. Often this stage could include search and rescue and the provision of important life-saving and protective services. When the situation stabilises, this is called the rehabilitation, reconstruction and recovery phase (Johns Hopkins and International Federation of the Red Cross and Red Crescent Societies, 2008; Joyce et al., 2009; United Nations Office for Disaster Risk Reduction, 2009). In this book, I consider the whole cycle of emergency preparedness, acute relief/response and recovery/rehabilitation/reconstruction. While there are specific stages illustrated in Figure 3.1 and recognised by humanitarian agencies, the transition from one phase to another is often not clear, especially in situations of mass displacement due to chronic conflict. History of conflict has shown that refugee situations can last a long time, with an average length of 17 years (Their World, 2016).

The severity of an emergency and whether outside assistance is required is generally measured according to the widely agreed upon formula:

Risk = Hazard × Vulnerability / Capacity

A situation would be considered a humanitarian crisis or emergency generally when the hazard (i.e. earthquake, conflict, flood) is very severe, the vulnerability is equally high in the country and the capacity to deal with this is low. The highest level of emergency response support is provided by the UN system when a crisis is labelled level 3 or L3. At this level, the whole humanitarian support system is activated, including a high influx of coordination support, staff and finances. The Emergency Relief Coordinator (ERC) is in charge of designating a crisis to this level (IASC, ND). The ERC is also UNOCHA's Under-Secretary General for Humanitarian Affairs. He/she leads the Inter-Agency Standing Committee (IASC), and is responsible for the oversight of all emergencies that require UN humanitarian assistance. He/she, in consultation with the IASC principles, basis his/her analysis on five criteria: scale, complexity, urgency, capacity and reputational risk (ibid.). *Scale* refers to the number of people affected or potentially affected, number of countries and areas of a country affected. *Complex* situations will have multiple barriers such as widespread injury and death, increased violence that is continuing to escalate, internal displacement, external displacement, massive damage to infrastructure, multiple ethnic, religious and tribal groups, security risk of staff, etc. *Urgency* refers to how critical humanitarian response is to saving lives, the crude mortality rate, etc. *Capacity* is about the government and civil society's ability to respond. In the majority of large-scale emergencies classified as L3, the government and civil society are often fractured and/or very weak before an emergency occurs. This can be one of the root causes of a crisis escalating to a L3 level emergency. *Reputational risk* refers to what might happen if the humanitarian system does not respond based on media and public attention and visibility, expectations on the humanitarian system by donors, the public and national stakeholders (ibid.). When the international community did not respond to prevent the Rwanda crisis, it resulted in genocide, the death of millions of people and massive displacement. The humanitarian community was ill-prepared to handle the massive displacement and needs of people. This is widely considered a failure of the international community.

In 2014, South Sudan was declared an L3 emergency as it met all five criteria: large-scale internal and external displacement, complex situation with multiple warring tribes and ethnic groups, urgency to support the situation to keep a new country going, a weak government and civil society and huge reputational risk of not responding. The designation of South Sudan as an L3 country continues in 2019. The risk is high in South Sudan also because the hazard or the war has been far reaching throughout the country and the vulnerability to affect the whole country and its neighbouring countries is high while the capacity to deal with the crisis has been extremely low. South Sudan had many vulnerabilities from its previous long war with what is now Sudan, long-standing poverty, low education and literacy levels, and a fragile new government. While at this stage there is not a need for search and rescue, the emergency phase is prolonged. People are still in refugee and IDP camps and are still often not meeting their basic needs, including ECD.

Inter-Agency Standing Committee and the cluster system

Established in June 1992, in response to the United Nations General Assembly Resolution 46/182 on the strengthening of humanitarian assistance, the IASC is the main humanitarian inter-agency coordination mechanism. The IASC was established as a global entity that brings together key UN and non-UN humanitarian partners (IASC). It has a secretariat with UN staff in Geneva, Switzerland and New York, United States (ibid.). While there are multiple members of the IASC, most represent various United Nations agencies such as United Nations Children's Fund (UNICEF), United Nations High Commissioner for Refugees (UNHCR), World Health Organization (WHO), Food and Agriculture Organization (FAO), United Nations Office for the Coordination of Humanitarian Affairs (OCHA), United Nations Development Programme (UNDP), World Food Programme (WFP), United Nations Population Fund (UNFPA) and UN-Habitat). In all declared emergencies, whether they are classified as L3 or not, the IASC can activate the humanitarian coordination structure. Figure 3.2 illustrates the key players in a country-level humanitarian coordination architecture.

As seen from Figure 3.2, UNOCHA is at the centre of the whole humanitarian coordination architecture. They enter a country when there has been an emergency declared. With protracted crises, UNOCHA may remain in a country for many years or it may exit once a disaster ends and there is a transition to recovery and development. As mentioned previously, UNOCHA's Under-Secretary General for Humanitarian Affairs is the Emergency

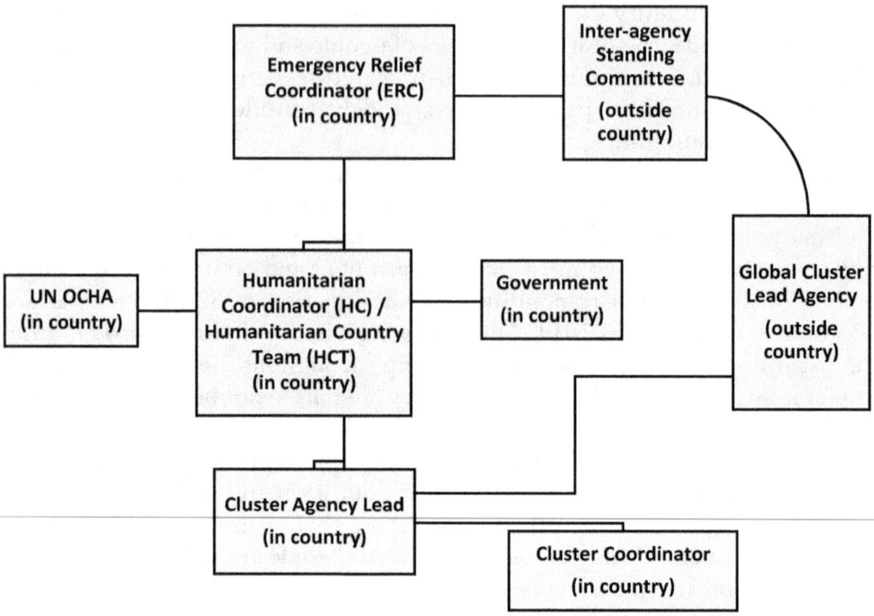

Figure 3.2 Coordination architecture in the cluster approach.
Source: Based on UN OCHA.

Relief Coordinator. As the lead for the IASC, the ERC is responsible for the oversight of all emergencies and a central focal point for governmental, inter-governmental and non-governmental response activities. The ERC can appoint a Humanitarian Coordinator (HC) and Humanitarian Country team (HCT), which will lead the implementation of a response. These positions are housed by UNOCHA. The staff work closely with government ministries, but also the IASC cluster leads for the various sectors. IASC cluster leads coordinate and lead response efforts from a sector perspective. Table 3.1 outlines the various IASC thematic clusters and who leads them.

Table 3.1 indicates that most cluster leads are UN agencies (IASC, ND). Education is the only cluster that has a non-governmental organisation (NGO)—Save the Children. There are huge implications for an agency to take on this role. It requires a commitment of its own resources to support emergency response, even where they may not be present. These lead agencies are always the default agencies or the Provider of Last Resort (IASC, ND).

Member agencies (i.e. local and international NGOs) are a part of sectoral clusters. There is an inter-cluster coordination team that helps facilitate collaboration between the various clusters. However, in my personal experience, this does not work very well. During humanitarian crises, clusters are so busy focusing on an immediate response for their specific sector that inter-cluster coordination is often not prioritised. This creates siloed

Table 3.1 IASC Clusters

IASC cluster	*Cluster lead*
Health	WHO
Nutrition	UNICEF
Education	UNICEF and Save the Children
Protection	UNHCR
Food security	WFP and FAO
Logistics	WFP
Shelter	IFRC/UNHCR
Water, sanitation, hygiene	UNICEF
Camp coordination and camp management	UNHCR/IOM
Early recovery	UNDP
Emergency telecommunications	WFP

Source: UNOCHA.

approaches to humanitarian interventions which does not always meet the needs of affected populations nor is it cost effective. This is changing slowly in certain humanitarian crises, but there is still a long way to go. The HCT includes representatives of NGOs, UN agencies and cluster lead agencies. The HC is sometimes also the Resident Coordinator (RC). In non-emergency contexts, UNDP may have a Resident Coordinator. When an emergency is declared in a country, that person may become the HC or another person could be appointed.

Humanitarian financing mechanisms

Humanitarian and development pots of money are usually separate—different staff, different criteria for financing, different disbursement procedures. Staff from the same donor agencies may not even talk or coordinate. This has been the norm for many years and has reinforced a siloed approach to the humanitarian and development continuum. As illustrated in the disaster cycle (Figure 3.1), the shift from a humanitarian to development situation is not black and white, especially with conflict-affected protracted situation such as the South Sudan crisis. This siloed approach is changing with a greater realisation that emergency and development funding need to coordinate, especially in situations of mass internal or external displacement. The IASC currently has a task team focused on bridging the humanitarian and development divide, but significant progress is still needed (IASC). In this section, I outline the key humanitarian funding mechanisms. While multiple pots of money are available, ECD colleagues or other implementers do not always take advantage of them to increase financing for ECD in emergencies. By understanding what financing options are available and how to access them, ECD staff can better target them for advocacy which can hopefully increase overall investment for ECD in emergencies.

Tools for humanitarian funding: FLASH and CAP

At the onset of an acute emergency, there are two critical tools that are used to articulate immediate needs: FLASH Appeal and the Consolidated Appeals Process (CAP) (Education Cluster, ND; Stoddard, 2008). Some of these result in direct financial disbursement. FLASH Appeals are coordinated by the sectoral clusters and used for rapid release of funds for the first three to six months of an emergency. After an initial rapid assessment is conducted within the first 24 hours or so of an emergency, FLASH Appeals can be submitted. Funding through FLASH Appeals is usually confirmed within the first one to two weeks of an emergency. Financial support usually goes to sectoral cluster lead agencies. CAP comes into effect after the FLASH Appeal. It is used to aid organisations to plan, coordinate, implement and monitor large-scale humanitarian action in a given country or region. It responds to the needs in a Common Humanitarian Response Plan and usually supports interventions for 12 months. Cluster coordinators lead the process of putting forward proposals for the FLASH Appeal and CAP. Agencies that are involved with sectoral clusters from the beginning will know the timing of when the CAPs need to be submitted and can prepare concept notes for this. Those that are not involved in the clusters may not know about when CAPs are due and could miss the funding opportunity. Based on personal experience being present at the early stages of an emergency response when clusters first meet can provide insight not only into the process and timing, but can provide the opportunity to influence what is funded. ECD staff or those interested in obtaining funds for ECD in emergencies at the immediate outset of an acute crisis should stay involved in a few different clusters—education, child protection, health and nutrition. Different aspects of ECD in emergencies can be presented as part of a CAP proposal for any of these clusters. For example, early learning/pre-school can be integrated into any education proposal while play, learning and psychosocial support for children 0–5 years can be framed as a child protection intervention in child-friendly spaces. Maternal newborn and child health can be integral to any health or nutrition proposal. Parenting support can be integrated into all of the sectors as this intervention should have aspects of education/learning (education), preventive health (health), child and maternal nutrition and breastfeeding (nutrition), psychosocial support and prevention of violence (child protection).

While appeals processes do not guarantee funding, as they are not actual funding mechanisms, but rather a way of articulating immediate humanitarian needs through the lens of various sectors, some donors will only fund projects that are in the FLASH/CAP appeals. The reason for this is that it indicates that the implementing agency is actively coordinating and collaborating with others. It is therefore important for those that want to raise money for ECD to be present in cluster meetings at the immediate outset of an emergency and ensure a project around ECD in emergencies is integral to submissions for various clusters. In my personal experience, active involvement with the cluster system has resulted in financing for ECD in emergencies programming.

Major financing mechanisms in emergencies

While there are the FLASH and CAP appeals processes, there are some main humanitarian funding mechanisms. These include the Central Emergency Response Fund (CERF), Common Humanitarian Funds (CHF) which are also known as the Country-based Pooled Funds (CBPF), and the Emergency Response Funds (ERF) (Education Cluster, ND; Stoddard, 2008; UNOCHA, 2019). These are typically allocated by the HC in a country based on advice from the HCT, or by in-country committees (Education Cluster, ND). Usually only a fraction of the request is funded so it is not only important to understand the criteria for funding projects but also the in-country priorities so the right language can be used to integrate ECD in emergencies. The in-country priorities are based on needs, but also the personality and interests of UNOCHA, the HC and the HCT. In many humanitarian situations, the understanding of what is ECD and why it is important in emergencies remains low. When there are so many important priorities, the language that fits with in-country priorities is the best way to raise funds for ECD in emergencies.

The CERF is a global unearmarked pooled funding mechanism managed by the CERF secretariat that sits at UNOCHA (Education Cluster, ND; Stoddard, 2008; Welsh, 2019). It covers initial funding for most urgent life-saving projects in the appeals, but also for under-funded emergencies (Education Cluster, ND). CERF was approved in 2005 and started operating in 2006 when the United Nations realised an imbalance in funding various types of emergencies such as the Indian Ocean tsunami of 2004 and the Darfur refugee response (Welsh, 2019). It was initially a $50 million loan facility, but quickly became a $450 million grant facility that could met needs of humanitarian crises wherever and whenever needed (ibid.). The top five all time donors for CERF are the governments of the United Kingdom, Sweden, Norway, the Netherlands and Germany. However, since 2006, over 120 countries have given the CERF. While most of the funding is from governments, the CERF secretariat has been working to identify ways to diversity its donor base. More recently, the private sector, foundations, philanthropies and individual donors have also contributed to CERF (ibid.).

There are two windows of disbursing funds through the CERF: Rapid Response and Under-funded emergencies (Welsh, 2019). About two-thirds of the funds go to the Rapid Response window which can be disbursed within 24 hours when leveraged against agency reserves of funding (Stoddard, 2008; Welsh, 2019). In 2018, this window provided $500 million of support for the initial stages of multiple emergencies around the world (ibid.). Life-saving criteria and time-critical response are crucial in order for the HC to trigger CERF funding for the Rapid Response window.

The second window within CERF is the Under-funded emergencies which aims to fill key gaps in international funding (Welsh, 2019). Many protracted crises are included in this, especially those waning in their donor support and media attention. The South Sudan crisis and the South Sudanese refugees in Uganda qualified in 2018 for CERFs. Provision of funds within this window of CERF occurs twice a year. Decisions for funding under-funded crises are based on a CERF index which analyses the risk and vulnerability of a situation and the funding landscape and gaps (ibid.).

The advantages of the CERF include the fact that it is a source of upfront, unearmarked funds that can be used within 24 hours of an acute emergency (Stoddard, 2008; Welsh, 2019). It allows for the coordination required to determine prioritisation of needs (ibid.). It can also fill gaps and address inequities in funding across emergencies and meet unmet needs (Stoddard, 2008). Drawbacks to CERF include the fact that funding does not go directly to NGOs who would be best placed to launch a rapid response (ibid.). By passing through UN agencies only, it also increases money spent on overheads and can cause time lags for the response (ibid.).

The CHF/CBPF is a second main funding mechanism during crisis situations (Education Cluster, ND; Stoddard, 2008; UNOCHA, 2019). It is a country-level pooled funding mechanism, coordinated through UNOCHA, that provides advanced multilateral funding for a country-wide emergency response plan while underpinning and incentivising humanitarian coordination (Education Cluster, ND; UNOCHA, 2019). Unlike the CERF, CHF/CBPF is an available funding source for international and local NGOs (Stoddard, 2008). The fund pools together unearmarked money into a single location (UNOCHA, 2019). The money can come from governments, private foundations or corporations (ibid.). The potential drawbacks of the CHF/CBPF are if there is a weak HC, the financing allocations could be based on inter-agency politics rather than merit/appropriateness (ibid.). Additionally, NGOs have indicated continued challenges with accessing funds vs. the time they spent on preparing their proposals. This is a good mechanism for donors who have limited funds and lack the in-country capacities to administer grants (ibid.).

The third main humanitarian financing mechanism is the ERF. The ERF is a country-level functional/thematic pooled funding source (Stoddard, 2008; Education Cluster, ND). It has been found to be effective in responding to small-scale, sudden-onset needs such as floods or other natural disasters within a larger humanitarian context (Stoddard, 2008). NGOs can directly access the funds and they are based on needs identified by each sector and cluster. A drawback to this fund is when an agency coordinating the cluster (UNICEF and Save the Children in the case of the Education cluster, for example) is also the recipient of funding (ibid.). ERF can also be an important source of funding if there is no CHF or CBPF.

Other humanitarian financing mechanisms

Beyond the above-mentioned financing mechanisms, there are bi-lateral agencies that have humanitarian arms and other pots of money. While none of them specifically fund ECD in emergencies, a case can be made for them to invest in the early years. These mechanisms include Education Cannot Wait (ECW) and the European Commission's Education in Emergencies initiative.

ECW is a new global fund dedicated to education in emergencies and protracted crises (ECW, ND). It brings together governments, humanitarian actors and development efforts to deliver a more collaborative and rapid response to the educational needs of children and youth aged 3–18 years affected by emergencies. The fund supports the whole range of the disaster cycle from the immediate onset to recovery phases. The fund aims to reach all crisis-affected children and youth with safe, free and quality education by 2030 (ibid.).

ECW, which is currently hosted at UNICEF in New York, was established in 2016 during the World Humanitarian Summit (ECW, ND). Myriad humanitarian and development actors, and public and private donors, decided to join hands to reposition education as a priority on the humanitarian agenda, usher in a more collaborative approach among key stakeholders in countries and catalyse additional funding to ensure that every crisis-affected child and young person is in school and learning (ibid.). Additionally, in September 2016, the New York Declaration for Refugees and Migrants—signed by 193 countries—highlighted education in emergencies as a cornerstone of the international response (UNHCR, 2016).

Current financial contributors to ECW include the governments of the United States, United Kingdom, EU, Canada, Denmark, Norway, the Netherlands, France and Australia. Dubai Cares and the Global Business Coalition for Education are two other non-government partners (ECW, ND).

ECW aims to achieve its mission by:

1 Inspiring political commitment so that governments and donors prioritise education in humanitarian situations.
2 Catalysing additional financing to help close the $8.5 billion funding gap needed to reach 75 million children and youth affected by crisis and emergencies.
3 Planning and responding collaboratively to support programmes that enable humanitarian and development actors to work together on shared objectives.
4 Strengthening capacity to respond to crises, nationally and globally, including the ability to coordinate emergency support.
5 Improving accountability by developing and sharing knowledge, including collection of more robust data in order to make better-informed investment decisions, and knowledge of what works and does not.

ECW has three funding windows: First Emergency Response window, Multi-year Resilience window and Acceleration Facility window (ECW, ND). ECW's First Emergency Response investment window supports education programmes immediately in sudden-onset or escalating crises.

ECW invests approximately 25% of its total budget to this window. The Multi-year Resilience investment window addresses long-term needs through multi-year (three to four years) joint programmes in protracted crises, enabling humanitarian and development actors to work together on delivering collective education outcomes. Projects funded within this window will be aligned with a country's Education plan and will focus on five priority outcomes: Increased Access, Increased Equity and Gender Equality (particularly for girls and children with disabilities), Continuity in Learning (ensuring children remain in school), Protection from Harm (ensuring all learning spaces are safe, healing environments for children) and Increased Quality (ensuring children learn through relevant curriculum, strong teachers and sufficient learning materials). Multi-year Resilience projects may also be jointly funded with the Global Partnership for Education that supports the development and implementation of National Education sector plans. The third funding window is the Acceleration Facility window which will support research and data collection, advance best practices and promote innovation, learning outcomes and gender-targeted interventions.

As of March 2018, ECW invested $81 million in 14 crisis-affected countries and through 42 implementing partners. The disbursements have mostly included allocations through the First Emergency Response window. To date, these funds have supported access to quality education for more than 650,000 children and youth of which 48% were girls (ibid.).

According to a member of the ECW Steering Committee, while the strategy includes educational support for children aged 3–18 years, few Humanitarian Response Plans or proposals have focused on ECD. Implementing partners in countries and OCHA, who coordinates the development of the Humanitarian Response Plan, have not been demanding the inclusion of ECD. When speaking with some International NGO staff in emergency affected countries, often their proposals are written by proposal developers and not technical staff. These individuals mentioned that technical NGO staff struggle to convince their own colleagues internally that there should be a focus on ECD. Therefore, change for ECD financing will need to come from various levels—from donors (top) and also from implementers (bottom).

In 2012, the EU received the Nobel Peace Prize. They decided to use the funds to launch an initiative to fund education in emergencies (European Commission, ND). This was a huge win for the education in emergencies community who have been and continue to fight for greater investment in children's learning. The EU has started with allocating 1% of their total humanitarian financial support in 2015 to education in emergencies (ibid.). Over the last few years, they have steadily increased their investment—5% in 2016, 6% in 2017, 8% in 2018 (ibid.). The total amount invested in education in emergencies reached €201.5 million between 2012 and 2017, which included €34 million through the EU Facility for Refugees in Turkey and €23.5 million through the Emergency Support Instrument. This has directly supported 5.5 million children in 52 countries (ibid.). The EU plans to increase their investment even further to 10% of their total humanitarian financing in 2019 (ibid.). With this significant investment, the EU is now shaping global policy on education in emergencies and influencing other donors to contribute.

While funding through the EU is focused on education which is often equated with primary and secondary education and not early learning opportunities for three to six years olds, some EU projects have funded preschool learning in emergencies. This has happened when ECD is prioritised in the country and a case is made for how it will help children's learning outcomes in primary grades. The potential for increasing investment for ECD, in particular early learning and parenting support in emergencies, is tremendous.

While humanitarian situations are increasing with more displaced individuals, there has been steady progress for ECD in emergencies support. Humanitarian work is more recognised as a profession, an architecture is in place to respond to emergencies and numerous financing mechanisms exist. The potential for ECD in emergencies to gain visibility, greater prioritisation and financing is present. What is needed is a top-down and bottom-up approach to (1) increase awareness of what is ECD and why it is important in emergencies, (2) coordinate efforts around ECD in emergencies (not necessarily with a new IASC cluster) and (3) strengthen the ability of implementing agencies to frame ECD so that it fits country, donor and sector/cluster priorities. In the next chapter, I delve into the context of the South Sudan crisis.

References

Ade, W. (1982). "Professionalization and its implications for the field of early childhood education", *Young Children*, 37(3), 25–32.

Anderson, A. and Roberts, B. (2005). "The inter-agency network for education in emergencies", *Forced Migration Review*, 22, 8–10.

Beech, H. (2018, January 1). "Rohingya children facing 'massive mental health crisis'", *New York Times*, www.nytimes.com/2017/12/31/world/asia/rohingya-children-myanmar.html, last accessed 1 January 2018.

Burnham, G. (2008). "Disaster definition", *In The Johns Hopkins and Red Cross Red Crescent Public health guide in emergencies*, https://reliefweb.int/sites/reliefweb.int/files/resources/Forward.pdf, last accessed 8 August 2018.

Davey, E., Borton, J. and Foley, M. (2013). *A History of the Humanitarian System: Western Origins and Foundation*. London: Humanitarian Policy Group, Overseas Development Institute.

Education Cluster (ND). http://educationcluster.net

Education Cannot Wait (ND). www.educationcannotwait.org/the-fund

Engle, P. et al. (2007). "Child development in developing countries 3 strategies to avoid the loss of developmental potential in more than 200 million children in the developing world", *The Lancet*, 369, 229–242, London.

European Commission. (ND). Retrieved 2 July 2018, https://ec.europa.eu/echo/what/humanitarian-aid/education-emergencies_en

Ferris, E. and Solis, M. (2013). *Earthquake, Tsunami, Meltdown – The Triple Disaster's Impact on Japan, Impact on the World*. Washington, DC: Brookings Institute.

Gostelow, L. (2009). "The sphere project: The implications of making humanitarian principles and codes work", *Disasters*, 34(4), 316–325.

Grantham-McGregor, S. et al. (2007). "Developmental potential in the first five years for children in developing countries", *The Lancet*, 369, 60–70, London.

Kagawa, F. (2005). "Emergency education: A critical review of the field", *Comparative Education*, 41(4), 487–503.

Johns Hopkins and International Federation of the Red Cross and Red Crescent Societies (2008). "Disaster definitions", In *Public Health Guide in Emergencies*. Johns Hopkins University and International Federation of Red Cross and Red Crescent Societies,

www.jhsph.edu/research/centers-and-institutes/center-for-refugee-and-disaster-response/publications_tools/publications/_CRDR_ICRC_Public_Health_Guide_Book/Forward.pdf

Joyce, K. et al. (2009). "Remote sensing and the disaster management cycle", In Jedlovec, G. (Ed.) *Advances in Geoscience and Remote Sensing*. London: IntechOpen Limited, 317–346.

IASC (ND). 2 July 2018, http://interagencystandingcommittee.org/

Lake, A. (2017). "Statement by UNICEF Executive Director Anthony Lake on the situation in Yemen", UNICEF, www.unicef.org/media/media_101460.html, last accessed 17 May 2019.

Martin, S. (2006). "Forced migration and professionalism", *International Migration Review*, 35(1), 226–243.

Moensch, M. (2007). *Costs and Benefits of Disaster Risk Reduction, Information Note 3, Global Platform for Disaster Risk Reduction*. Geneva: UNISDR.

Nicolai, S., et. al., (2016). *A common platform for education in emergencies and protracted crises: Evidence paper.* London: Overseas Development Institute.

O'Flaherty, M. and Ulrich, G. (2010). "The professionalization of human rights field work", *Journal of Human Rights Practice*, 2(1), 1–27.

Paulmann, J. (2013). "Conjunctures in the history of international humanitarian aid during the twentieth century", *Humanity: An International Journal of Human Rights, Humanitarianism, and Development*, 4(2), 215–238.

Rey Marcos, F. (2010). "Thoughts about the professionalization of the humanitarian sector", *Voice Out Loud*, 1, 8–9.

Sinclair, M. (2002). *Planning Education in and after Emergencies*. Paris: UNESCO IIEP.

Slim, H. (1995). "The continuing metamorphosis of the humanitarian practitioner: Some new colours for an endangered chameleon", *Disasters*, 19(20), 110–126.

The Sphere Project: Humanitarian Charter and Minimum Standards in Disaster Response (2011). www.sphereproject.org/content/view/91/58/lang,english/, last accessed 28 November 2010.

Stoddard, A. (2008). *International Humanitarian Financing: Review and comparative assessment of instruments*. US Office of Foreign Disaster Assistance: Washington, DC, www.ghdinitiative.org/assets/files/Resource%20Center/Humanitarian%20Financing/Funding%20Management/34.%20International%20Humanitarian%20Financing%20Review%202008.pdf, last accessed 8 August 2018.

Swithern, S. (2015). *Global Humanitarian Assistance Report 2015*, http://devinit.org/wp-content/uploads/2015/10/GHA2015P_Friendly2.pdf, last accessed 8 August 2018.

Their World (2016). *Safe Spaces: The Urgent Need for Early Childhood Development in Emergencies and Disasters*. London: Their World.

UNESCO (2015). *Humanitarian Aid for Education: Why It Matters and Why More Is Needed, Education for All Global Monitoring Report*, Policy Paper 21. Paris: UNESCO.

United Nations Office for Disaster Risk Reduction (2009). www.unisdr.org/we/inform/publications/7817, last accessed 18 May 2016.

UNOCHA (2018a). *World Humanitarian Data and Trends 2018*. New York and Geneva: UNOCHA.

UNOCHA (2018b). *Global Humanitarian Overview 2018: Six Months on*, www.unocha.org/story/global-humanitarian-overview-2018-six-months

UNOCHA (2019). Country-Based Pooled Funds Fact Sheet, https://reliefweb.int/sites/reliefweb.int/files/resources/CBPF%20Factsheet%20March%202017_EN.pdf, last accessed 17 April 2019.

UNHCR (2016). *New York Declaration for Refugees and Migrants*, www.unhcr.org/en-us/new-york-declaration-for-refugees-and-migrants.html, last accessed 8 August 2018.

UNHCR (2017a). *Global Trends: Forced Displacement in 2017*. Geneva: UNHCR.

UNHCR (2017b, March 17). "South Sudan's refugee crisis now world's fastest growing, Uganda and region in critical need of help", www.unhcr.org/en-us/news/briefing/2017/3/58cba77f4/south-sudans-refugee-crisis-worlds-fastest-growing-uganda-region-critical.html

UNHCR (2017c, August 17). "South Sudan refugees in Uganda pass 1 million mark, UNHCR renews call for help", www.unhcr.org/599457a34.html

Walker, P. (2003). "What does it mean to be a professional humanitarian?" *The Journal of Humanitarian Assistance*, https://sites.tufts.edu/jha/archives/73, last accessed 25 July 2019.

Welsh, T. (2019). "CERF: The fund that functions 'like the ambulance for the UN'", www.devex.com/news/cerf-the-fund-that-functions-like-the-ambulance-for-the-un-94731, last accessed 24 April 2019.

Willemse, J. (2010). "The evolution of the NGO sector – a historical perspective", *Voice Out Loud*, 11, 10–11.

4 South Sudan

Decades of conflict with little respite

A father from Lakes state in South Sudan told me "We have been fighting for so long. We want peace and we want our children to learn to be peaceful." The people of South Sudan have endured a long war that has yet to find a durable solution. The decades-long conflict in South Sudan started long before there was even a country called South Sudan. This chapter delves into the history and context of war in South Sudan. It provides the backdrop for this book's research.

In the beginning it was just Sudan

South Sudan, one of the newest countries in the centre of Africa, is landlocked and bordered by Uganda, Ethiopia, Kenya, Democratic Republic of Congo and Central African Republic. While it is rich in oil, it has been entrenched in conflict and violence for generations, making it one of the least developed countries in the world (BBC, May 2014). This new nation has been stuck in conflict since the 1950s when it was first a part of Anglo-Egyptian Sudan under joint British-Egyptian rule (BBC, 2016a, 2016b; Iyob and Khadiagala, 2006; Jok, 2011). In 1956 Sudan gained independence from the joint British-Egyptian rule and made Khartoum the new capital of Sudan. While the country gained independence, existing tensions between various tribes remained and exacerbated as the northern tribes had a hold on the seat of power in Khartoum. Tribes and ethnic groups from the northern, southern and western parts of the country have different cultures and generally different religions (many tribes in the north are Muslim and often with lighter skin, the tribes in the south are mostly Christian or Animist and often with darker skin and the tribes in the west are Muslims, but have darker skin colour) (Iyob and Khadiagala, 2006). Figures 4.1 and 4.2 show the location of various ethnic and religious groups. While in Sudan, the majority group are Arabs and the majority religion is Islam, the main ethnic/tribal groups in South Sudan are Dinka and Nuer and the main religions Christianity and Indigenous faiths.

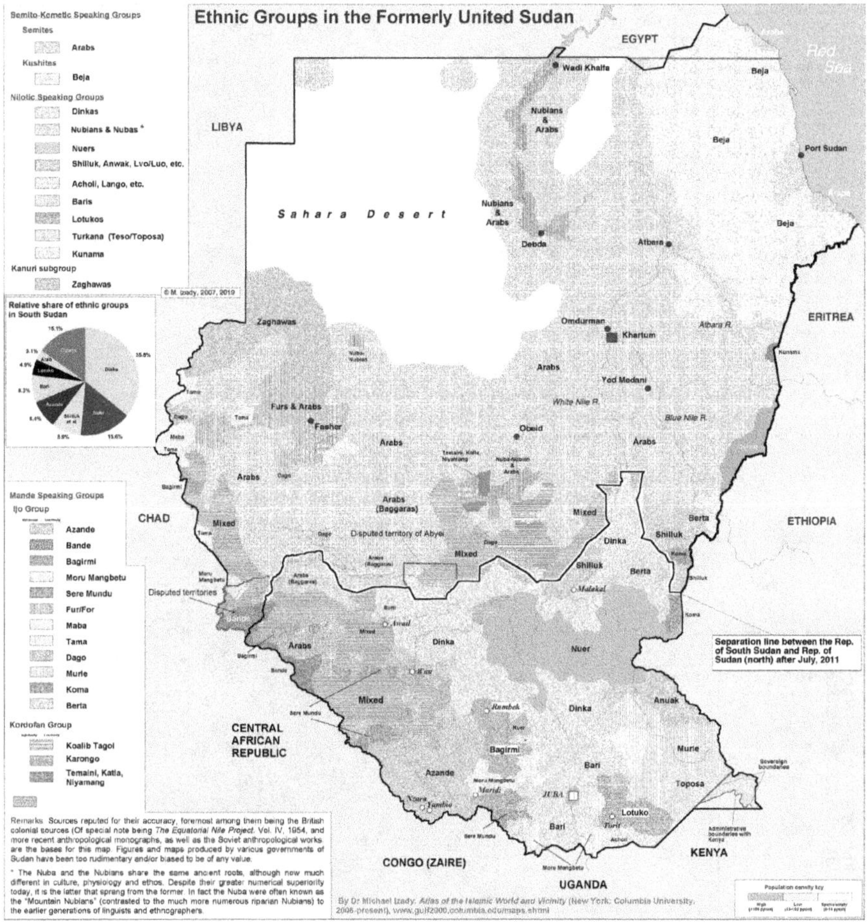

Figure 4.1 Ethnic Groups in the Formerly United Sudan.

The differences in culture, religion and ethnicity created tension between the various tribes once the capital of Sudan was established in the Arab and Muslim-dominated northern city of Khartoum. As the new government of Sudan started, many people in the southern (now South Sudan) and western (Darfur) parts of the country felt marginalised (ibid.). Their needs were not being addressed and they were not benefiting greatly from an independent Sudan (ibid.).

The Sudan Household Survey of 2006, when South Sudan and Sudan were one country, indicates stark disparities in education, infant mortality, household food consumption and water and sanitation (Ministry of

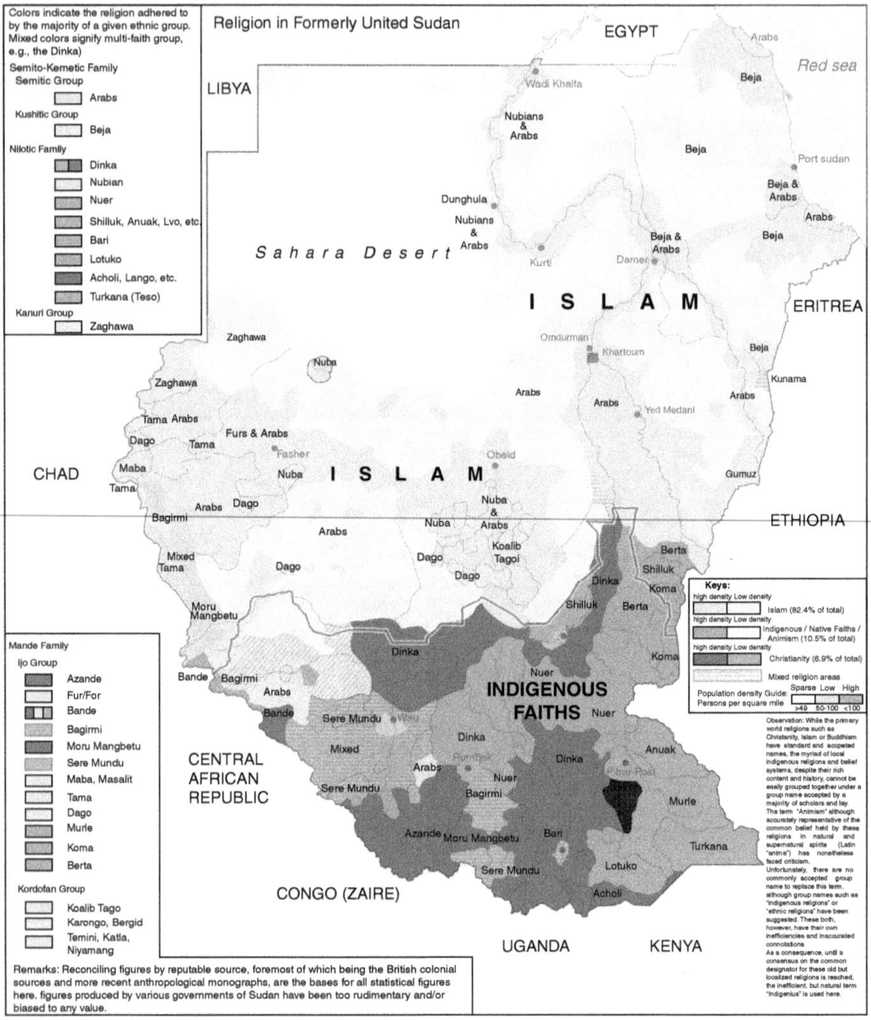

Figure 4.2 Religion in the Formerly United Sudan.

Health, Government of Southern Sudan, 2006). Table 4.1 summarises the differences.

In education, the majority of what is now South Sudan had less than 5% of children who completed primary school whereas in the northern part of the country the percentages ranged from 11% to 30% with a majority falling in the range between 21% and 30% (ibid). With regard to infant mortality, the greatest concentration of infant mortality was in the states of South Sudan and one part of Darfur, next to the border with Chad. The Household Survey reveals that in the states of South Sudan, one state at the South Sudan border

Table 4.1 Sudan and South Sudan

	Sudan	**South Sudan**
Primary school completion	Majority 21–30%	Majority <5%
Infant mortality (Deaths <one year old, per 1,000 live births)	Majority <50–70	Majority 71—over 100
Poor household food consumption	Majority <10–20%	Majority 21–40%
Improved water and sanitation services	Majority	Majority <5%

and two parts of Darfur on the west of the country had between 21% and 40% of households with poor food consumption. The majority of households indicated that the range was mostly at 31% and greater. Lastly, questions regarding access to clean water and sanitation indicated that in South Sudan, the percentage of households using "improved" water and sanitation facilities was <5%. The city of Juba was the only part of South Sudan whose range was 5–10% of households (ibid).

These disparities in services provided and lack of development focus in the south underpinned the rationale for rebel groups in the southern part of the country to start a war with the north (BBC, 2013).

This was the beginning of many years of civil war in Sudan between the northern, southern and western parts of Sudan. The first Sudan Civil War lasted between 1955 and 1972 (BBC, 2016a; BBC, 2016b; Iyob and Khadiagala, 2006; Jok, 2011). In 1972, a peace agreement was signed in Addis Ababa where the President of Sudan gave some autonomy to the southern part of the country (BBC, 2016a; BBC, 2016b; Iyob and Khadiagala, 2006; Jok, 2011). However, in 1978 oil was discovered in Unity State which is part of the southern part of Sudan (and which is currently a part of the country of South Sudan). Sudanese President Jaafar Nimeiri then abolished South Sudan's autonomy, prompting the eruption of violence and another civil war between the northern and southern parts of the country under the leadership of John Garang and the Sudanese People's Liberation Movement (SPLM) and the armed wing Sudanese People's Liberation Army (SPLA). This second civil war in Sudan between the north and the south lasted between 1983 and 2005 (BBC, 2016a; BBC, 2016b; Jok, 2011).

Autonomy for the south

A Comprehensive Peace Agreement (CPA) was signed in January 2005 which included a permanent ceasefire, autonomy for the south, a power-sharing government involving representatives from the SPLM in Khartoum and a South Sudanese referendum on independence in six years (BBC, 2016a; BBC, 2016b; Jok, 2011). In July of that year, a new constitution gave the south a large degree of autonomy. Further, John Garang, the former rebel leader of the SPLA was sworn in as Vice-President of Sudan. Soon after being sworn in as Vice-President, John Garang was killed in a plane crash, which sparked violent clashes in Khartoum between supporters of Garang from the south and those from the north that did not support Garang. Salva Kiir Mayardit succeeded Garang as the leader of the SPLA.

In September 2005, violence abated and a power-sharing government was formed in Khartoum. Soon after in October, an autonomous government, dominated by former rebels from SLPM/SPLA, was formed in South Sudan, in line with the January 2005 peace agreement. Even with this agreement and power-sharing deal, smaller scale violence continued between Arab militias from the northern part of the country and those from the southern part of the country—SPLA. This occurred mostly in the southern towns of Malakal and Abyei, which have important resources such as oil. The northern and southern parts of the country continued with fighting and cease fires until 2011 when a referendum about the future of the southern part of the country was held (BBC, 2016a).

Independence yet conflict continues

In 2010, then President Omar Bashir said he would accept any result of the referendum even if the south voted for full independence (BBC, 2016a; BBC, 2016b). On 9 July 2011, 99% of Sudanese in the southern part of Sudan voted for full independence. I was in Juba at the time the results were announced. While there was fear that violence could break out, the city remained calm. Many people I interacted with were excited and optimistic about the new country and its future. As the country became independent from British and Egyptian rules, national institutions remained weak, and the physical infrastructure remained inadequate to meet the needs of its people (Smith, 2017). Due to years with little access to educational opportunities, the capacity of many of its people remained limited. A few South Sudanese colleagues said that they had always been marginalised and not given leadership opportunities in Sudan. So, they were worried South Sudanese would not be able to peacefully govern their new country. These sentiments predicted what was to come to the new country. Approximately 60 ethnic groups divided into separate tribes remained in the country. These groups were separated into varying geographic pockets. The new border between the north and the south put the oil-rich town of Abyei right in the middle, which has continued to cause tensions and fighting as both countries want the economic benefits of the oil. Further, tensions and violence have continued all along the border areas and in Unity, Upper Nile and Jonglei states. In January 2012, South Sudan declared a humanitarian emergency for Jonglei state after approximately 100,000 fled due to clashes between rival ethnic groups—mostly the Dinka and Nuer tribes. Some of these people crossed into other countries, while some remained internally displaced in South Sudan, settling in states such as neighbouring Lakes. In February 2012, Sudan and

South Sudan signed a non-aggression pact while also dealing with remaining secession issues. The oil-rich town of Abyei is part of the disputes between Sudan and South Sudan; oil is drilled out of South Sudan while pipes to export it go through Sudan. Sudan shut down the oil pipes saying South Sudan had not paid their fees for transporting the oil through Sudan. In August of that year, another 200,000 people from the disputed areas in Sudan near the borders with South Sudan fled into South Sudan to escape fighting. Discussions aiming to resolve these disputes ended in March 2013 so oil could continue to be pumped and both countries could continue to profit. All troops from Sudan and South Sudan were withdrawn and the area was made into a demilitarised zone (ibid.).

2013 South Sudan internal crisis

While South Sudan gained its independence in 2011 and disputes between Sudan and South Sudan continued for two years, South Sudan faced another crisis, but this time within its borders (ibid.). Due to a power struggle within the government, President Salva Kiir Mayardit (who is from the Dinka tribe and leader of the SPLM) dismissed the cabinet and Vice-President Riek Machar (who is from the Nuer tribe). Civil war erupted in mid-December 2013 when President Kiir accused ex-Vice-President Machar of plotting to overthrow him. Through this, Kiir and Machar have divided the country along sectarian lines. Machar and the rebels seized control of several regional towns in South Sudan. Fighting between government troops and rebel factions erupted, killing and injuring thousands of people, and pushing more than 2.5 million people to leave their homes. During this time, South Sudan was divided into 10 states or regions as seen in Figure 4.3.

Figure 4.3 South Sudan Administrative States.

In August 2014, peace talks began in Addis Ababa, Ethiopia and a year later in August 2015, President Salva Kiir signed an internationally mediated peace deal called the Agreement on the Resolution of Conflict in South Sudan (ARCSS) where Riek Machar was re-instated as Vice-President (Smith, 2017). In October of 2015, President Kiir announced his decision to change the map of South Sudan—from 10 states to 28 states (The Stimson Center, 2016).

Re-emergence of conflict in 2016

While a peace deal was signed and Machar was sworn in as the first Vice-President of a new unity government of South Sudan in April 2016, both sides were pushed into a deal that they did not fully agree with. In July 2016, Machar was sacked again and returned to exile. Fighting has continued. Violence which started primarily between the Dinka and Nuer tribes of Kiir and Machar in the eastern and northern parts of South Sudan has now spread quickly to Juba and the states below it which have different ethnic groups and tribes, including the Madi, Acholi, and Bari (ibid.; Smith, 2017). This area was previously peaceful and not greatly affected when fighting erupted in 2013. However, since the re-emergence of violence, the southern part of South Sudan has been severely affected (Smith, 2017). Fighting is increasing at an alarming rate and touching many more aspects of people's lives. Long-held grievances that tribes did not deal with through violence are now using this as a means to be heard, to get revenge. Small arms are proliferating, criminality is increasing, political and economic elites are stoking ethnic division through inflammatory rhetoric to build constituencies and consolidate power. Children are also being recruited and used by militias and armed groups, which now number over 40 throughout the country. Between January and May 2017, there was a two-thirds increase in violence against civilians and nearly 1.5 times more communal ethnic conflict-related incidents (ibid.). As violence and tensions are increasing, tribes are becoming further isolated which is strengthening this circle of violence. Research conducted in Juba and Bor found that 45% of people had interacted fewer than three times per week with a member of a different tribe (Smith, 2017). The isolation is fuelling tension and reinforcing ethnic and tribal stereotypes. The myriad drivers of conflict are mutually reinforcing each other in an environment of impunity without the rule of law and ethnic isolation and division.

In December 2016, a United Nations commission on human rights team who visited South Sudan said they saw a process of ethnic cleansing in several parts of the country, a claim that President Salva Kiir denied (OHCHR, 2016). Adding to the conflict, tension and spread of violence beyond the Nuer and Dinka tribes, was a famine which was declared in February 2017 (BBC, 2017b). The United Nations describes the famine as a man-made catastrophe caused by civil war and economic collapse of South Sudan (ibid.). As fighting intensified, crops were destroyed and cattle killed. The forced displacement and insecurity caused disruptions in traditional planting seasons and agriculture activities, which has resulted in a lower yield of food. With less food being grown, the prices have spiked, making it difficult for many families in the lowest socio-economic group to purchase it (Smith, 2017). The southern parts of the country and the former Unity state were particularly affected. Approximately six million people in South Sudan by August 2017 were considered severely food insecure and about 100,000 estimated to be on the verge of starvation (Smith, 2017).

As of December 2017, the famine subsided and South Sudan was no longer declared to be in a state of famine (BBC, 2017a; BBC, 2017b). However, thousands of people have already been displaced, and violence has not abated.

Before independence, there were few representatives from the south in the Khartoum government. Conversations I had with South Sudanese and Westerners that work for non-governmental organisations (NGOs) said that because South Sudanese did not have many opportunities to be a part of the Khartoum government, few people in an independent South Sudan know how to run a country. This, from their perspective, has contributed to the challenges that South Sudan has faced in building a strong and independent government and has contributed to internal conflict in 2013 and 2016.

Mass displacement in Northern Uganda

Since 2013, it is estimated that over 50,000 people were killed and over 4 million were displaced within South Sudan and its neighbouring countries (Smith, 2017). According to the United Nations High Commissioner for Refugees (UNHCR), by December 2017, there were 2,466,027 refugees and asylum seekers from South Sudan in Uganda, Ethiopia, Kenya, Democratic Republic of Congo, Central African Republic and Sudan (UNHCR, 2017). In South Sudan itself, it estimated that there are approximately 1.9 million internally displaced persons (IDPs) and 280,000 refugees, mostly from South Kordofan and Blue Nile regions of Sudan (ibid.). UNHCR's statistics indicate that there are now more than 1,065,094 South Sudanese refugees in the camps/settlements in Uganda (UNHCR, 2017). This makes Uganda the host to the largest percentage of South Sudanese refugees (ibid.). Much of this occurred during the re-escalation of conflict in 2016 where refugees fled from the southern parts of South Sudan close to the Uganda border.

Figure 4.4 shows the map of Uganda divided into four parts: Central (where the capital of Kampala is), Eastern, Western and Northern.

When there was civil war in Uganda, it was concentrated in the northern part of the country. With difficulties in South Sudan and Democratic Republic of Congo, there are currently refugees from both these countries in the northern part of Uganda. Figure 4.5, based on UNHCR data, illustrates the various locations of South Sudanese refugee camps/settlements in the north-western part of Uganda.

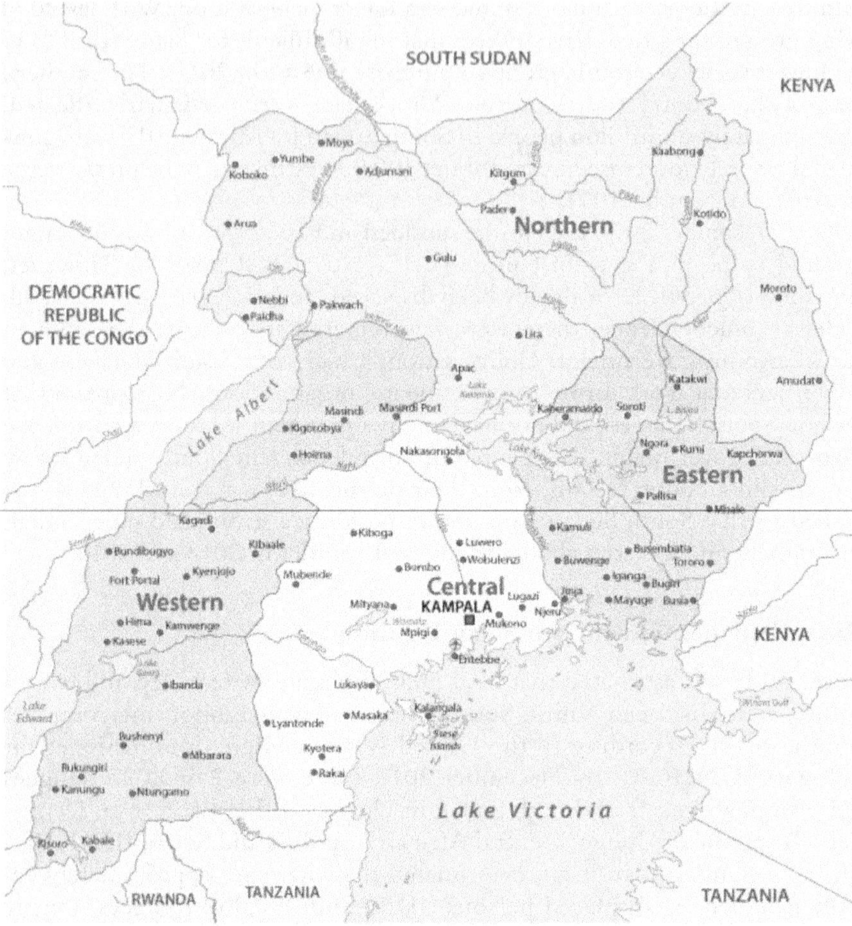

Figure 4.4 Map of Uganda.

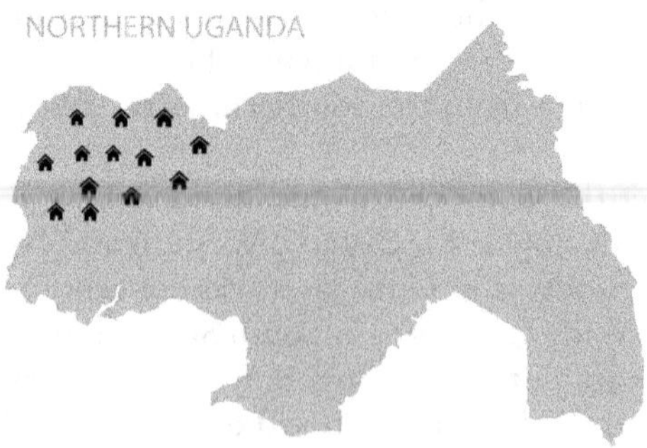

Figure 4.5 South Sudan refugee settlements in Uganda (as of 2017).

There are currently 14 refugee settlements around the catchment areas of Yumbe, Arua and Adjumani: Arua being the most western, Yumbe being the most northern and Adjumani being the most eastern. They are not like refugee camps one might see in other conflict and displacement situations where people are given a tiny spot of land for a tent. The Ugandan government has allowed the South Sudanese refugees settle on this land and while people have settled near each other, some have space to plant vegetables and move around. Most people in the camps/settlements have created semi-permanent to permanent shelter usually made from mud and bricks. The camps/settlements include Ayilo I, Ayilo II, Boroli, Maaji 1, Maaji II, Maaji III, Palorinya, Baratuku, Nyumanzi, Pagrinya, Bidibidi, Imvepi, Lobute and Rhino.

After the 2013 conflict, the majority of South Sudanese refugees in Uganda, Ethiopia and Kenya came from Jonglei, Unity and Upper Nile states, which had large numbers of people from the Dinka and Nuer tribes. The majority of the South Sudanese refugees where research for this book was conducted are in the Adjumani catchment area. Most of these people come from Jonglei state which was a Nuer stronghold. This is why most of the South Sudanese refugees from Jonglei state are Dinka as they had to flee attacks against them. Seventy-one per cent of refugees during the initial influx which started in 2013 are from Jonglei state and in particular from the town of Bor, which is the capital of Jonglei state, and Pibor another large town in the state. A smaller percentage of South Sudanese refugees in Uganda during this time came from Upper Nile and Unity states in the northern part of the country and from Central Equatoria where the capital Juba is located.

As conflict re-escalated in 2016, a second influx of South Sudanese refugees went mostly to Uganda in new catchment areas near the towns of Yumbe and Arua. As these refugees were displaced from different parts of South Sudan, mostly from the states formerly known as Central and Eastern Equatoria, the ethnic and tribal makeup of the newer refugees is different from those currently in the Adjumani area. The major tribes in the Yumbe and Arua are from the Bari, Madi, Acholi and other tribes found in Central and Eastern Equatoria.

Uganda: a safe refuge in a conflict-affected country

Uganda itself has its own history of conflict and displacement, which has also influenced the conflict in South Sudan. During the mid-1980s, many Acholi people in northern Uganda felt marginalised, abused and excluded from Uganda's development (Berber and Blattman, 2013). For two decades following independence, the Acholi people had political dominance, but this changed when Yoweri Museveni came into power (ibid.). A 'Holy Spirit Movement', rebellion led by Alice Lakwena, started during this time to fight the oppression of the northern part of Uganda (which has majority from the

Acholi tribe) (Invisible Children website, accessed 2016). When Alice Lakwena was exiled from Uganda, Joseph Kony took over and changed the name of the group to the Lord's Resistance Army (LRA) (ibid.).

The LRA fought a low-scale war against President Museveni and his government; however, civilian support for the LRA was meagre (Berber and Blattman, 2013). Kony had only a few hundred fighters in his ranks, so these people raided people's homes, taking food, medicine and forcibly recruiting youth along the way at night (ibid.). From 1988 to 1994, the LRA kidnapped and forcibly recruited several thousand children and youth to be child soldiers in their ranks. They forced these young people to kill and mutilate their own family members and neighbours (ibid.). This rebellion might have died out on its own if it had not been for the Sudanese government, who in 1994 began arming the LRA. Further they gave them territory in Sudan where they could build bases. The Sudanese government did this in retaliation for President Museveni's support of the southern Sudanese rebels—SPLA. The Khartoum government's support for the LRA reinvigorated the group and as a result attacks and abductions of children escalated. Over this period of war between the LRA and the Ugandan government, it is estimated that 60,000 to 80,000 children, mostly adolescent boys, were abducted and forced to be soldiers in the LRA. Adolescent girls were taken as well to become fighters, servants and "wives." Estimates indicate that when fighting ceased about 82% of these abductees escaped and survived. The LRA's fighting peaked in 2002 when the Ugandan army drove them from their base in Sudan to Uganda. Intense fighting continued through 2004 when they were defeated. Since 2004, the LRA, while still in existence, is small and mobile. The LRA are thought to be moving through the western parts of South Sudan, eastern parts of Central African Republic and principally in eastern Democratic Republic of Congo (Berber and Blattman, 2013; Raghavan and Whitlock, 2013). Abductions in Uganda stopped in 2005 where there was peace (Berber and Blattman, 2013).

Adjumani, Uganda: research location

While the LRA's terror was mostly confined to northern Uganda, Adjumani, where many South Sudanese refugees are currently staying, was not untouched. It still remains a conflict affected and poor part of Uganda. This is the context that the refugees displaced after the 2013 conflict have gone and the context in which the research was conducted.

Adjumani is located in Uganda's West Nile region, west of Gulu, Lira and Kitgum, where much of the LRA fighting occurred. It also borders what is now South Sudan; the porous border has meant that people go back and forth between the two countries. The majority ethnic group among Ugandans in Adjumani is the Madi tribe, which also live in the southern part of South Sudan (Okello and Ng, 2006).

Adjumani district is home to one of the largest refugee populations in Uganda, being affected by the LRA fighting and war between the SPLA and the Khartoum government in Sudan (Okello and Ng, 2006; UNHCR, 2002). While some camps were set up for Sudanese displaced during the SPLA's war with the Khartoum government, IDPs affected by fighting between the LRA and the Ugandan army received little humanitarian support. Most displaced families were not registered and placed in camps. There are many reasons for Adjumani being overlooked by humanitarian actors, especially those displaced during the LRA fighting. First, while Adjumani is a part of the greater northern Uganda region, it is administratively part of the West Nile region. The LRA war was thought to be an "Acholi" problem and because Adjumani's ethnic majority is "Madi," there was not much focus given. Because the government did not move the displaced Ugandans into camps, they were not visible by humanitarian actors. Lastly, the scale of the internal displacement was not comparable to other parts of Uganda, including Gulu, Lira and Kitgum (east of Adjumani) (ibid.).

Further, Adjumani borders South Sudan and has many people from the Madi tribe, who also live in southern South Sudan near the border. As the border between Sudan and Uganda was and continues to be porous, Sudan People's Liberation Army (SPLA) regularly went into Adjumani and operated from there (ibid.).

Status of Early Childhood Development in South Sudan and Uganda

Early Childhood Development (ECD), or Early Childhood Development and Education (ECDE) as it is referred to by the South Sudanese government, is a new concept and still requires a lot sensitisation among the general population (UNESCO, 2015). In the past, availability of early learning classes and opportunities have been limited and dominated by the private sector. This was because the Sudanese government and then the South Sudanese government did not have the resources or capacities to tackle this issue when they could not meet the needs of primary education. During these years, those children that accessed pre-primary or ECDE activities were in urban areas and ones whose families could afford to pay the required fees (ibid.).

In 2012, in order to combat this and support greater access to early learning throughout South Sudan, the government passed the Education Act 2012, which mentions two years of early learning as an introduction to the schooling experience for children aged between three and five years (Ministry of Justice, 2012). Additionally, the General Education Strategic Plan (GESP) 2012–2017 also prioritises the access and quality of ECDE. The national government has now also established a national curriculum for ECDE. These classrooms, as is stipulated in the Education Act 2012 and GESP, have to be part of existing primary schools as nursery or kindergarten classrooms (ibid; UNESCO, 2015).

The most recent 2013 statistics indicate that there are currently 652 schools with ECDE classrooms and 1,774 ECDE classrooms nationally (Ministry of Education, Science and Technology, 2015; UNESCO, 2015). These spaces, which are now mostly government or community owned and operated, provide 77,312 children aged three to five years access to early learning activities. Community owned and operated classrooms are often supported by faith-based groups or the private sector. ECDE currently in comparison with primary, secondary and other types of education has among the highest gender parities. Among the total enrolled children, 52.2% are boys and 47.6% are girls. There are 2,286 ECDE teachers nationally (ibid).

While there are policies, legislation and a national curriculum in place, and while there has been an expansion of early learning services in South Sudan, the government continues to struggle with providing early learning opportunities, especially outside urban areas and for the most marginalised children. ECDE has not been allocated enough funding from the government in its annual national education budget. In places where fighting has been on and off (including Jonglei state), the access to education overall is small and access to ECDE is even smaller. The Education Cluster in South Sudan found that over 70% of the 1,200 schools in Jonglei, Unity and Upper Nile states, where the conflict has been most severe, have been closed since the onset of the crisis (Education Cluster, 2015). Further, the Education Cluster found that at least 91 schools in the three states have been occupied by armed groups or used as shelters (ibid.). Many parts of Jonglei state have virtually no ECDE services (Plan International Education Assessment, 2015). Though there are policies and legislation for ECDE, there is no policy framework to guide the establishment and management of ECDE centres. Further, there are no policy guidelines to assist in raising more funds.

In addition to issues of access, especially for the rural parts of the conflict-affected states of Jonglei, Unity and Upper Nile, quality is also low. Textbooks and other teaching and learning materials are in short supply. Often 25 children share 1 textbook. As ECDE is still a new concept in South Sudan, there is little support from local governments and the systems they manage (South Sudan, EMIS) and communities. Out of the existing 2,286 ECDE teachers only about 37% of them have received training on the national curriculum and how to work with young children to promote their learning. Some of the existing teachers only speak Arabic and now the curriculum is changing over to promoting English in schools. The government has plans to establish short and long courses for strengthening the capacity of ECDE teachers through teacher training institutes in the country. However, implementing this has been challenging due to insufficient funds and continued insecurity in the country.

Uganda in contrast has made larger leaps in providing ECD to its children. In 2016, the Ugandan Ministry of Gender, Labour and Social Development led the development of the "National Integrated Early Childhood Development Policy of Uganda" (Ministry of Gender, Labour and Social Development,

2016)). The Integrated Early Child Development (IECD) policy will be in effect from 2016 to 2021. This is the first national policy focused on ECD that has been agreed upon by various government ministries—the Ministry of Gender, Labour and Social Development, Ministry of Education, Ministry of Health and the Ministry of Finance, Planning and Economic Development. The ministries have agreed to work together to support children from conception to eight years in the areas of maternal and child health and nutrition (including prenatal and post-natal care for mothers and early infant stimulation), sanitation, protection against abuse, exploitation and violence and early childhood care and education (including pre-school and community-based childcare). This policy also includes family strengthening support and in particular support for parents and primary caregivers. The IECD policy aims to harmonise the goals and strategies across sectors and levels from national, district and community levels to ensure greater coordination and integrated and inclusive services. The IECD policy highlights a particular focus on the most marginalised and vulnerable children in Uganda; this includes support at the national level for young refugee children. While this is a great step for Uganda's and refugees' children, it is only a national-level policy and does not yet have a clear implementation plan or financing. UNICEF Uganda is currently working closely with the government to help them implement this policy, including raising the money to finance its implementation.

Both South Sudan and Uganda have experienced decades of conflict. While some pockets, such as northern Uganda, have peace, the remnants of war remain. Additionally, both countries have recognised ECD, but still have a long way to go before high-level talk and policies can impact the lives of young children and especially young refugee children. The research for this book was thus conducted within this backdrop of years of violence and few ECD services where a whole generation of people had few opportunities for education and even fewer chances of succeeding economically. Some of their children have only seen war, displacement and refugee camps. According to refugee leaders and ECD caregivers in the settlements around the Adjumani catchment area, many said that they were happy to at least have basic services in Uganda, even if they are not sufficient. Their children have a chance to obtain education, which many did not have in South Sudan, especially not for three to five years olds.

The next chapter explores the last part of the background and context of this book. Chapter 5 analyses child and human development and how its intersection provides a new lens and theoretical underpinning to understand ECD in emergencies.

References

BBC (2013). "South Sudan on precipice of civil war, Obama warns", www.bbc.com/news/world-africa-25459615, last accessed 30 September 2015.

BBC (2014). "South Sudan: What is the fighting about?", www.bbc.com/news/world-africa-25427965, last accessed 5 March 2019.

BBC (2016a). "South Sudan County Profile", www.bbc.com/news/world-africa-14069082, last accessed 28 May 2016.

BBC (2016b). "South Sudan profile – Timeline", www.bbc.com/news/world-africa-14019202, last accessed 28 May 2016.

BBC (2017a). "South Sudan famine: What is happening and why?" last accessed 28 July 2019, www.bbc.co.uk/newsround/39107125

BBC (2017b). "South Sudan no longer in famine", last accessed 28 July 2019, www.bbc.com/news/world-africa-40352926

Berber, B. and Blattman, C. (2013). "The logic of child soldiering and coercion", *International Organization*, 67(1), 65–104.

Education Cluster (2015). *Education Cluster Strategic Response Plan 2015*, https://reliefweb.int/report/south-sudan/education-cluster-strategic-response-plan-2015, last accessed 5 March 2019.

Government of Uganda. http://health.go.ug/sites/default/files/FINAL%20NIECD%20Popular%20Version%20Approved%20by%20Acting%20P.S%20%20%20%20%20%20%20Mpagi.pdf

Invisible Children website. http://invisiblechildren.com/conflict/history/, last accessed 16 June 2016.

Iyob, R. and Khadiagala, G. (2006). *Sudan: The Elusive Quest for Peace*. Boulder, CO: Lynne Rienner Publishers.

Jok, J.M. (2011). "Diversity, Unity, and Nation Building in South Sudan", Washington, DC: US Institutes of Peace, www-preview.usip.org/sites/default/files/Diversity,%20Unity,%20and%20Nation%20Building%20in%20South%20Sudan%20(Jok).pdf

Ministry of Education, Science and Technology (2015), *Education Statistics for the Republic of South Sudan*, Juba: Government of South Sudan, last accessed 28 July 2019, http://www.altaiconsulting.com/wp-content/uploads/2016/03/SSEMIS_2015_National.pdf

Ministry of Gender, Labour and Social Development (2016), National Integrated Early Childhood Development Policy of Uganda, Kampala: Government of Uganda, last accessed 28 July 2019, https://health.go.ug/sites/default/files/FINAL%20NIECD%20Popular%20Version%20Approved%20by%20Acting%20P.S%20%20%20%20%20%20%20Mpagi.pdf

Ministry of Health, Government of Southern Sudan (MOH-GOSS) (2006), "South Sudan Household Survey", *South Sudan Medical Journal*, Juba: Government of South Sudan, last accessed 28 July 2019, http://www.southsudanmedicaljournal.com/research/southern-sudan-household-survey.html

Ministry of Justice, Government of South Sudan, Laws of South Sudan, General Education Act, 2012, Juba: Government of South Sudan, last accessed 28 July 2019, https://planipolis.iiep.unesco.org/sites/planipolis/files/ressources/general_education_act_2012.pdf

OHCHR (2016). "UN human rights experts says international community has an obligation to prevent ethnic cleansing in South Sudan", www.ohchr.org/EN/NewsEvents/Pages/DisplayNews.aspx?LangID=E&NewsID=20970, last accessed 5 March 2019.

Okello, M.C. and Ng, J. (2006). *Invisibly Displaced Persons in Adjumani District*, Refugee Law Project, Working paper No. 19, Makerere University, Uganda. www.refugeelawproject.org/files/working_papers/RLP.WP19.pdf

Plan International Education Assessment (2015). unpublished document.

Raghavan, S. and Whitlock, C. (2013). "Hunt for Joseph Kony, elusive African warlord, is halted", *Washington Post*, www.washingtonpost.com/world/hunt-for-elusive-african-warlord-halted/2013/04/03/833cc0dc-9c81-11e2-9219-51eb8387e8f1_story.html?utm_term=.44d1a128bdf0, last accessed 5 March 2019.

Smith, K. (2017). *Building a Constituency for Peace in South Sudan*. Washington, DC: Search for Common Ground.

The Stimson Center (2016). "The 28 States System in South Sudan", www.stimson.org/sites/default/files/fileattachments/Stimson_StatesBriefingNote_9Aug16.pdf

UNESCO, Ministry of Education and Training (2015). *Education for All 2015 National Review Report: South Sudan*, http://unesdoc.unesco.org/images/0023/002316/231645e.pdf

UNHCR (2002). "UNHCR condemns rebel attack on refugee settlement in Uganda" www.unhcr.org/cgi-bin/texis/vtx/search?page=search&docid=3d2c49314&query=LRA

UNHCR (2017). http://data.unhcr.org/SouthSudan/regional.php, last accessed 16 February 2016.

5 Nexus of Vygotsky and Human Capability Approach

This last chapter in the background and context of the book looks at the intersection of two theoretical areas: child development and human development, within a humanitarian context. These two theoretical areas of work have traditionally been separate and not considered as overlapping. The human development camp has focused on broader issues of human development in developing countries while those working on child development/learning have focused on children. Further, the exploration of these theories in a humanitarian context, which focuses on the broader socio-political aspects of a country, is also new. While practically in the implementation of early learning and development programmes in humanitarian contexts may sometimes have these theoretical underpinnings, there is not a clear recognition and understanding of them and how they together can strengthen programmes on the ground. By clearly bringing these two theoretical frameworks together in a humanitarian context, academics, and practitioners alike, can better understand how to further conduct research in this area and how to improve the quality of programmes on the ground. Through the exploration and analysis of the various theories within the child and human development paradigms, I bring together two key theories: Vygotsky's Socio-cultural theory and the Human Capability Approach. I will argue that both of these theories together provide the best lens for understanding the situation of South Sudanese refugees in Uganda and early learning and development programming in emergencies.

Child development

Child development, and in particular, Lev Vygotsky's Socio-cultural theory, is the first theoretical area of exploration in this book. This section starts with an investigation of the foundations, debates and critiques which have allowed the Socio-cultural theory to gain more recognition and prominence today. It provides a clear link to why the Socio-cultural theory is best positioned to frame one's understanding and work on Early Childhood Development (ECD) in emergencies.

Child development is defined as a continuous process of change where a child slowly masters more complex levels of moving, thinking, feeling and interacting with and in the world (Gray and Mac Blain, 2015). Learning can be defined as an acquisition of knowledge or skill (ibid.). The first conceptualisation and theororisation of child development and learning are unclear, but the roots have links to the seventeenth- and eighteenth-century life in Europe and thinking and writings of philosophers John Locke (1632–1704) and Jean-Jacques Rousseau (1712–1778) (Bruer, 1999; Das Gupta, 1994; Gray and Mac Blain, 2015; Thomas, 2005).

As life in eighteenth-century Europe became more industrialised, the role of women and the care for children also changed. Previously, many women spent a lot of time on farms or doing hard labour for the families' survival. Children were cared for in a communal manner, by older siblings, other family members not working or community members (Bruer, 1999). It was not primarily the mother's role to care for and raise children; it was a community role. With urbanisation, women from bourgeois families no longer had to work in fields and had more time to care for their children. They assumed the roles of shaping the future of their infants. It soon became a natural role for women and those that did not care for their infants were considered not doing a mother's duty. This cultural mind-set of what the role of mothers is has become an ingrained part of what we understand and believe to be critical for children's development (Bruer, 1999).

While John Locke and Jean-Jacques Rousseau were influenced by these changes in women's role in the eighteenth century and others before them such as Aristotle and Socrates, their writings are some of the earliest that bring up the issue of children's development and learning from very different points of view. Locke proposed that children at birth were blank slates or "tabula rasa" and what they became and how they developed and learned were based on their experiences and the external environment (ibid.). Locke believed that while each child was different with varying temperaments and personalities, they were not born with knowledge (Das Gupta, 1994). Interaction with parents and the world through a "serve and return" interaction, which is now widely acknowledged as critical to young children's development and learning, was important for children's learning (National Scientific Council on the Developing Child, 2004). He saw parents as key to moulding children and helping them gain knowledge (Das Gupta, 1994). Nurture or external forces were more crucial to children's development, according to Locke, and the driving force in development (ibid.). While Locke believed that children had varying capabilities and these could be influenced by the external environment, and particularly parents, he did not deny that there are limits to what the influence could be (Cole and Cole, 1997). So, while Locke believed that two children at age 6 months could develop differently and that their external environment can help them accelerate or slow down their development, he did not deny that a small child of this age could do the same as a child of five years (ibid.).

Locke's contribution to the thinking around the importance of a child's external environment influenced Ivan Pavlov (1849–1936) and John Watson (1878–1958) which resulted in a new school of thinking known as behaviourism where life experiences and the external environment were critical to influence children who were blank slates (Gray and Mac Blain, 2015).

This translated into teaching in the classroom that was based on rote learning, drill and memorisation, a practice that continues today in many classrooms around the world (ibid.).

Like Locke, Jean-Jacques Rousseau also argued that the differences among people generally were primarily due to their varying life experiences, but he disagreed with Locke in his view of children and the role of adults in influencing children's development (Cole and Cole, 1997). Rousseau emphasised the role of nature or internal influences and genetics as key drivers of children's development (Das Gupta, 1994; Thomas, 2005). Rousseau's thinking and writing have also been foundational for modern developmental theories that focus on maturation, evolutionary stages of development (Das Gupta, 1994). In the maturation/evolutionary perspective, a child develops according to an innate biological timetable. They can develop independently from environmental influences and not simply moulded by adults or others in their environment. Stages of development identify specific periods when these innate, biological things occur over time that drive a child's development (ibid.). Marilyn Fleer (2006) points out that before the 1800s, age was not a criterion for organising people, often because people were not aware of their age (Fleer, 2006). However, many modern child development theorists, based on Rousseau's emphasis on Biological maturation, use chronological age as boundaries for children's capacities and place greater emphasis on heredity and biology (O'Neill et al., 2013). Age is used as the criterion for measuring or benchmarking what might be the expected level of biological development of the child, what a child is physically and mentally capable of doing. Children's capabilities fall within confines of heredity and biology.

The debate of whether nature or nurture has a greater impact on a child's development and learning has influenced many to investigate and expand upon these ideas and develop modern child development and learning theories. Even strong supporters of the nature or nurture perspective agree that both have influences on children's development, but where child development theories differ is to what extent nature or nurture affects children's development (Das Gupta, 1994). Two ways this has been considered in the nineteenth century and first half of the twentieth century include hereditary, establishing the boundaries of potential development, and environment, determining where, within those boundaries, a child's actual development occurs. Another perspective says that while both heredity and environment influence children's development, the extent to which this does will differ by characteristic. For traits such as eye colour, the influence of environment factors, such as nutrition, may not be as strong as nutrition's influence on cognitive ability (Das Gupta, 1994).

Four broad frameworks

Four broad frameworks indicate the contributing factors of nature and nurture and have been the basis of child development theories (Cole and Cole, 1997).

These are not always named in the same manner in the literature, but the ideas presented in them are generally the same. There is the Biological-maturation or evolutionary framework (based on Jean-Jacques Rousseau's work) that places significantly greater emphasis on the contribution of biology and heredity. As children mature internally and grow older by age, development will slowly unfold and allow children to have the capacity to do more. The environment plays a secondary role in shaping a child's development (Cole and Cole, 1997).

The second major framework is Environmental-learning (based on John Locke's work) which attributes greater contribution of the child's environment over his/her biology, heredity and internal maturation (ibid.). These two frameworks were the earliest perspectives which then moved the thinking towards Constructivist and Socio-cultural perspectives. The Constructivist framework takes a middle ground, understanding the great importance of biology, heredity and internal maturation and the child's external environment. While nature and nurture are not necessarily equal in the child development theories that follow the Constructivist framework, there is greater balance between the two.

A Constructivist view provides children with a greater role in shaping their own development than do the Biological-maturation and Environmental-learning frameworks (Cole and Cole, 1997). The fourth main framework for child development theories is the Socio-cultural framework (also known as Cultural-context and Socio-historical). This framework includes biological and environmental factors, but also adds a third variable—the culture in which the child is born and how it has been passed down through previous generations (Cole and Cole, 1997; Smidt, 2009). This framework evolved from Constructivism and has many similarities. Similar to the Constructivists, those that follow the Cultural-context or Socio-historical framework believe that children influence their own development by actively engaging with the world. However, they differ from other perspectives in that they believe that the culture and history of the place a child lives affect the biological and environmental factors that influence children's development. Activities, patterns and cultural beliefs passed down from earlier generations affect how children interact with their current environment and how their biological and heredity potential comes out or does not come out when a child is developing (ibid.). For example, research in New Guinea found that children have the same universal ability to grasp basic number concepts as children in France or the United States (Saxe, 1981, 1994). However, due to the requirements of their culture, they learn these concepts in a very different way and use numerical concepts for different things. In New Guinea, the research found that children learned numerical concepts by counting body parts (ibid.). Research in Brazil indicated that street children that did not attend school also developed mathematical skills based on their everyday life of buying and selling, but these children had difficulties when the concepts and problems are presented in a school like format (Nunes et al., 1993). In these examples, culture has influenced the conditions under which biological and environmental factors interact.

Humanitarian situations such as the South Sudan conflict and displacement in Ugandan refugee camps present a similar situation where children's culture and their situation mean that there are different cultural expectations and opportunities. These cultural and contextual differences affect a child's development. Understanding this as it is articulated in Vygotsky's Socio-cultural theory is critical to designing, monitoring and evaluating early learning and development programmes in emergencies.

See Figure 5.1 for a summary of the four broad child development frameworks.

For many years, the Biological-maturation and environmental perspectives dominated child development until Jean Piaget challenged these ideas.

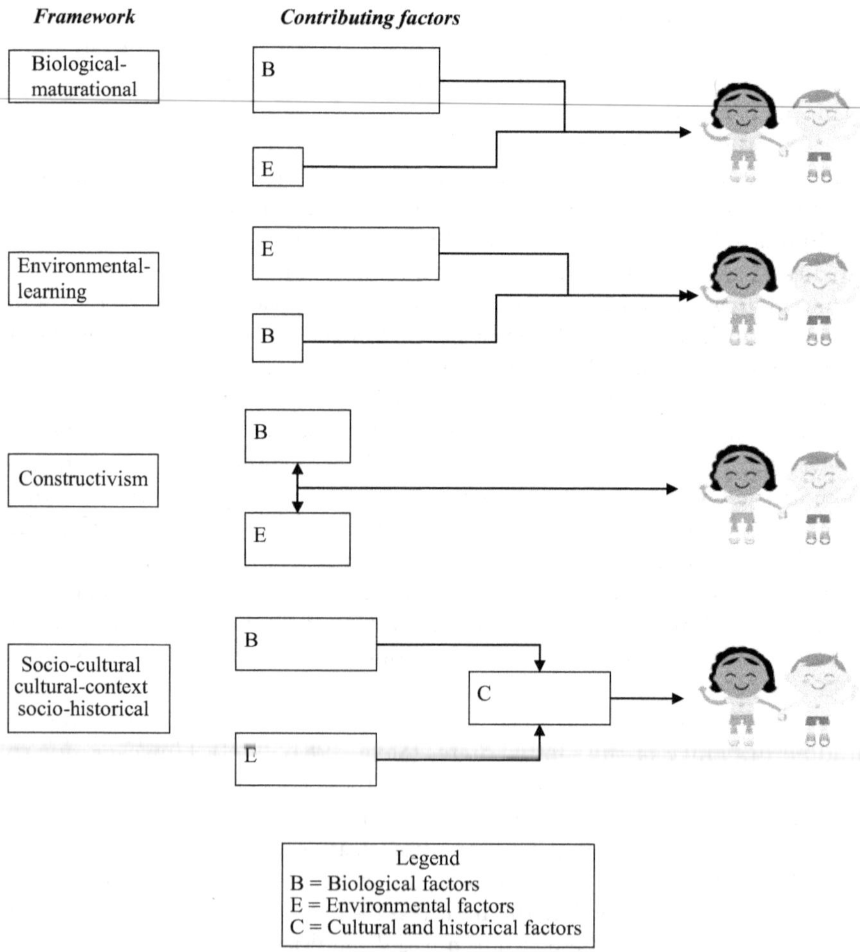

Figure 5.1 Four broad child development frameworks.
Source: Adapted from Cole, M. and Cole, S., 1997; Gray, C. and Mac Blain, S., 2015.

Jean Piaget's constructivist approach to child development

Jean Piaget (1896–1980), a Swiss scientist, was the first to be critical of earlier approaches to child development saying especially that repetition and memorisation did not mean a child actually understood what he/she was learning (Gray and Mac Blain, 2015). He believed that children were not passive recipients of learning based on their external environments, but the interaction between the child as active in his/her learning and the inputs to the child from the external environment are what helped children learn (ibid.). Piaget offered one of the first theories about the emergence and development of children's thinking—cognitive development. He was the first to introduce the idea of discovery learning through practical activities (Gray and Mac Blain, 2015). His theory termed *constructivism*, which stated that humans generate or "construct" knowledge and meaning from an interaction between their experiences and their ideas, was the first major challenge to behaviourist theories because it placed importance on the child as integral to his/her learning. Further, he believed that the construction of knowledge was through a step-by-step process of actions rather than an inventory of information (Thomas, 2005). Piaget maintains that the environment does not influence children in the same way at all ages. The influence of the environment, rather, depends on the child's current stage of development (Cole and Cole, 1997). Through this research, Piaget engaged in child-centred experiments and used observation and testing of real children which was also not done so much during this time. Rather than working in a laboratory as many other scientists did during this time, he observed children in their natural environment and listened to what they said (Gray and Mac Blain, 2015). He believed that he could better understand children and how they are developing by listening to them (ibid.). This concept of children's voices and active participation and involvement in their own learning and development has endured and is integrated in many child development and early learning programmes. His work led him to conclude that children's thinking is different from adults' and that younger children think differently from older children (Gray and Mac Blain, 2015). From birth, children's thinking evolves and changes with age and experience as the brain grows and creates more connections. Their thinking begins before they have the language to express their thoughts.

Language, Piaget believed, was a tool used to develop and enhance thinking (ibid.). These claims were considered revolutionary in Piaget's time. Many of Piaget's contemporaries did not accept his ideas about children's evolving thinking and cognitive development. Despite this, Piaget continued his work to further refine and develop his theory over 50 years. Through his work, he offered a model of how children's thinking develops. Piaget thought that the process of cognitive development followed specific phases from birth until adolescence (Cole and Cole, 1997; Gray and Mac Blain, 2015; Huitt and Hummel, 2003). He was a staged theorist who believed that one had to go through certain phases: infancy, early childhood, middle childhood and adolescence and that each phase builds on the other (Cole and Cole, 1997).

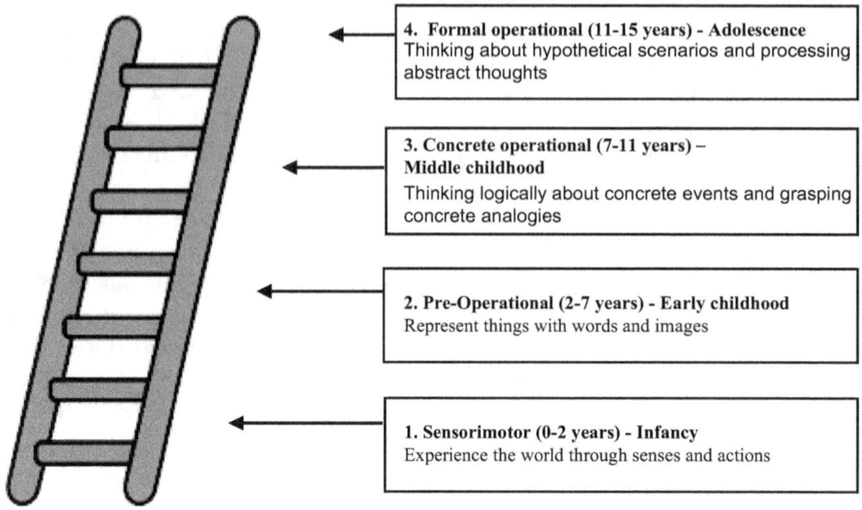

Figure 5.2 Piaget's stages of cognitive development.
Source: Adapted from Cole, M. and Cole, S., 1997; Gray, C. and Mac Blain, S., 2015; Huitt, W. and Hummel, J., 2009.

As a child develops, he/she cannot go back to an earlier stage (Gray and Mac Blain, 2015; Huitt and Hummel, 2003). Figure 5.2 illustrates Piaget's four key stages of cognitive development: sensorimotor, pre-operational, concrete operational and formal operational.

Criticisms of Piaget

Piaget advanced the growth of a new area of study known as "child development" (Gray and Mac Blain, 2015). He was the first theorist to explain, through research, the internal processes of children's thinking at different ages. Additionally, he offered researchers new tools to examine different aspects of a child's development. Further, he also was one of the first scientists to place the child at the centre of his studies where their voices were critical to his research, understanding and ultimately the development of this theory.

While Piaget's contribution advanced the study of child development, there were many critiques of his work. Piaget did extensive research to formulate this theory, but they were based primarily on case studies and were therefore descriptive (Huitt and Hummel, 2003). While he did correlations and used experimental methods, they did not always support the claims that underpin his theory (ibid.). Further, some people said that there was a lack of clarity in some of his concepts. Research scientist Sutherland and others claimed that Piaget's role of equilibrium in children's learning lacked clarity and was impossible to either prove or disprove (Gray and Mac Blain, 2015).

Meadows (1993) argued that the language Piaget used in his tests on children was too complicated for young children and tested what they could not do rather than what they could do. She claimed that the wording was deliberate and chosen to make it difficult for children, thereby underestimating children's ability to complete the task (Meadows, 1993). Other researchers argue that the small sample sizes of most of Piaget's research studies and the fact that most of the samples included white, middle-class children with university-educated parents were limitations (Gray and Mac Blain, 2015). This is especially an argument that comes from those that believe in a stronger role of culture in shaping a child's cognitive development (Cole and Cole, 1997; Gray and Mac Blain, 2015).

Another major critique of Piaget's work was his claim that cognitive development happens in discrete stages (Gray and Mac Blain, 2015). As a child had to go through the various stages, his work could not explain why some children were delayed in reaching these stages or advanced and surpassed these stages faster, especially in non-Western contexts (Cole and Cole, 1997; Gray and Mac Blain, 2015). Piaget also believed that once a child progressed to a higher part of the ladder or the next stage, he/she could not go back down to a lower stage. Evidence of children in adverse situations such as emergencies has disproved this. Children in these situations can temporarily regress developmentally and this is normal (Donahue-Coletta, 1992; Duncan and Arnston, 2004; IASC, 2007; Pine et al., 2005). Piaget believed that because children had to go through various stages based partially on their Biological maturation, learning could never be accelerated. However, he could not explain why some children learn things faster than others, especially when they had exposure and stimulation (Gray and Mac Blain, 2015). Meadows (1993) disagreed with this claim and through her research found that it was possible to teach pre-school children who were three and four-year-old to perform concrete operational tasks, which according to Piaget occurs between seven and 11 years old (Meadows, 1993). Shayer and Adey (2002) found further evidence that it was possible to accelerate a child's cognitive development and learning through their research with five-year olds (Shayer and Adey, 2002).

Over the years, Piaget shifted his thinking around the universality of the stages and in particular formal operational thinking (Cole and Cole, 1997; Piaget, 1972). He did say that in "extremely disadvantaged conditions, [formal operational thought] will never really take shape" (Piaget, 1972, 7). Goodenough (1953) conducted research to provide evidence that formal operational thought *can* occur even in non-literate communities (Goodenough, 1953). His research focused on Polynesia and Micronesia. Formal tests that Piaget used may have concluded that these people had not developed formal operational thought, but Goodenough found that they could solve complex problems in a non-scientific manner when they developed a compass for navigation based on the stars (ibid.). Further, Piaget considered that children progress through the stages at different speeds, depending on the quality and frequency of intellectual stimulation available in their environment (Cole and Cole, 1997; Piaget, 1972). The conclusion he came to towards the end of his life was that most people do get to the last stage of formal concrete operations, but they reach this stage in different areas depending on their aptitudes and professional specialisations such as advanced studies or apprenticeship for various trades (Cole and Cole, 1997; Piaget, 1972).

Further, Piaget believed that all children, irrespective of culture and race, would follow the same stages as illustrated earlier (Gray and Mac Blain, 2015). This aspect of his theory did not consider potential variations in culture, context, and history and how that could affect a child's development. Other than providing the child with a stimulating environment, Piaget's theory places little emphasis on the role of the teacher (ibid.). This was another major criticism of Piaget's work and brings us to the fourth major child development framework that was pioneered by the work of Lev Vygotsky.

Lev Vygotsky's Socio-cultural theory for children's development

Lev Vygotsky (1896–1934) was a Russian psychologist and a contemporary of Jean Piaget. He too critiqued the Biological-maturation and Environmental perspectives of child development. He knew of Piaget's work and agreed with aspects of it. However, a critical difference between the work of Vygotsky and Piaget is the importance Vygotsky placed on the influence of culture on a child's development. Vygotsky was one of the first researchers to delve more deeply into the influence of a child's external environment, including his/her culture, the role of the teacher and how that affects a child's thinking and overall development (Gray and Mac Blain, 2015). Vygotsky and Piaget both put children at the centre and as active constructors of their own knowledge and development so that both fall under the umbrella of constructivism (Cole and Cole, 1997; Gray and Mac Blain, 2015; Smidt, 2009). However, Vygotsky was a social constructivist who believed that it was important to consider the quality and nature of a child's environment, his/her age, culture and life experiences before drawing any conclusions about his/her development (Gray and Mac Blain, 2015). Culture and the beliefs and values that come from it shaped a child's development in addition to his/her biology and the general external environment (Cole and Cole, 1997; Gray and Mac Blain, 2015; Smidt, 2009). Each culture, he believed, had its own values and beliefs, which affect a child's development from the beginning as the baby interacts and grows within an environment (Gray and Mac Blain, 2015; Smidt, 2009). For example, a child that is talked to a lot as an infant will learn to talk faster and have larger vocabularies compared with a child who is not talked to. Piaget was a constructivist who believed that the development of cognition was the result of mental construction (ibid.). He saw development of thought and cognition occurring in the child as he/she interacted with the environment (ibid.). Piaget did not consider the potential impact that culture could have on a child's development (ibid.). Piaget had a single logic underlying adult thought, whereas Vygotsky and others in the socio-cultural camp believed that there are variations in the context of adult activity and so there is no homogeneity in adult thought processes (Cole and Cole, 1997).

Vygotsky believed that development was essentially a social process hugely influenced by the culture in which a child lived (Gray and Mac Blain, 2015). While he and Piaget agreed that children were born with the basic building blocks of cognition, visual recognition, memory, attention and speed of processing, Vygotsky believed that a child's development is a result of interaction between children and their social environment (Gray and Mac Blain, 2015). The quality of the environment and the values in the culture shaped what a child learned, how he/she developed and therefore his/her capabilities (ibid.). Further, Vygotsky believed that children's cultural development appears at the social level (between people) and at the individual level (within the child) (Vygotsky, 1978). Piaget also believed in the influence of the external environment, but believed that children need to go through certain steps in their development. He believed children need to mature over time in order to reach certain capabilities (Cole and Cole, 1997; Smidt, 2009). Further, Piaget believed development to be unidirectional, whereas Vygotsky saw it as being bi-directional. Piaget's stages of development follow a chronological order and it is essentially the same in every child no matter where he/she is from and what culture or situation he/she lives in (Cole and Cole, 1997; Gray and Mac Blain, 2015). Vygotsky rejected what he believed to be Piaget's biological and individualistic reductionism (Ageyev, 2003). He did believe that children need to go through stages, but he was not as rigid as Piaget was in his stages (Cole and Cole, 1997; Gray and Mac Blain, 2015; Smidt, 2009). While children normally move forward in their development, they could move backwards when they face something new or difficult (Gray and Mac Blain, 2015). Once a child gains experience he/she can then progress forward again (ibid.). In humanitarian situations, there are often cases of children regressing in their development due to high levels of stress and difficulties they face (Donahue-Coletta, 1992; Duncan and Arnston, 2004; IASC, 2007; Pine et al., 2005). This regression is considered a normal reaction to severe stress that can be experienced in an emergency situation (ibid.).

Vygotsky's Socio-cultural theory has three core assumptions (Cole and Cole, 1997). The first assumption is that activity generates thinking (ibid.). Children's activities help construct the contents of their minds. Action and interaction within a culture create thought. Mental development is a process of children's internalising the results of their transactions with their environment. Katherine Nelson (1981) suggests that as a result of children's participation in various activities that are valued by the culture, children acquire generalised event representations or "scripts" (Nelson, 1981). Scripts are guides to different activities in a child's world. They help children understand who participates in this type of activity, their role, the objects used for this activity and the sequence of actions that make up the event (ibid.).

For example, a baby learns about bath time by taking a bath, experiencing what happens, who is involved, what you do during a bath, etc. This process allows a child to make mental representations and figure out what is likely to happen next time they are in familiar circumstances (ibid.). Vygotsky believed that humans rarely experience their environment without the lens of their culture (Cole and Cole, 1997). The second assumption is that development advances by dialectical exchanges (Cole and Cole, 1997). The influence of Marx and Hegel in this aspect of his thinking is evident. Hegel's dialectical formula for logical thought includes an assertion (thesis) and opposite (antithesis) which when they interact result in a revised conclusion (synthesis). Marx applied this to the development of societies while Vygotsky applied this to the development of children (ibid.). The third assumption in Vygotsky's Socio-cultural theory is that development is a historical process within cultural contexts (Cole and Cole, 1997). He believed that understanding how and why children develop requires the society's cultural background within history which means that it can be different even from society to society and generation to generation (ibid.). A culture during a particular time in history provides unique opportunities and demands. A child's own past dialectical confrontations determine how prepared he/she is to resolve upcoming problem situations (ibid.).

Vygotsky believed that the unevenness of development that comes from this exchange within a culture and within a period of time that have unique values and expectations is influenced by culture in five ways (Cole and Cole, 1997). First, one's culture arranges the occurrence and non-occurrence of certain activities (ibid.). This means that a child cannot learn about and develop capabilities in something you have not observed, heard about or been able to interact with in your life. For example, children in South Sudan usually do not wear clothes with buttons or zippers. While the ability to use buttons and zippers is a part of Western child development tests that look at fine motor skill development, this is not something that South Sudanese children should be expected to do since they rarely ever interact with buttons or zippers. Additionally, South Sudanese children from villages most likely will not have stairs in their homes, so requiring them to be able to walk up stairs in a child development test is not culturally relevant. Further, a one year old child in Nepal may be toilet trained early as there is a dearth of disposable diapers, whereas in the United States, a child may not learn this until he/she is 3–4 years old. Second, one's culture determines the frequency of basic activities (Cole and Cole, 1997). For example, Balinese children may be skilled dancers by age 4, whereas Norwegian children may be skilled skaters or skiers. If a particular activity and skill are valued in the culture and the child has many opportunities to practice it, he/she will develop that capability earlier and/or better than children in other cultures where it is not valued in the same way (ibid.). There is also evidence that children who have more exposure to and practice in reading books or having books read to them will be more capable and proficient readers (Fountas and Pinnell, 1996; Graves et al., 2007). Culture can also impact a child's development through the connections and associations they make between activities (Cole and Cole, 1997). For example, a child moulding clay in a nursery in the United Kingdom could be developing the muscles in his/her fingers and hands, using his/her imagination to create something, and associating the activity with fun and play. A child moulding clay in another society may associate that activity with making pottery, digging in a quarry, firing the clay and selling it in a market. The child may not necessarily see this as fun and play as the child from the United Kingdom does (ibid.). Culture can also decide on the difficulty of children's roles and this can affect their development and their capabilities (ibid.). For example, in many African countries, children as young as five years are expected to care for their baby and toddler siblings or girls as young as 10 are expected to make meals, carry heavy buckets of water, and search for firewood. In many Western contexts, five-year-old children would not be expected to do this. Lastly, culture can shape a child's development by emphasising activities that promote widely held cultural values (ibid.). In Indonesia, it is very important for children to know their morning prayers. Many children who went through Plan Indonesia's ECD programmes could recite their morning prayers (Plan International, 2011). This was something families were very happy about. They associated the programme with their child's ability to know their morning prayers (ibid.).

Humanitarian situations add an additional layer of complexity to the interaction of culture, time and children's development. In these situations, culture, access and opportunities may change, thereby impacting children's development. For example, while conflict, war and displacement are generally not thought of as positive, good things can come from them such as access to early learning services. Among the child participants for this research, a very small percentage ever had access to early learning in their village in South Sudan. Through an informal conversation I had with a Plan International South Sudan staff, he sent his family to Uganda for safety, but also because he knew they would receive services they would never receive in their village in South Sudan. While funding for ECD in emergencies is very low in comparison to the need and to sectors such as food, water, shelter and health, it can be more than what refugees got in their home countries (Arnold, 2004; UNESCO, 2006). From my professional experience of implementing education and early learning programmes in emergencies, there are many instances when girls access early learning and education services for the first time. Further, as there are often fewer competing obstacles for girls, they sometimes attend in higher numbers than boys. These differences in context can change cultural views and therefore expectations and opportunities for children. This all contributes to children's development and capabilities. The Socio-cultural theory provides an appropriate framework to understand and apply this to ECD in emergency programmes.

Parents, siblings, peers, teachers and significant objects such as favourite books or toys are the "cultural tools" necessary to help a child develop his/her thinking in his/her cultural environment and time in history (Gray and Mac

Blain, 2015; Smidt, 2009). Cultural tools are things or the signs or symbols that humans within groups have developed over time in order to help them think about and reflect on their values, ideas, principles and practice (Smidt, 2009). They influence our perceptions, understandings and experiences of the world (Gray and Mac Blain, 2015). Language is a key cultural tool (Gray and Mac Blain, 2015; Smidt, 2009). For example, there are huge differences between English and Spanish in that Spanish has many more verb forms and ways of expressing emotion and experience. This affects a child's development, thinking and manner of expressing him/herself. Nursery rhymes, fairy tale stories, folklore, music and art are also cultural tools (Gray and Mac Blain, 2015). In emergency situations, new cultural tools may be introduced from other countries. As children interact with and use cultural tools, slowly they become internalised, natural and normal (Smidt, 2009).

Initially a child will have "lower order thinking" that involves unconscious biological functions such as memory, attention and intelligence (Gray and Mac Blain, 2015). These processes are not value free and are influenced by our feelings and emotions, in the context of a particular culture (ibid.). Higher-order thinking, which involves conscious deliberate intentions and action such as problem solving and logical reasoning, is where children should get to as they develop (ibid.). The way for children to get to that, Vygotsky believed, was through mediated social collaborative activity. He said that this type of activity can be thought of as the bridge that can help children get from one type of thinking to another. Cultural tools, as mentioned earlier, can be part of the mediated, social collaborative activity (ibid.).

Zone of proximal development

A key concept in Vygotsky's theory that is used a lot among teachers and early childhood educators in pre-school and primary schools in many countries is the "Zone of Proximal Development" (ZPD) (Ageyev, 2003; Cole and Cole, 1997; Gray and Mac Blain, 2015; Smidt, 2009; Vygotsky, 1978). This concept brings together the use of "cultural tools" and mediated social collaborative activities (Gray and Mac Blain, 2015; Smidt, 2009). Vygotsky said that ZPD is "those functions which have yet to mature but are in the process of maturing…'buds' or 'flowers' of development rather than 'fruits' of development" (Vygotsky, 1978, 86). The ZPD is the belief that a child at any stage of their development is at a point where he/she has the capabilities of doing something on his/her own without any support. This could be something that he/she internalised from the use of cultural tools and through the participation of mediated social collaborative activities. However, in order for a child to get to the next level of learning, teaching with support or "scaffolding" (a term coined by those building on Vygotsky's work) needs to occur in the ZPD. Scaffolding methods help teachers and early childhood educators provide a safe and protective structure in which children can extend their capabilities (Wood et al., 1976). ZPD is an area where a child can be capable of doing something with support of a teacher, peers or some expert "other" because it puts a child a little bit out of his/her comfort zone (Gray and Mac Blain, 2015). Real learning happens when a child is outside of his/her comfort zone, but in a safe space where he/she can begin to extend his/her capabilities (ibid.). Beyond the ZPD is an area that a child at a particular stage of his/her development does not have the capabilities of doing even with support from a teacher or an expert "other" such as parents of peers (ibid.). In many classrooms in the United States, the activity of "guided reading," which usually occurs between kindergarten and second grade, is aimed at exactly what Vygotsky said—to help a child become more capable readers (Fountas and Pinnell, 1996; Graves et al., 2007). Figure 5.3 illustrates how Vygotsky saw the ZPD.

Play was critical in all of these processes according to both Vygotsky and Piaget, because this was the way children could interact with the real world, learn about it in a safe space (Cole and Cole, 1997; Gray and Mac Blain, 2015; Smidt, 2009). For Vygotsky, imaginary play is a precursor to abstract thinking (Gray and Mac Blain, 2015). Whereas Piaget believed that the development of play occurs naturally, Vygotsky believed that there is an influence of adults and the culture in how children play, which therefore affects their thinking and development (Cole and Cole, 1997; Gray and Mac Blain, 2015). Play creates a ZPD for a child and allows him/her to act and behave in ways they do not normally do, more like adults (Cole and Cole, 1997). Freund (1990) in her

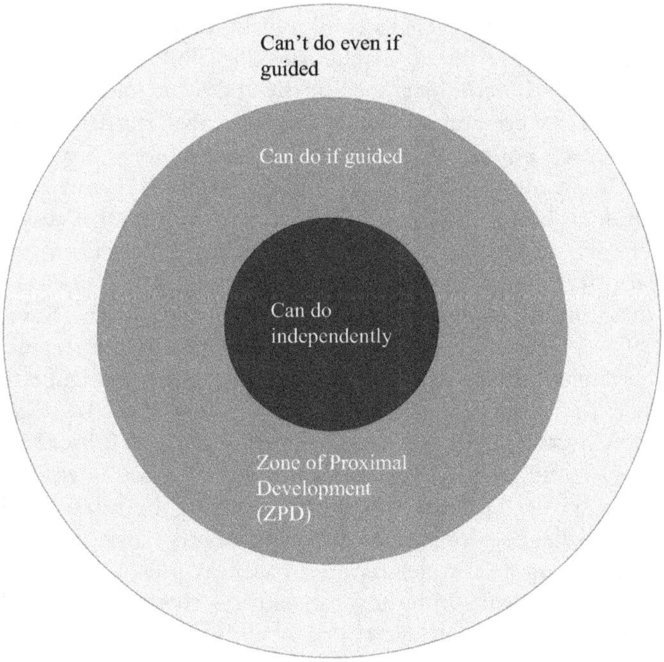

Figure 5.3 Vygotsky's zone of proximal development.
Source: Adapted from Vygotsky, L. S. (1978).

research of three- to four-year olds revealed that children who had support in doing their activity had greater understanding and capability than doing it alone (Freund, 1990). Freund gave the children a doll house and furniture and asked them to place the furniture throughout the doll house. Some children did the task on their own, which is in line with Piaget's approach of discovery learning, whereas other children had an adult helping them. There were children from both groups that were capable of doing the task, but those that had adult support came away with a stronger understanding of a house, furniture, where things go, their functions and why certain things go in certain locations (ibid.). In play or in other activities, Vygotsky believed that having an asymmetric relationship between children and other children or children and adults fosters a transfer of knowledge from the more knowledgeable one to the less experienced one (Gray and Mac Blain, 2015). Having a symmetrical relationship, Vygotsky believed, was like solving the problem alone where there would not be as much learning (ibid.). In modern classrooms in the United States, teachers and early childhood educators often form groups of children of mixed capabilities. The aim of this is exactly what Vygotsky mentions; it creates asymmetrical relationships that allow children to rise to a higher level.

Criticisms of Vygotsky's work

While Vygotsky changed understanding of child development by including the influence of culture and values, there are many criticisms of his work. Vygotsky was alive during Piaget's time, but he died young, and so did not have a chance to expand fully on his theories nor conduct many experiments. The experiments he did conduct, specifically about the ZPD, had small samples where the data were ambiguous, where advanced statistics were missing and where there was not clarity on how he controlled for individual variables (Ageyev, 2003). Vygotsky's work was influenced by Marxism and much of it was kept hidden by the Soviet Union, which means that it was not available to other parts of the world, especially the English speaking world until after his death. It was not until the 1960s that Vygotsky's work started to be translated into English and was read by those outside of the Soviet Union (Smidt, 2009). Vygotsky assumed that social and cultural experiences are always positive for children's development when there is evidence that social and cultural experiences can also be negative (Gray and Mac Blain, 2015). Additionally, Vygotsky believed that thought could not fully exist without spoken language (ibid.). If this was the case, then a child is devoid of thought until he/she can speak. Children usually begin saying their first words around age 1, but brain science provides evidence of infants having an exponential explosion of thinking and understanding of the world (Conel, 1959). They may not be able to speak, but they can express themselves in other ways (ibid.). Vygotsky did not consider children with disabilities who were deaf and therefore could not speak. He did not consider the role of other types of expression of thought such as sign language (ibid.). There is also criticism that some aspects of Vygotsky's messages were lost in translation and did not fully capture the essence of his ideas (Smidt, 2009).

By the mid-1980s, Vygotsky's theoretical approach and key ideas about the role of the environment and in particular culture became more popular than Piaget's theories (Gray and Mac Blain, 2015; Smidt, 2009). Since then, many modern approaches to education, including early childhood education, are underpinned by Vygotsky's ideas. In the area of international education, the idea of the central role of one's culture in shaping and influencing how a child learns is now integral to programmes in developing countries.

Despite these criticisms, it has not prevented contemporary academics and practitioners to base their work on the central tenets of his theory. The next section lays out some of the adaptations of Vygotsky's Socio-cultural theory and how some academics have taken forward and further developed some key aspects of his work.

Child development perspectives based on Vygotsky

Vygotsky has influenced many people to reflect upon, critique and expand upon his work. Some theorists, researchers and educationalists include Urie Bronfenbrenner, Barbara Rogoff, Mariane Hedegaard, Marilyn Fleer, John Dewey and Maria Montessori (Cole and Cole, 1997; Gray and Mac Blain, 2015). In this section, I highlight the contributions of some of the key perspectives that build part of the theoretical foundation for my own research.

Urie Bronfenbrenner has been one of the most influential contributors and most widely cited in development and humanitarian work as he expanded Vygotsky's Socio-cultural theory to develop his Ecological Systems theory. Bronfenbrenner's Ecological Systems theory is known by many practitioners and used to understand children's development and well-being in emergency contexts. He was heavily influenced by Lev Vygotsky and took the role of nurture and the child's external environment further than Vygotsky (Bronfenbrenner, 1979; Gray and Mac Blain, 2015). In Bronfenbrenner's perspective, there is a relationship and influence between the child and his/her external environment that goes beyond the parents and teachers as Vygotsky mentioned (ibid.). Bronfenbrenner identified five levels that interact with the influence how a child develops: microsystem, mesosystem, exosystem, macrosystem and chronosystem. As seen in Figure 5.4 of Bronfenbrenner's Ecological Systems theory, the child is in the middle. Surrounding him or her is the microsystem, which includes his/her parents, friends, school and other groups within the immediate vicinity of the child. The microsystem is where the child has his/her regular daily interactions with the social world. The mesosystem is one layer away from the child and includes the interactions between the microsystem and the exosystem. The exosystem includes friends of the family, neighbours and other services. Beyond the exosystem is another layer that influences children's development; this is the macrosystem which includes the major attitudes and ideologies of a culture. For example, a culture where girls' education is not prioritised can affect how a girl develops and the types of opportunities she has to increase her skills and capabilities. The last layer in the Ecological Systems theory is the chronosystem. This layer includes socio-historical conditions and time since life events. As Vygotsky mentioned, the values of a culture can change from society to society and from generation to generation (Gray and Mac Blain, 2015; Smidt, 2009). This could include the historical memory of war or natural hazard that destroyed the child's village and because these types of events can affect a whole society, it can affect the child's overall development. What Bronfenbrenner includes in Figure 5.4 is the interaction between the various layers and how they can all continuously influence each other. Vygotsky did not explicitly include the continuous interaction of the child with his/her external environment or culture.

In many countries that have been inflicted with war and conflict for decades such as Sudan, South Sudan, Uganda, Liberia, Sierra Leone, Democratic Republic of Congo, Afghanistan, Iraq and Syria, children are being born during these times which is affecting their opportunities, the values that culture places on children's education and therefore their capabilities. For example, a 2015 report published by Save the Children, American Institutes of Research and CfBT Education Trust found that literacy rates in Syria before the large scale conflict used to be at 95% with almost all Syrian children

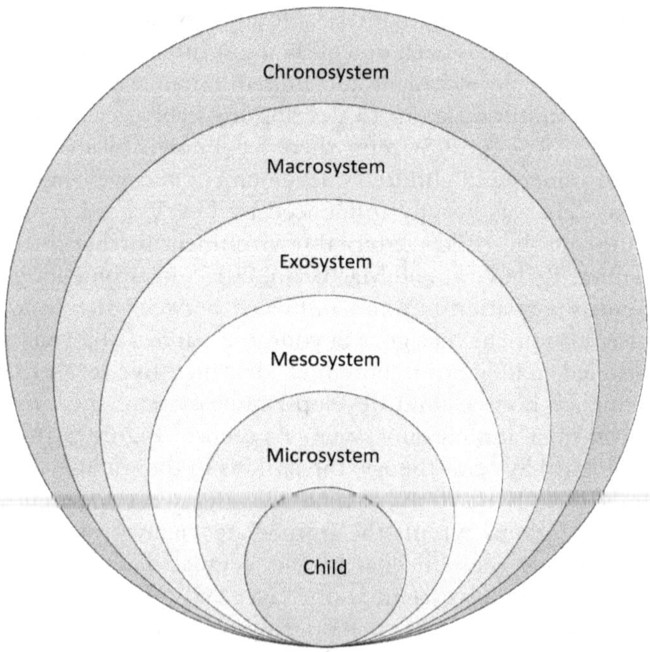

Figure 5.4 Bronfenbrenner's Ecological Systems theory.
Source: Adapted from Bronfenbrenner, Urie (1979).

enrolled in primary school (Save the Children, CfBT and American Institute of Research, 2015). However, years later, almost three million children are no longer in school and Syria is now estimated to have one of the lowest enrolment rates in the world (ibid.). In the city of Aleppo, where there has been a great deal of fighting, enrolment rates in education are around 6% while a majority of children currently living in neighbouring Jordan and Turkey have no access to education (ibid.). This change in the external environment of conflict-affected children is already having huge impacts on their capabilities. As this is happening on a large scale in the Syrian society, it will affect this and the next generation of Syrians and their capabilities.

While Bronfenbrenner expanded the cultural and societal influences on children's development through the conceptualisation of the Ecological Systems theory, Barbara Rogoff, Marilyn Fleer and Mariane Hedegaard began investigating the applicability of these theoretical frameworks. They critiqued the long held evolutionary perspective of child development that looked at capabilities developed by chronological age and without the influence of culture.

Barbara Rogoff, an educator (1998, 2003), bridges the fields of psychology and anthropology and has been heavily influenced by Vygotsky. She investigated cultural variation in learning processes and settings, with a particular interest in investigating learning, collaboration and shared problem solving in communities where children do not have lot of access to school (Gray and Mac Blain, 2015; Rogoff, 1998; Rogoff, 2003). She believes that individuals develop as participants in their cultural communities, engaging with others in shared endeavours that build on cultural practices of many generations (Rogoff, 2003). Children attempt to acquire culturally defined ideals of mature thought and action through this interaction with their culture (ibid.). Culture structures the child while a child's individual actions redefine the culture, so Rogoff sees development as a two-way dynamic process and the reason why culture in one society can change from one generation to another (ibid.). Rogoff (2003) further believes that cultural differences go to the family level which accounts for differences among people in the same community (ibid.). Her research has focused on finding the common patterns and variations in different communities and finds evidence for the fact that there is not just one way for children to develop (ibid.). However, at the same time, she has found that there are some regularities in children's development (ibid.).

Rogoff studied children in Oceania, the United Kingdom, Zaire and other countries (Rogoff, 2003). For example, three-year-old Kwara'ae children in Oceania can be caregivers to younger siblings, but in the UK it is illegal to leave a child under 14 years without adult supervision (ibid.). Infants in the Efe community in Zaire can use machetes safely while in the US middle-class adults often do not trust young children with knives (ibid.). Rogoff also found differences between European-American heritage children and Indigenous-heritage children of North and Central America, specifically with how they pay attention to and learn from events around them, and how they collaborate in ongoing endeavours. She concluded that children's attention and learning were connected to the extent of their families' familiarity with learning traditions that seem to be common in their cultures, especially customs related to Western type of schooling. Rogoff also found that when children were integrated into everyday activities with their parents and given opportunities to observe and try to do things, they were able to more quickly learn those activities and therefore increase their capabilities (ibid.).

Rogoff sees three levels of the socio-cultural context: (1) apprenticeship, (2) guided participation and (3) participatory appropriation (Rogoff, 1990, 1995, 2003). These three planes of analysis are inseparable and mutually occurring at once as a child learns. While one of the planes may be the focus at a specific time, the others would always be present in the background (Rogoff, 1995). Apprenticeships allow a child to be a novice and through practical experience learn a new skill (ibid.). Guided participation is the means by which adults shape young children's development through collaboration built upon shared understanding in routine problem-solving situations (Cole and Cole, 1997; Rogoff et al., 1998; Smidt, 2009). The role of parents as guides or as instructors and the extent to which they allow children's participation in various types of cultural activities can affect the child's development and capabilities (Rogoff et al., 1998). Children learn and develop through both observation and hands on participation in activities in their culture (ibid.). Rogoff believed that guided participation as a process may be universal, but there are variations in the expectations and the goals communities have for their children's development (Rogoff et al., 1998). Participatory appropriation is the process by which individuals change through their involvement in an activity within their culture, in the process of becoming prepared for subsequent involvement in related activities (Rogoff, 1995).

Rogoff rejected Piaget's stages of development and the placing of children in age-specific grades (Rogoff, 2003). Organising children by ages is a relatively new phenomenon as this was not the case in the United States and other countries until the last half of the 1800s (ibid.). Children used to be organised around level of understanding rather than age batches. Rogoff said ages and onsets of capabilities are a cultural product. Children who are able to engage in more mature activities can more quickly gain those capabilities than those who are excluded from activities that adults or older children engage in. Maria Montessori's approach draws on this idea and in the Montessori learning model and schools, children of multiple ages are put together in one class so that younger students can observe, participate in the same activities as older children and learn from them (Gray and Mac Blain, 2015).

Marilyn Fleer also investigated the applicability of the Socio-cultural theory in various cultural contexts (ibid.). Learning by doing is often the assumption in most Western early childhood programs, but Marilyn Fleer in her research in 2002 found that for Indigenous Australian children learning by observation without explanation is also very important (ibid.). Marilyn Freer and Mariane Hedegaard (2010) took Vygotsky and Rogoff's work a step further by relating society and community with the concept of institutional practice (Fleer and Hedegaard, 2010; Ridgway, 2010). They explore the role of those institutions, children's participation in them and how this can shape children's development and capabilities (Fleer and Hedegaard, 2010; Ridgway, 2010).

For all three of them, culture, whether it be the broader societal culture as Bronfenbrenner highlights or the level of the institution the child is in or the family or the generation, it is a critical element in a child's development and is key to determining children's capabilities (Bronfenbrenner, 1979; Rogoff, 2003). Their work shows the influence of different types of cultures on children's development. It also shows that Piaget's perspective of chronological age determining a child's development and capabilities is not quite correct when one investigates other cultures. This research therefore builds on this previous work and applies a Socio-cultural theory to early-years programming in the context of Uganda with South Sudanese refugees. The key focus on "culture" in this theoretical perspective is what makes it the most appropriate theoretical framework for this research. The next section will go deeper into what aspects of a child are developed when we say child development.

Child development domains

The theories presented provide a macro-level picture of how a child develops. In this section, I present the domains of child development as this will be part of the data collection for this research. There are many ideas of the domains of child development. The four key areas that are often adopted and considered are: Physical, Socio-emotional/Psycho-social, Cognitive and Language/Communication. Figure 5.5 shows the interconnectedness of these domains

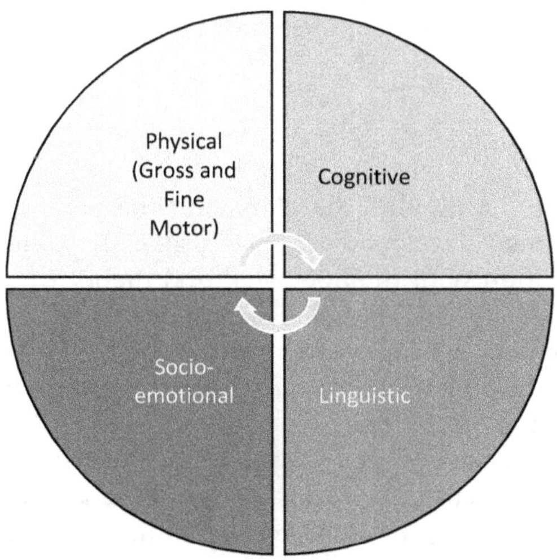

Figure 5.5 Child development domains.

and how they can influence one another (Fernald et al., 2009; Williamson and Robinson, 2006). These domains are also context specific and in some cultures spiritual development or other aspects may be equally important to the four domains mentioned here (Williamson and Robinson, 2006)

Physical development includes the change in physical appearance of the body, change in movement patterns and brain growth. It means the progress of a child's control over his/her body. There are two types of motor skills: (1) *Gross (or large) motor skills* involve the larger muscles including the arms and legs. Actions requiring gross motor skills include walking, running, balance and coordination; (2) *Fine (or small) motor skills* involve the smaller muscles in the fingers, toes, eyes and other areas. Actions that require fine motor skills include drawing, writing, grasping objects, throwing, waving and catching. Large muscles develop before small muscles. Muscles of legs and arms develop before those in the fingers and hands. Children learn how to perform gross (or large) motor skills such as walking before they learn to perform fine (or small) motor skills such as drawing.

Cognitive development abilities are associated with memory, reasoning, problem-solving thinking and expressing. These are the capabilities through which a child expresses his/her thoughts and feelings.

Linguistic development includes the abilities of talking/expressing and understanding of words and sentences. Initially babies produce different sounds and then begin to produce their first real words. At the age of 18 months, children begin to use two words sentences. Around the age of two, children begin to produce short, multi-word sentences.

Socio-emotional/psycho-social development means social interactions and the ability to show emotions. The ability to show empathy, express feelings, sharing, expressing gratitude, being helpful, express and control anger express happy and sad feelings are all part of social and emotional development.

These domains of child development will be considered, adapted and then applied in this research.

Human development

In addition to considering child development, the book also includes perspectives from human development. Specifically, the Capability Approach is used in combination with the Socio-cultural theory to create a new lens through which ECD among South Sudanese refugees in Uganda and ECD in humanitarian situations generally can be understood. The new lens strengthens the theoretical base upon which future programming, research and government policy can be established.

Within the human development camp, there are two key theoretical approaches that will be examined in this section: Human Capital Theory and the Human Capability Approach. Whereas Human Capital Theory focuses more on people's capabilities as they contribute to economic growth, the Human Capability Approach looks at people developing capabilities and functionings based on their own context as an end in itself. It does not have the goal of economic growth. While both of these theoretical approaches have their merits and limitations, the Human Capability Approach is used to frame the questions of this research.

Human Capital Theory

For many years, development of a country and its people has been centred on its economic growth—on the human capital that people have. Human capital refers to the capabilities of human beings that contribute to economic growth (Eide and Showalter, 2010). These capabilities can be developed in people through investments in areas such as education, health, nutrition and on-the-job training (Eide and Showalter, 2010; Sweetland, 1996). Early concepts of human capital were explored by economists, including Adam Smith, John Stuart Mill, Alfred Marshall and Irving Fisher (Eide and Showalter, 2010; Reynolds et al., 2010; Sweetland, 1996).

Economists from the University of Chicago, led by Gary Becker and Theodore Schultz, further developed these early concepts and pioneered the Human Capital Theory (Becker, 1962; Robeyns, 2006; Schultz, 1961; Unterhalter, 2009). Human Capital Theory is about how investments in people can lead to economic benefits for individuals and countries (Sweetland, 1996). These investments can increase individuals' future ability to earn income and drive economic growth, thus increasing people's well-being (Eide and Showalter, 2010). Because the focus of the Human Capital Theory is on economic returns, policy makers would choose between different types of investments and select the ones with the greatest rate of return.

Education is consistently considered a main investment for increasing human capital through both formal and informal activities. Education can be formal in nature at schools from pre-primary through secondary levels. It can also be informal through early stimulation and play at home, on-the-job training and apprenticeships or vocational education and training (Becker, 1962, 1993; Schultz, 1961; Sweetland, 1996; Unterhalter, 2009). In education, this theory recognises its main role in increasing human capital (Robeyns, 2006; Unterhalter, 2009). Education is important in creating and strengthening skills and acquiring knowledge that will allow a person to be economically productive in society (ibid.). This framework considers the access to educational opportunities as key to increased economic output, but does not consider that education must be of high quality in order to have results in children's capabilities (Unterhalter, 2009). All children that enter education will not necessarily exit it with the same skills (ibid.). Further, knowledge and skills that come through education contributes to health, nutrition and other aspects of one's growth and development. Someone who understands which healthy foods to eat, how to prevent or treat certain diseases, how to improve their ability to work and generate economic benefits will have the knowledge and skills to do so (Sweetland, 1996). This notion of education for the building of human capital provided attention to people as central to development efforts when previously the focus was only on macro-level economic development (Robeyns, 2006).

Novel Prize-winning Economist James Heckman and other economists broadened the Human Capital Theory to include applications to early childhood education, psychology and public health (Reynolds et al. 2010). James Heckman was one of the first economists to investigate human capabilities developed during early childhood. His research found that capabilities could be developed during this period of a child's life and that the greatest returns on investment were found with pre-school programmes over primary and secondary school and remedial programmes for older children (Carneiro and Heckman, 2003; Heckman, 2006). Even one extra year of pre-school could increase a person's future productivity by 10–30%, depending on the country and context (Van der Graag and Tan, 1998). Children who are ready to enter school due to preparations made during ECD programmes have been shown to be less likely to drop out or repeat a year (Arnold, 2004). Evidence from numerous long-term studies indicates that children who complete primary and secondary school are less likely to be involved in crime, drugs or other destructive behaviour and more likely to succeed in finding work (Arnold, 2004; Van der Graag and Tan, 1998). Further, Heckman (2006) found that investing in positive early educational experiences costs less than remedial programs or treatment for children later in life (Heckman, 2006).

A seminal longitudinal study on the cost benefit of ECD programming was conducted with the High Scope Perry Preschool programme in the United States. It targeted economically disadvantaged African American children. The study found a cost-benefit ratio of 7:1 when the participants were 27 years old and 13:1 when they were 40 years old (Barnett, 1996; Belfield et al., 2006). This means that for every $1 invested for ECD programming, there was a $7 or $13 worth of savings and benefit to society (ibid.). When compared to people who had no early childhood experience, graduates of the High Scope Perry Preschool had higher levels of education, higher earning potential and in many cases salaries, higher likelihood of stable family lives, better health and lower rates of criminality (Arnold, 2004). The evaluations also indicated greater benefits for girls (ibid.). Cost-benefit studies in developing countries have similar returns. A study in Bolivia and Colombia had a rate of return of 3:1 while one in Egypt had a return of 5.8:1 (Arnold, 2004). All of these cost-benefit studies found the greatest returns on the most disadvantaged children. As emergencies cause greater challenges and make children more vulnerable, there are reasons to believe that cost-benefit or cost-effectiveness studies of high-quality ECD programmes in humanitarian situations would have similar, if not better, returns on investment. Unfortunately, to date, no such analysis has been done to provide that evidence.

While the Human Capital Theory has allowed for cost-benefit and cost-effectiveness studies to be conducted and provide quantitative information for policy makers to base their budgetary decisions on, there are a number of weaknesses to this model (Robeyns, 2006). First, this theory sees education only as way to increase knowledge and skills that would increase a worker's productivity, wages and broader economic development (ibid.). This approach does not consider cultural, social and non-quantifiable aspects of life and a person's well-being (ibid.). It assumes that the way to a person's well-being and happiness is through economic stability and wealth. The theory further assumes that people act for economic reasons only. The Human Capital framework does not consider that someone may value other things in life over monetary wealth. The theory cannot explain why a person spends time learning a new language when it may not be needed for him/her to obtain a job or higher wages or why a person may prefer a lower paying job if it provides flexibility for a woman to also care for her family.

A second problem with the Human Capital Theory is that it values only the quantifiable aspects of education (Robeyns, 2006). Knowledge and skills gained through education that can be measured and quantified for the direct or indirect contribution to economic productivity are considered in this model. Quantifying and measuring investments can be very useful for policy makers deciding where to put their money; however, it does not tell the whole story of the importance of ECD and education programmes. While investments in education can have quantitative and economic results, they can also have qualitative improvements that are important for one's life such as an understanding how the political process works and how to participate in it or knowledge that is just for the sake of learning and understanding rather than making money (Robeyns, 2006; Sweetland, 1996). A child who learns how to live with people with different perspectives would contribute to a more tolerant society (Robeyns, 2006). A woman who learns about good nutrition and preventable diseases can help keep her family healthy even if she cannot use this knowledge to make money. The Human Capital Theory does not address qualitative and non-economic benefits of ECD and education and the effects it can have for improving people's well-being. Moreover, the Human Capital Theory does not provide any way of measuring these non-economic benefits (ibid.).

A third problem with the Human Capital Theory is that because it is focused on economic productivity as an end result, it could deter investments in education and ECD that may not lead to the highest economic returns (Robeyns, 2006). This is particularly relevant for girls' and women's access to educational opportunities. Dreze and Sen (2002) write about how the "gender division of labour" or social and cultural expectations of girls and women affect the perceived benefits of educating them (161–162). In many cultural contexts, girls and women are responsible for taking care of the home, family members and domestic duties. They may not be allowed to work outside of the home, so educating them may not bring about the same monetary returns to the family and society as boys and men. And because they are not always perceived to contribute to economic productivity, they are often excluded, from an early age, from important ECD and education services. Cumulative disparities that can start prenatally and in the first years of life result in lifetime consequences (Walker et al., 2011).

Human Capability Approach

The Human Capital Theory defines successful development when there are high rates of economic growth, which has merit to answer particular questions. However, it is not sufficient to address the questions of this research. The Human Capability Approach widens the view of development from the Human Capital Theory and views development and well-being in a multidimensional way (Alkire and Deneulin, 2009; Robeyns, 2006).

Starting in the 1970s, Amartya Sen, Nobel Laureate in Economics, challenged the scope of the Human Capital Theory and saw it to be too narrow to fully understand development and well-being. Sen does not see economic growth as the end and main purpose of development and well-being, but sees people at the centre and the reason for doing any sort of development work (Alkire and Deneulin, 2009; Walker and Unterhalter, 2007). He believes that economic growth is not the only way to measure a person's quality of life nor can this be illustrated through a single numeric scale (Nussbaum, 2005, 2011). Economic growth is a sub-set of development and well-being and one of many aspects that need to be considered when assessing a person's quality of life (Alkire and Deneulin, 2009, 26). This is especially true for those, such as females, who could benefit less from a nation's prosperity due to cultural barriers (Nussbaum, 2005).

Sen does not deny the Human Capital Theory, but goes further and says that a person's well-being is not just about high income or ensuring they have a right to something, but that it is "a person's ability to do valuable acts or reach valuable states of being; [it] represents the alternative combinations of things a person is able to do or be" (Sen, 1993, 30).

A second core aspect of Sen's conceptualisation of the Capability Approach is it is important to base definitions of development, well-being and quality of life on what people themselves value and this could be different in various cultural contexts and among different groups of people (Alkire and Deneulin, 2009; Walker and Unterhalter, 2007). The idea of capabilities is about a person's freedom and "the range of options a person has in deciding what kind of life to lead" (Dreze and Sen, 2002, 11). People themselves should be active agents in their own development and that starts with defining what that means (Walker and Unterhalter, 2007). Some people may value a capability that is not valued in another culture. According to Sen, people should be able to choose what defines a valuable life (Alkire and Deneulin, 2009; Robeyns, 2006; Walker and Unterhalter, 2007).

A third core concept of the Capability Approach is that of capabilities and functionings. Sen sees capabilities and functionings as different. Functionings are achieved outcomes such as reading and talking while capabilities are the potential to achieve these outcomes (Walker and Unterhalter, 2007; Unterhalter, 2009). Capabilities would include having been taught to read, having books or newspapers available to read. It focuses on the process rather than the end result. One may need multiple capabilities in order to have one functioning or outcome (ibid.). For example, in education, a functioning could be passing a test whereas the capability would be about how well the student has understood the concept and how this understanding could be applied to other functionings as well (ibid.).

Sen's conceptualisation of the Capability Approach is incomplete as it does not define what capabilities should be assessed for well-being, development and high quality of life (Alkire and Deneulin, 2009). He leaves this definition vague as he believes that people themselves should decide this. Unfortunately, there are a few problems with this. First, there are numerous perspectives and possible definitions within one country as different racial, ethnic or religious group may value different things. Second, in many cultural contexts people are not able to voice their viewpoints or they may omit certain capabilities that by society at large are valued. Further, certain groups, if they have the power to define capabilities to value, may push only their views and not others (ibid.).

Martha Nussbaum confronted these challenges in her work taking the thinking and discourses of the Capability Approach further (Alkire and Deneulin, 2009; Nussbaum, 2005, 2011). Nussbaum uses a stronger rights-based lens in combination with the Capability Approach to construct a theory of basic social justice by proposing ten central human capabilities (ibid.). These include (1) life, (2) bodily health, (3) bodily integrity, (4) senses, imagination and thought, (5) emotions, (6) practical reason, (7) affiliation, (8) other species, (9) play and (10) control over one's environment (Nussbaum, 2005, 2011). While Sen believes that fixing a pre-determined set of capabilities undermines people's agency, Nussbaum believes that existing structures of inequality and discrimination present in all countries will influence and shape what people value and deem relevant (Alkire and Deneulin, 2009). She further believes that in order to ensure people's basic rights and freedoms, some central capabilities must be set. These capabilities can be the basis of assessing the quality of life in a country (Nussbaum, 2011).

Sen identifies education as central and crucial to well-being and Nussbaum agrees with this (Saito, 2003; Terzi, 2007; Walker and Unterhalter, 2007). However, neither fully investigated education within the Capability Approach. Sen expresses the relevance of education towards well-being in terms of levels of literacy (Terzi, 2007). Saito, Unterhalter, Walker and Terzi are some who have taken this discussion further. Terzi (2007) considers education as a basic capability in that the absence of being educated would harm or significantly disadvantage the person in society (Terzi, 2007). Further, she states that being educated plays a significant role in developing other capabilities. This is particularly important for children as the lack of education and the foundational informal and formal learning that comes from it cannot be compensated for later in life (ibid.). Terzi (2007), like Nussbaum, puts forward a set of basic capabilities; however, Terzi's capabilities are specifically for education (Terzi, 2007). These include literacy, numeracy, being social and participating, learning disposition, physical activity, science and technology and practical reason (ibid.).

A weakness of the Capability Approach is that it usually does not have the quantitative empirical data required for rates of return analyses (Unterhalter, 2009). While the Capability Approach can help establish correlations, many policy makers want the quantitative data and rates of return to help them make decisions (ibid.). Another weakness of the Capability Approach is that Sen developed it as a broad theory that still requires further reflection, investigation and clarification on its applicability. While Nussbaum, Unterhalter and Walker explored issues of gender and education as it pertains to the Capability Approach and Terzi investigated how the Capability Approach might support children with disabilities (Terzi, 2008), very little has been written or explored with respect to early childhood and the Capability Approach.

Saito (2003) critiqued Sen's Capability Approach and was one of the first to ask how the Capability Approach could be applied to children, since children needed their parents' help in making decisions (Saito, 2003). Children, she believes, are not mature enough to make their own decisions (ibid.). Sen's response to Saito's reflection was that "when you are considering a child, you have to consider not only the child's freedoms now, but also the child's freedom in the future" (Saito, 2003). Her main argument for compulsory education is that it will give the child more freedom when he/she is older (Saito, 2003).

Jerome Ballet, Mario Biggeri and Flavio Comin (2011) are some of the first researchers to explore the many questions that still remain about children and the applicability of the Capability Approach. They began this pioneering work in 2004 with the establishment of a thematic group as part of the Human Development and Capability Association (Biggeri et al., 2011). Ballet, Biggeri and Comin ask several questions such as how the Capability Approach can be used to assess policies aimed at children's well-being, how capability can change with age, how children's ability to participate in their own development and well-being change with their age and maturity. They also ask if children are indeed able to define their own capabilities and how these capabilities can then be converted into functionings or outcomes (ibid.). Ballet, Biggeri and Comin conclude that the Capability Approach can theoretically underpin the conceptualisation and measurement of child well-being and can support policy decision-making.

Article 12 of the Convention on the Rights of the Child (CRC) highlights the importance of children's participation. This does not have a lower age limit where children can participate based on their capacities and stage of development (Biggeri, 2007). There is evidence that even very small children are capable of understanding and to which they can contribute thoughtful opinions (Ballet et al., 2011; Biggeri, 2007). However, based on their age and maturity, these capabilities evolve and so children may not be able to reach the highest levels of active participation in early childhood (Ballet et al., 2011). Biggeri (2007) involved children from middle childhood and adolescence in

Italy, India and Uganda in establishing their own models of valued capabilities and child well-being (Biggeri, 2007). However, this exercise has not been tested with young children who are below eight years of age.

Biggeri and Mehrotra (2011) explored how to choose domains of children's well-being and came up with a preliminary list of capabilities relevant for children. They went through a process with child development experts of first preparing an open-ended discussion about a list of capabilities for children. They then compared this list with others' lists of capabilities, including Nussbaum and Robeyns, and reflected upon the work of United Nations (UN) agencies. Their preliminary list of capabilities includes 14 domains (ibid.). The main limitations of this approach are that they did not include children in the process nor does it align with children's development at different ages.

Di Tommaso (2006) conceptualises and develops a framework for Indian children's well-being using the Capability Approach; however, she focused only on children six to 12 years old (Di Tommaso, 2006). She follows Robeyns' method to identifying appropriate capabilities. She uses Nussbaum's general list of capabilities, Robeyns' list of capabilities for gender inequality in Western countries and Phipps' list of capabilities for Canadian children as a general guide for establishing a children's capability framework for Indian children. Di Tommaso then selected relevant capabilities based on economic literature on Indian children. She then pilot tested this draft set of capabilities by engaging academics specialised in the Capability Approach and development in India. A limitation of this study was that Di Tommaso did not explore capabilities for children younger than six years old. Early childhood includes conception to eight years and children younger than six years would have different capabilities. Further, Di Tommaso did not use any participatory approaches to engage children or community members in India. Engaging academics can provide some insight into Indian culture, but not as it could if community members were actively involved in helping to develop this capability framework (ibid.).

Many gaps remain in furthering the investigation of children and the Capability Approach. First, while there are some references to child development theories in some of the work done on children and the Capability Approach, it is weak. Child development theories, and particularly Vygotsky's Socio-cultural theory, can provide insight into how children develop based on their external environment and therefore help create a Capabilities framework that is appropriate for the South Sudanese cultural context. In addition to simply using capabilities set forth in Nussbaum, Robeyns and other academics writing about the Capability Approach, the use of Vygotsky's Socio-cultural theory can provide added insight into capabilities that could be most appropriate for young South Sudanese children. Second, few studies have been conducted involving children in the establishment of capabilities and no studies have included young children below eight years of age. A strong child development lens and the inclusion of children, their parents and other caregivers' views could strengthen the process of establishing a relevant framework for children's capabilities. Further, much more testing and application needs to be done in order to determine whether the Capability Approach can be operationalised for young children. Lastly, no studies have looked at the use of the Capability Approach in emergency situations. Humanitarian situations add levels of complexity and challenges in measuring children's development and well-being that range from the fact that there are short projects to the security situation, etc. Therefore, many programmes do not collect rigorous and quantitative data on children's development in emergency situations. The lack of rigorous data and the lack of tools to measure child development in emergency contexts are huge gaps in academic literature, policy papers and practitioner guides and tools. A capability theory of ECD, based on a child development framework, may help government and donor decision makers invest more financial and human resources in this area. Additionally, it could support non-governmental organisations and the UN in designing and implementing the Capability Approach to ECD in emergency programmes. This book will therefore take discourses on child development and the Capability Approach further by testing its application to early learning and development in emergencies among South Sudanese refugees in Uganda in Parts II and III of this book. Part II (Chapter 6) explains how an ECD in development model was adapted and implemented in the South Sudanese refugee context.

References

Ageyev, V. (2003). "Vygotsky in the mirror of cultural interpretations", Ch. 20 In Kozulin, Al et al. (Eds.) *Vygotsky's Educational Theory in Cultural Context*. Cambridge: Cambridge University Press, 432–450.

Alkire, S. and Deneulin, S. (2009). "The Human development and capability approach", Ch. 2 In Deneulin, S. and Shahani, L. (Eds.) *An Introduction to the Human Development and Capability Approach*. London: Earthscan, Taylor and Francis, 3–21.

Arnold, C. (2004). "Positioning ECCD in the 21st century",. In Hanssen, E. and Zimanyi, L. (Eds), Coordinators' Notebook: An International Resources for Early Childhood Development. No. 28, 1–34., Toronto: The Global Consultative Group on Early Childhood Care and Development, Ryerson University: Canada.

Ballet, J., Biggeri, M. and Comim, F. (2011). "Children's agency and the capability approach: A conceptual framework", Ch. 2. In Mario, B., Jerome, B. and Flavio, C. (Eds.), *Children and the Capability Approach*. New York: Palgrave MacMillan, 22–45.

Barnett, S. (1996). *Lives in the Balance, Age-27 Benefit-Cost Analysis of the High/Scope Perry Preschool Program*. Ypsilanti, MI: High Scope Press.

Becker, G. (1962). "Investment in human capital: A theoretical analysis", *The Journal of Political Economy*, 70(5), 9–49.

Becker, G. (1993). *Human Capital: A Theoretical and Empirical Analysis with Special Reference to Education* (3rd edition). Chicago and London: The University of Chicago Press.

Belfield, C.R., Nores, M., Barnett, W.S. and Schweinhart, I. (2006). "The High Scope Perry Preschool Program: Cost-benefit analysis using data from the age 40 follow up", *Journal of Human Resources*, 41(1), 162–190.

Biggeri, M. (2007). "Children's valued capabilities", Ch. 10. In Melanie, W. and Elaine, U. (Eds.), *Amartya Sen's Capability Approach and Social Justice in Education*. New York/Oxon: Palgrave MacMillan, 19–214.

Biggeri, M. and Mehrotra, S. (2011). "Child poverty as capability deprivation: How to choose domains of child well-being and poverty", Ch. 3. In Mario, B., Jerome B. and Flavio, C. (Eds.), *Children and the Capability Approach*. New York: Palgrave Macmillan, 46–75.

Bronfenbrenner, U. (1979). *The Ecology of Human Development: Experiments by Nature and Design*. Cambridge, MA: Harvard College.

Bruer, J. (1999). *The Myth of the First Three Years: A New Understanding of Early Brain Development and Lifelong Learning*. New York: The Free Press.

Carneiro, P. and Heckman, J. (2003). *Human Capital Policy,* NBER Working Paper 9495, National Bureau of Economic Research, Cambridge, MA.

Cole, M. and Cole, S. (1997). *The Development of Children* (3rd edition). New York: W.H. Freeman and Company.

Conel, J. L. (1959). *The Postnatal Development of the Human Cerebral Cortex*. Cambridge, MA: Harvard University Press.

Das Gupta, P. (1994). "Images of childhood and theories of development", In Oates, J. (Ed.) *The Foundations of Child Development*. Hoboken, NJ: Wiley-Blackwell, 1–48.

Di Tommaso, M.L. (2006). "Measuring the well-being of children using a capability approach: An application to Indian data", Centre for Household, Income, Labour and Demographic Economics Working Paper, University of Turin.

Donahue-Coletta, N. (Ed.) (1992). *Understanding Cross-Cultural Child Development and Designing Programs for Children*. Washington, DC: PACT.

Dreze, J. and Sen, A. (2002). *India: Development and Participation*. Oxford: Oxford University Press.

Duncan, J. and Arnston, L. (2004). *Children in Crisis: Good Practices in Evaluating Psychosocial Programming*, Washington, DC:Save the Children.

Eide, E.R. and Showalter, M.H. (2010). "Human capital", In Peterson, P., Baker, E. and McGaw, B. (Eds) *International Encyclopedia of Education* (3rd edition). Oxford: Academic Press, 282–287.

Fernald, L. et al. (2009). *Examining Early Child Development in Low-Income Countries: A Toolkit for the Assessment of Children in the First Five Years of Life*. Washington, DC: World Bank.

Fleer, M. (2006, June). "The cultural construction of child development: Creating institutional and cultural intersubjectivity", *International Journal of Early Years Education*, 14(2), 127–140.

Fleer, M. and Hedegaard, M. (2010). "Children's development as participation in everyday practices across different institutions", *Mind, Culture, and Activity*, 17, 149–168.

Fountas, I. and Pinnell, G. (1996). *Guided Reading: Good First Teaching for All Children*. St. Louis, MO: Turtleback Books.

Freund, L.S. (1990). "Maternal regulation of children's problem-solving behavior and its impact on children's performance", *Child Development*, 61(1), 113–126.

Goodenough, W.H. (1953). *Native Astronomy in the Central Carolines*. Museum Monographs. Philadelphia: University Museum, University of Pennsylvania.

Graves, M., Juel, C. and Graves, B. (2007). *Teaching Reading in the 21st Century.* Irving, TX: Pearson.

Gray, C. and Mac Blain, S. (2015). *Learning Theories in Childhood.* London: Sage Publications.

Heckman, J. (2006). *Return on Investments: Cost vs. Benefits.* Chicago: University of Chicago. www.childandfamilypolicy.duke.edu/pdfs/10yranniversary_Heckmanhandout.pdf, last accessed 15 January 2016.

Huitt, W. and Hummel, J. (2003). "Piaget's theory of cognitive development", *Educational Psychology Interactive.* Valdosta, GA: Valdosta State University, last accessed 26 July 2019, http://www.edpsycinteractive.org/topics/cognition/piaget.html.

IASC (2007). *IASC Guidelines for Mental Health and Psychosocial Support in Emergency Settings.* Geneva: IASC.

Meadows, M. (1993). *The Young Child as Thinker: The Cognitive Development and Acquisition of Cognition in Childhood.* London: Routledge.

National Scientific Council on the Developing Child. (2004). *Young Children Develop in an Environment of Relationships.* Working Paper No. 1. www.developingchild.net

Nelson, K. (1981). "Social cognition in a script framework", In Flavell, J.H. and Ross, L. (Eds.) *Social Cognitive Development.* Cambridge: Cambridge University Press, 97–118.

Nunes, T. et al. (1993). *Street Mathematics and School Mathematics.* Cambridge: Cambridge University Press.

Nussbaum, M. (2005). "Capabilities as fundamental entitlements: Sen and social justice", In Agarwal, B., Humphries, J. and Robeyns, I. (Eds.) *Amartya Sen's Work and Ideas: A Gender Perspective.* Abingdon: Routledge.

Nussbaum, M. (2011). *Creating Capabilities: The Human Development Approach.* Cambridge, MA: Belknap Press of Harvard University Press.

O'Neill, S., et al. (2013). "A cultural-historical construction of safety education programs for preschool children: Findings from SeeMore Safety, the pilot study", *Australasian Journal of Early Childhood,* 38(2), 74–84.

Piaget, J.P. (1972). "Intellectual evolution from adolescence to adulthood", *Human Development,* 15, 1–12.

Pine, D., Costello, J. and Masten, A. (2005). "Trauma, proximity, and developmental psychopathology: The effects of war and terrorism on children", *Neuropsychopharmacology,* 30, 1781–1792.

Plan International (2011). *Benefits of Early childhood care and development in Emergencies: Indonesia, Pakistan, Bangladesh,* Unpublished report.

Reynolds, A., Rolnick, A., Englund, M. and Temple, J. (2010). "Early childhood development and human capital", In Reynolds, A., Rolnick, A., Englund, M. and Temple, J. (Eds.), *Childhood Programs and Practices in the First Decade of Life: A Human Capital Integration.* New York: Cambridge University Press, 1–26.

Ridgway, A. (2010). "How can cultural-historical theory be used as a methodological dialectic?", *European Early Childhood Education Research Journal,* 18(3), 159–176.

Robeyns, I. (2006). "Three models of education: Rights, capabilities and human capital", *Theory and Research in Education,* 4, 69, Sage Publications.

Rogoff, B. (1990). *Apprenticeship in Thinking: Cognitive Development in Social Context.* New York: Oxford University Press.

Rogoff, B. (1995). "Observing sociocultural activity on three planes: participatory appropriation, guided participation, and apprenticeship", In Wertsch, J.,

Del Rio, P. and Alvarez, A. (Eds.), *Sociocultural Studies of Mind*. London: Oxford University Press, 139–164.

Rogoff, B. (1998). "Cognition as a collaborative process", In Damon, W. (Chief Ed.), Kuhn, D. and Siegler (Eds.), *Cognition, Perceptions and Language: Handbook of Child Psychology* (5th edition). New York: Wiley & Sons, 679–744.

Rogoff, B. (2003). *The Cultural Nature of Human Development*. Oxford: Oxford University Press.

Rogoff, B., Mosier, C., Mistry, C. and Göncü, A. (1998). "Toddlers' guided participation with their caregivers in cultural activity", In Woodhead, M., Faulkner, D. and Littleton, K. (Eds.), *Cultural Worlds of Early Childhood*. Routledge: 225–249, London.

Saito, M. (2003). "Amartya Sen's capability approach to education: A critical exploration", *Journal of Philosophy of Education*, 37(1), 17–33.

Save the Children, CfBT, and American Institute of Research (2015). *The Cost of War: Calculating the Impact of the Collapse of Syria's Education System on the Country's Future*. London: Save the Children.

Saxe, G.B. (1981). "Body parts as numerals: A developmental analysis of numeration among the Oksapmin in Papua, New Guinea", *Child Development*, 52, 306–316.

Saxe, G. (1994). "Studying cognitive developments in sociocultural context: The development of a practice-based approach", *Mind, Culture and Activity*, 1, 135–157.

Schultz, T. (1961). "Investment in human capital", *The American Economic Review*, 51(1), 1–17.

Sen, A. (1993). "Capability and well-being", In Nussbaum, M. and Sen, A. (Eds.) *The Quality of Life*. Oxford: Clarendon Press, 30–53.

Shayer, M. and Adey, P. (Eds.) (2002). *Learning and Intelligence: Cognitive Acceleration across the Curriculum from 5 to 15 Years*. Buckingham: Open University Press.

Smidt, S. (2009). *Introducing Vygotsky: A Guide for Practitioners and Students in Early Years Education*. New York: Routledge.

Sweetland, S. (1996). "Human capital theory: Foundations of a field of inquiry", *Review of Educational Research*, 66(3), 341–359.

Terzi, L. (2007). "The capability to be educated", In Walker, M. and Unterhalter, E. (Eds.), *Amartya Sen's Capability Approach and Social Justice in Education*. New York: Palgrave Macmillan, 25–43.

Terzi, L. (2008). *Justice and Equality in Education: A Capability Perspective on Disability and Special Educational Needs*. New York: Continuum Publishing.

Thomas, M. (2005). *Comparing Theories of Child Development* (6th edition). Wadsworth, OH: Thomson Learning.

UNESCO (2006). *Education for All Global Monitoring Report 2007. Strong Foundations: Early Childhood Care and Education*. Paris: UNESCO.

Unterhalter, E. (2009). "Education", Ch. 9. In Deneulin, S. and Shahini, L. (Eds.) *An Introduction to Human Development and Capability Approach*. London: Earthscan, Taylor and Francis, 207–227.

Van der Graag, J. and Tan, J.P. (1998). *The Benefits of Early Childhood Development Programs: An economic Analysis*. Washington, DC: World Bank.

Vygotsky, L.S. (1978). *Mind in Society: The Development of Higher Psychological Processes*. Cambridge, MA: Harvard University Press.

Walker, M. and Unterhalter, E. (2007). "The capability approach: Its potential for work in education", In Walker, M. and Unterhalter, E. (Eds.), *Amartya Sen's Capability Approach and Social Justice in Education*. New York: Palgrave Macmillan.

Walker, S. et al. (2011). "Inequality in early childhood: Risk and protective factors for early childhood development", *The Lancet*, Child Development 1 series, 378, 1325–1338, London.

Williamson, J. and Robinson, M. (2006). "Psychosocial interventions, or integrated programming for well-being?" *Intervention*, 4(1), 4–25.

Wood, D., Bruner, J.S. and Ross, G. (1976). "The role of tutoring in problem solving", *Journal of Child Psychology and Psychiatry*, 17(2), 81–100.

Part II

Early Childhood Development in emergency programming

Part I of this book painted a picture of the scenario for Early Childhood Development (ECD), humanitarian contexts, the impact of emergencies on young children and why investment is needed in the early years during crises. Britto et al. point out that while there is a growing understanding and consensus globally about "what" is ECD and "why" it is important, a huge gap remains in "how" to implement such programmes across existing systems and varying contexts so they are of high quality, scalable and sustainable (Britto et al., 2018). In speaking with Dr Kofi Marfo of the Aga Khan University's Institute of Human Development, he said, "[t]he child development research we currently have represents the cultures and contexts of only 5% of the world." As part of this, it is still unclear how to bundle various aspects of nurturing care that children need—responsive caregiving, health, nutrition, safety and protection and early stimulation and learning (ibid.). Further, as Murphy, Yoshikawa and Wuermli uncover in a review of existing evidence on implementation research for ECD in humanitarian contexts, there is still a critical gap in understanding not only which programmes are effective and show positive outcomes, but why, how and in which circumstances (Murphy et al., 2018). A huge gap remains in understanding how to implement ECD models in developing countries and especially in humanitarian contexts.

Part II of this book begins to address these concerns. Chapter 6 investigates the adaptation and implementation of an ECD model for South Sudanese refugees in Uganda. It details, based on qualitative research, what aspects of the model were easy to implement and which were not. Further, it delves deeply into how a development model can be adapted, and what needs to be considered during adaptation. The chapter ends with guidance for design and implementation of future ECD in emergency programming.

6 Adaptation of a development model for a humanitarian context

ECD ranges from prenatal services that focus on pregnant women to newborns to children up to eight years who are in early primary grades. The ECD Nurturing Care Framework outlines the five critical components young children need to survive and thrive: opportunities for early learning, responsive caregiving, security and safety, good health and adequate nutrition (WHO, UNICEF and World Bank, 2018). The Nurturing Care Framework components can be implemented in myriad ways based on who runs projects, the context and available financing. While ideally all ECD interventions should integrate all of the aforementioned components of nurturing care, it is not always realistic to do so simultaneously or at the same depth due to insufficient financing or technical understanding. This challenge becomes even more difficult in humanitarian situations when interventions and staff leading sectors are largely siloed. This chapter delves deeper into one evidence-based ECD model—Community-Led Action for Children (CLAC)—which is heavily focused on opportunities for early learning and responsive caregiving, but has some elements of good health, adequate nutrition and security and safety. I first present the model in its original form as it was conceptualised and then analyse its design and implementation in a development and refugee context. The adapted model analysed in this chapter was then tested among South Sudanese refugees in Uganda (results in Chapter 9). The section presents one evidence-based ECD in emergency model that can be used in different humanitarian situations. I then draw upon lessons learned through this analysis and my years of professional work experience to summarise key tips for future ECD programming in emergencies. This guidance is aimed at humanitarian practitioners, but can be useful for development practitioners, policy makers, donors and others.

Framing of the implementation analysis

The analysis of implementation can look at various dimensions such as intended outcomes, dosage (duration, frequency and intensity), delivery (content, service provider, mode of delivery), fidelity, quality, sustainability, scalability, adaptation, cost benefit and cost effectiveness (Britto et al., 2018;

Murphy et al., 2018). During this research, I used qualitative methods to frame the analysis around these five areas: (1) intended outcomes, (2) content, (3) dosage (duration, frequency, intensity), (4) delivery (service provider and mode of delivery) and (5) adaptation. The qualitative data collection included Focus Group Discussions (FGDs), Key Informant Interviews (KIIs), existing Plan International documentation (both published and unpublished) and observation.

As the CLAC model provides broad implementation guidance and a humanitarian context requires adaptation, looking at its fidelity was not as important. The model was not looking to follow the original model exactly. Further, scalability and sustainability were hard to investigate as the emergency project had one-year funding and was not initially thought through before design and implementation in the refugee settlements. This is often a challenge for humanitarian practitioners—to think about scale and sustainability when they have short-term projects. Cost-benefit and cost-effectiveness analyses require quantitative approaches and costing data. I did not have full costing data to make this a possibility (Gustafsson-Wright and Boggild-Jones, 2018). Implementation analysis can also be done at a broader full model level or component level. I present the full model, but analyse the implementation by each component.

Community-Led Action for Children Model

The CLAC model, developed by Plan International, is one of many types of ECD models created and implemented in development and humanitarian contexts. It is a low cost, community-based ECD model that supports children, parents, teachers and government (Plan International, 2013). The model was first implemented in 2009 in Uganda and then in Kenya, Ethiopia, Zimbabwe, Mozambique, Zambia and other places in East Africa (ibid.). It is now piloted in other regions such as West Africa and humanitarian contexts such as South Sudan, refugee camps in Uganda and Ethiopia, Central African Republic, Jordan and others. The model draws on and builds from community expertise about childcare and development. It aims to empower communities and strengthen parent and/or caregiver capabilities so they can help their children reach their developmental potential and contribute to society in a positive way. While the groups are open to all parents, Plan targets the most vulnerable families such as single-headed households (especially female-headed households), those with the lowest levels of education, those from areas with fewer services and those in greatest economic need. This also includes an emphasis on families that have children with disabilities as it has been found that early intervention and support is even more critical for these children (ibid.).

The CLAC model is underpinned by Vygotsky's Socio-cultural theory and Bronfenbrenner's Ecological systems theory and is in line with the Global Consultative Group on Early Childhood Care and Development's (ECCD) Four Cornerstones Approach. It includes a strong emphasis on the bundling of two aspects of the ECD Nurturing Care Framework: opportunities for early learning and responsive caregiving. Integral, but having smaller prominence in the model, are three other aspects of the Nurturing Care Framework: good health, adequate nutrition and security and safety. Vygotsky's Socio-cultural theory places great importance on the child's external environment, including his/her parents and the culture in which a child lives (Vygotsky, 1978). The CLAC model uses existing culture and understanding of child development and care as the basis for parenting support and responsive caregiving. Bronfenbrenner's Ecological systems theory builds on Vygotsky's work and illustrates circles of support for a child, which includes his/her parents as primary and most important, but also includes the school and community environment, government policies and societal norms, expectations and policies (Bronfenbrenner, 1979).

Plan International's CLAC has four key components (Figure 6.1): (1) parenting education, (2) early learning, (3) transition to primary school and (4) advocacy to influence policy. Each of these four components will be analysed separately considering the following: (1) intended outcomes, (2) content, (3) dosage (duration, frequency, intensity), (4) delivery (service provider and mode of delivery) and (5) adaptation. Adaptation will be integral to the analysis of the implementation in the South Sudanese refugee context. Analysis of each component separately will allow practitioners that only want to implement a particular pillar to easily understand the approach and lessons learned.

These four components highlight the importance of the external environment and in particular the various levels as the Socio-cultural and Ecological system theories outline. Component 2 focusing on early learning looks at the individual child and his/her immediate teacher, whereas components 1, 3 and 4 look at the external environment and in particular at the level of parents, teachers and community and the broader national context. The broader national context would include society's expectations and milestones for children, cultural definitions and interpretations of various aspects of children's development and learning. These cultural expectations, norms and definitions trickle down to the other components and shape the implementation of a particular activity such as parenting education or early learning spaces

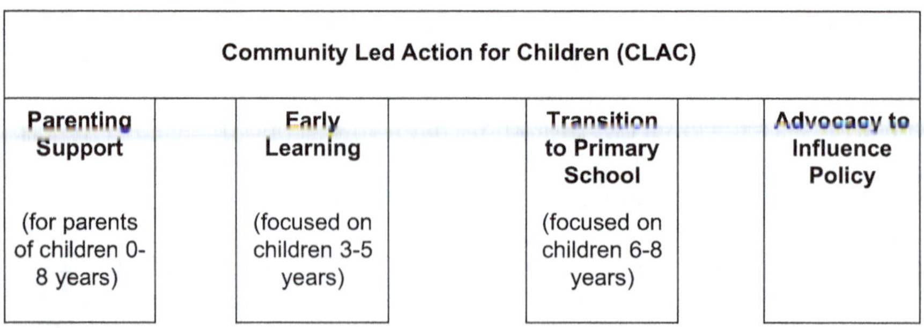

Figure 6.1 Community-Led Action for Children.

and curriculum. The approach in its original form bundles early stimulation/learning and responsive caregiving. Through KIIs, Plan Uganda staff indicated that they and other colleagues in East Africa, also implementing the CLAC model, have recognised that it needs to strengthen three areas: (1) health/nutrition inputs, (2) pre-natal support and (3) implementation in emergencies.

Implementation contexts being analysed

Development context: Lira, Uganda

The CLAC model is currently implemented in many parts of Uganda. Uganda is a low-income country where about 75–80% of children aged three to six years have no access to toys or learning activities (Singla et al., 2015). Additionally, 40% of children are stunted and 14% are underweight (ibid.). The analysis presented here investigates implementation of CLAC in Lira, Uganda. This is east of Adjumani in the West Nile region where South Sudanese refugees are settled. Lira is a conflict-affected area and was plagued with violent conflict for many years. It has a population of approximately 403,000 people and also has poor child development, health and maternal health (Singla et al., 2015). Currently, there is relative peace in Lira.

Emergency context: South Sudanese refugees in Uganda

South Sudan is also a low-income country with similar statistics to Uganda. The South Sudanese refugees are in multiple informal settlements in the West Nile region that lies westward from Lira. This research analysed the implementation of the CLAC model in settlements in the Adjumani area of West Nile.

Components of the model: implementation in development and emergencies

Component 1: parenting support

Original model

In all CLAC programmes, parenting education is a critical and central component to any support for young children. The *intended outcome* is to strengthen parents' skills and capabilities so they can provide optimal care and stimulation for their growing child or children. The intention of active skill building among parents is so they can support all of their children—from birth to the transition to primary school—at home and through everyday experiences.

The underlying belief of the CLAC model is that parents and other primary caregivers are the first and most important teachers in children's lives and their responsive caregiving is essential to young children's positive development outcomes. Bronfenbrenner includes parents as a child's first layer of protection and support (Bronfenbrenner, 1979). This activity aims to improve parents' knowledge and practical skills to improve child health, nutrition, learning and protection. As Vygotsky outlines, an adult or parent is crucial to helping children in their zone of proximal development (ZPD). They can provide the scaffolding a child needs as he/she slowly becomes competent and can independently do what is in the higher part of the ZPD (Gray and Mac Blain, 2015; Smidt, 2009).

Building adults' capabilities can therefore promote children's well-being. This theory of change reflects new research from Harvard University's Center on the Developing Child, which places support for parents as critical to children's positive development outcomes (Center on the Developing Child, 2013). Harvard's theory of change, known as Building Adult Capabilities for Children's Outcomes, is based on evidence that highlights the critical importance of developing certain executive function skills for success in adulthood (ibid.).

Some of these executive function skills include focusing attention, self-regulation, delaying gratification, being able to solve problems and being able to work cooperatively in teams (Center on the Developing Child, 2013; Center on the Developing Child, 2016). The development of these skills begins in infancy. While the flexibility and plasticity of this part of the brain accelerate during early childhood, it does not fully mature until a person is 25–30 years old. Continuing work with young adults, who may already be parents, will still allow practitioners to take advantage of important maturation that occurs in the adult brain. Stronger executive function skills can help parents better support their children. However, research from Uganda, Bangladesh and other countries reveal that simply giving advice and information to parents is not enough to see change in parent behaviours (Aboud, 2007; Center on the Developing Child, 2013; Yousafzai and Aboud, 2014). Active skill building, through coaching and practice, is critical (ibid.).

The ECD Nurturing Care Framework highlights the responsive caregiving piece (WHO, UNICEF and World Bank, 2018). This element is seen as the critical element for children's positive outcomes (ibid.). While originally the Nurturing Care Framework was developed to emphasise support for children from birth to three years of age, as this group has been more neglected than children three years and older, there is a recognition among the ECD community that Nurturing Care is important for children of all ages (Black et al., 2016; Britto et al., 2016).

CONTENT

In the original CLAC model, parent support emphasises five key areas related to child development: (1) food and nutrition (particularly the nutrition of local foods and how to prepare nutritious local foods for children), (2) handwashing and hygiene to prevent illness, (3) play and cognitive stimulation, (4) adult interaction and communication and (5) fostering love and respect within the family unit and among the community. Through parenting support, Plan included other aspects of the Nurturing Care Framework: health, nutrition and safety and security. While the five broad themes mentioned earlier are the entry point, parents can bring up any topic or issue of concern.

DOSAGE: DURATION, FREQUENCY, INTENSITY

The original CLAC model does not dictate the dosage of the parenting support because the theory of change is based on bottom up processes. In order to establish community ownership and longer term sustainability, the duration of each group session, the frequency of the meetings (i.e. monthly, bi-monthly) and the intensity (i.e. one hour, three hours) are to be determined by each individual community. This also ensures that the dosage is realistic for the community members, so attendance can remain high.

DELIVERY: SERVICE PROVIDER AND MODE OF DELIVERY

All parenting sessions are co-led by Plan staff and one or two parents from the community. The parents should be selected by the community. Initially, the sessions start off with Plan staff leading a bit more, but slowly transition to the parenting groups continuing on their own.

Beyond the parents in the groups, community ownership and active participation are critical to ensuring that the parenting groups continue on their own after Plan phases out. The community, therefore, should provide the meeting place (i.e. building or safe area), and actively select co-facilitators of the sessions. This allows for the process to build on the local culture and existing parenting strengths and achievements.

Plan implements parenting support through group sessions and 1:1 home visits. It usually facilitates the creation of new parenting groups among community members. The recommended guidance for the parenting groups is to cap the number to 30 people. Key community leaders are important actors that can help parents take the interventions forward and ensure longer term sustainability. Peer to peer support and practicing skills they learn about are key aspects of the parenting sessions. Parents can and are encouraged to bring their children, especially infants, so the child has continuous care and parents can practice activities they learn in the parenting groups with their children. Parents can also bring their older children and in this case, Plan and the community can jointly provide caregivers to play and take care of the children while their parents are in the group sessions. Both mothers and fathers can be in the parenting groups.

Implementation in a development context: Lira, Uganda

Intended outcomes: To strengthen parents' skills and capabilities so they can provide optimal care and stimulation for their child or children from birth to eight years.

While the CLAC model itself does not have specific outcomes for mothers' well-being, the implementation of this in Lira, Uganda focused on and measured maternal well-being as a secondary goal along with children's development (Singla et al., 2015).

CONTENT

While the global CLAC model does not specify the number of total sessions, Plan Uganda has a 12-session parenting curriculum. This is in line with the model's five thematic areas. The curriculum currently being implemented includes 12 sessions and 5 critical skills: (1) child nutrition and diet, (2) hygiene, (3) child development and play for learning, (4) two-way communication between adults and (5) family relationships (Singla et al., 2015). Among the 12 sessions, the first is an introductory session where people can get to know each other, to set the rules for the group, etc. The next six sessions focus on the child—his/her development, different play activities to promote psychosocial well-being and cognitive development, nutrition and health. Afterwards, the next four sessions focus on the mother and ensuring her care, psychosocial well-being and relationship with her spouse.

The approach for this parenting curriculum took time to develop and test. Many changes were made until it got to the approach and content that are being implemented in Lira today. Initially, Plan established a parenting curriculum that was based on theoretical frameworks of responsive parenting that promote child development (Singla et al., 2015). Responsive parenting includes interaction between the parent and child such as through two-way conversation and play (ibid.). Despite differences in cultural contexts, responsive parenting has been found to enhance cognitive and language development (ibid.). This curriculum has been tested and modified based on experience that Plan has had with its parenting programmes (Aboud, 2007; Aboud et al., 2013; Singla et al., 2015). According to Key Informants, initially the curriculum included more than 12 sessions (while still including the 5 core areas) and focused more on giving information. Slowly, Plan realised through evaluations and experience implementing that they needed to reduce the breadth of the curriculum and focus on depth and in particular on actively building parents' skills. This is line with research presented earlier conducted by Yousafzai and Aboud in Pakistan, Uganda, Bangladesh and other countries (Yousafzai and Aboud, 2014).

In Lira, each session started with a welcome song so people could meet each other and feel comfortable. The song was a local song and the facilitators selected which song they wanted to start the session with. Attendance was taken after the initial welcome song. The facilitators proceeded with a review of the previous session's key points and parents discussed any challenges they faced in implementing what they previously learned and any additional questions to help them improve the care and support parents provide for their children. A new topic of the day was introduced which included presentation of key content, but also practice on using the learning from the topic of the day. This could be related to cooking nutritious food or playing new games with children.

According to the KII and FGDs, there were huge changes in the relationship between spouses in a family. One mother in a parenting group in Lira said, "We talk more now. He helps me with the child care. He comes to the parenting sessions. It has improved our relationship and there is peace in the family." These sessions focus on combating against maternal depression and promoting harmony and a strong supportive family. The last of the 12 sessions is a concluding session. Where the community wants, they can continue meeting on their own. While these general themes are set, parents were able to bring up critical issues related to these topics. This allowed parents to help each other find solutions to the challenges they were facing.

DOSAGE: DURATION, FREQUENCY, INTENSITY

According to FGDs and KIIs, parents in each group decided on the frequency of the parent meetings, how long each one would be and where they would meet. Some in Lira chose monthly meetings, while others chose bi-weekly meetings. This process of parents making their own decisions is important for ownership and sustainability. The hope is that these groups continue on their own without Plan's support. In Lira, a majority of the groups decided to meet for about 60–90 minutes every month near their pre-school centres (Singla et al., 2015). FGDs, KIIs and research conducted by Singla et al. (2015) revealed that in most places one cycle of parenting sessions lasted about seven months; in other places, the parenting groups continued after the core parenting sessions were complete (ibid.).

DELIVERY: SERVICE PROVIDER, MODE OF DELIVERY

As with the original model, in Uganda, Plan staff co-facilitated parenting sessions with two volunteers from the community. These individuals were selected by the community due to the trust they already had and other volunteer work they had done for the community.

Plan held a community meeting to sensitise the community about child development and establishment of peer to peer parenting groups. Plan identified and worked with local leaders in the areas of implementation to form groups. Both women and men living in the community were invited to join the groups, but a priority was given to families with low maternal education and deemed as more vulnerable (Singla et al., 2015). Each group had approximately 20–35 members (including fathers). Plan Uganda staff made a special effort to actively involve fathers in the parenting groups. One participating father said, "Plan invited us to join. At first I didn't think it would be useful, but I have learned a lot. I see my child learning and it makes me happy." While Plan leads the parenting sessions, there are parent co-facilitators to help co-lead and eventually lead the groups without Plan's support. One parent facilitator said, "Plan approached me as I am known in the community and speak the local language. I did not know how to do it, but I thought I would try. The Plan staff helped me lead the sessions." The parent co-facilitators are not professionals, but know the community and have their respect, speak the local language, are enthusiastic, etc. (Singla et al., 2015). Helping parents understand this process and mobilising them to want to be involved took time as the concepts of early childhood education/development and the role of parents were new.

In order to provide holistic support to families, parents involved in the parenting groups also had their children three to five years in Plan supported early learning centres. These parents also had children of other ages, both older and younger than the pre-school age, but this approach allowed Plan to strengthen the capabilities of a child and his/her environment based on their own cultural context as Socio-cultural theory and Ecological systems theory promote. This approach also aligns with recent brain research conducted by Harvard University's Center on the Developing Child (Shonkoff, 2013). Parents were encouraged to bring their children with them to the parenting sessions so they could practice some of the things they learned with their children (i.e. games that promote cognitive development). Plan utilised an active learning approach that included peer support, role play, games, parent-child interactions, practice and problem solving (Singla et al., 2015). For example, during the sessions parents used word and toy games to play with their children, and created and acted out skits to practice communication and conflict resolution with their spouses. Colourful posters with the key messages connected to the topics of the five key areas were used during the sessions. Parents were encouraged to solve problems related to the new topic and practice what they learned. Parents were then provided with homework where they had to practice what they learned in the parenting session with their children, spouses and peers at home.

Along with group sessions, Plan conducted home visits to help parents overcome the challenges of implementing the things they learned during the sessions. The most vulnerable families were prioritised for home visits. Home visits were used to accompany the parenting sessions so facilitators could further help parents practice the skills they learned. Plan used a Home Visit Observation sheet to measure parent-child interactions during these visits.

KIIs mentioned that they saw huge differences in the interactions between parents and their children. Based on FGDs and KII, parents were more aware of their children's needs, were more committed to finding additional assistance when certain needs were not met and became strong advocates for their children and children in the community in general. There were also many active fathers in the parenting groups.

After the core parenting sessions, Plan connected some of the parents to existing Village Savings and Loan Associations (VSLA). According to KIIs, the idea was to help strengthen families' financial status, thereby benefiting their children. At the time of data collection, connecting parents with existing VSLA groups was new.

Implementation in an emergency context: South Sudanese refugees in Uganda

At the time of data collection, Plan was in the early stages of fully implementing this approach in Ayillo 2 so many parents had not participated in many sessions. In Ayillo 1, Plan had not yet started parenting education at all as the refugees had come to the camps only two weeks prior to the data collection.

INTENDED OUTCOMES

As with the implementation of parenting in Lira, within the refugee response programme, the main and secondary objectives remained the same. The primary objective was to strengthen parents' skills and capabilities so they could provide optimal care and stimulation for their child or children from birth to eight years. The secondary objective was to improve mothers' psychosocial well-being.

While in development contexts, mothers might be feeling stress due to different types of adversity (i.e. poverty), this stress can elevate during humanitarian crises. In the South Sudanese refugee context, many women were in the settlements without their husbands or experienced the loss of their husbands from the fighting. Many of these women were caring for multiple children alone in a new country. During FGDs and KIIs, many refugee women mentioned they were stressed—for example not knowing if their husband was dead or alive, if they would ever see him again, how they would survive without money in a new country, etc. So, focusing on aspects of psychosocial well-being was very important for these women. The parenting groups provided a safe space where women could come together, re-build social support networks that may have been broken due to the displacement. A number of women from FGDs mentioned that they had new friends and a new family in the settlements.

CONTENT

The emergency programme followed the same parenting manual (12 sessions with 5 core areas) as the programme in Lira followed. During KIIs, I asked why this was the case and the Plan staff mentioned that they had funding for this, but not the skills or sufficient experience to adapt the training package. So, as a first step they preferred to use the materials that were available and make changes as required in the future.

A critical aspect that parents raised, which was not prominent in the content of the parenting manual, was about positive parenting/discipline and promoting peace. Positive parenting referred to alternative methods of discipline that do not use physical violence. Promoting peace includes respecting diversity, teaching children non-violence ways to behave with others and solve problems, working collaboratively with children and people of all tribes and ethnic groups. As the majority of the ethnic groups in Adjumani were from the Dinka tribe, the population initially did not see the need to respect other ethnicities or learn to live together. However, I observed many people arguing and fighting—children and parents—both from the same tribes and those of different tribes. In a number of instances in the camps, I saw children fighting and then their parents started fighting, verbally and physically, with the other parents. FGDs and KII confirmed that many people tried to resolve problems through arguing and fighting. Many South Sudanese I met and talked to during this research process want this to change and hope for a better future. Positive discipline and promoting peace are areas Plan International need to address in its CLAC parenting programme, especially in conflict-affected fragile contexts, including refugee and internally displaced persons (IDP) situations. This is also a critical area for future ECD in emergency programmes.

DOSAGE: DURATION, FREQUENCY, INTENSITY

While in Lira, the parenting groups decided to meet once a month, in Adjumani, the groups decided to meet every two weeks. Eventually, the groups decided to change the frequency to every week. Each session lasted about two hours. In humanitarian situations where projects are shorter term, this adaptation to greater frequency fits better with the situation.

DELIVERY: SERVICE PROVIDER, MODE OF DELIVERY

As with Lira, community members were selected to work as volunteers, co-leading and co-facilitating parenting sessions. While parent co-facilitators were identified, at the time of data collection, they were not fully co-leading parenting sessions. The parents selected to be volunteers were women and they had no formal background in parenting support. However, they were active in the refugee settlement, motivated, had outgoing personalities and had the trust of the other parents.

According to KII and FGDs, the mobilisation and recruitment of parents to be group members and leaders followed a similar process as Lira with a few modifications. The groups were organised in a similar fashion, but where in Lira the groups were assembled while establishing the early learning centres, in Adjumani, the early learning activities began before parents were mobilised and organised. This was mostly due to limited financing, but also the fact that this activity was new to the Plan staff implementing the project. Plan held a meeting to let the community and leaders within it know about the start-up of parenting groups. Those that had children in early learning centres were prioritised for inclusion. Plan obtained approval from the refugee leaders of the camp. As with Lira, the space for the parenting sessions was decided by the community itself. In most circumstances, parents met in the ECD centres where children three to six years spent half a day to learn through play-based activities. However, parenting sessions can occur anywhere.

While parenting has started being implemented in the South Sudanese camps in Adjumani, at the time of data collection for this research, Plan had not started implementing the full spectrum of the parenting curriculum. While the same 12 modules from Lira were used, the parenting sessions in Adjumani did not have the same approach of using participatory methods that focused on practical skills building. Parents were encouraged to bring their children in order to practice some of the skills they learned. However, during the sessions, many parents did not bring their children. Part of this could be because the parenting session facilitators and Plan staff did not fully understand the CLAC approach and therefore did not actually implement it as it was intended to be where parents would be encouraged to bring children so they could practice skills they learned.

The original CLAC model and the implementation in Lira included home visits for the most vulnerable families that were identified as needing additional support. Home visits had not started in the refugee settlements at the time of data collection. During KIIs, Plan staff indicated that they had plans to begin this, but did not feel fully prepared technically to do so. Additionally, there were very few fathers who participated in the parenting sessions in the refugee settlements. Part of this is because there was a proportionally smaller percentage of adult men in the camps. However, among the men in the settlements, Plan staff mentioned that male involvement in caretaking was not normal and that they invited fathers, but they refused to come. These staff understood the importance of involving fathers and determined that they needed to create a better strategy for reaching refugee fathers.

Component 2: early learning

The original model

The CLAC model also includes early learning or pre-school education for children three to six years, usually through centre-based activities. This stage supports the transition from the home to a centre or place for learning and play. In some countries this is just one year of pre-school before children enter primary school. In other countries, the pre-school education services include two or three years.

INTENDED OUTCOMES

This component is focused on children's pre-literacy, pre-numeracy and other school readiness skills. While not an exclusive focus on socio-emotional skills, the approach is play based, where children can explore, be curious, ask questions, learn how to share with others and begin developing critical socio-emotional or twenty-first-century skills. Some of these critical skills include executive function such as the ability to focus and sustain attention, set goals, make plans, follow rules, solve problems, monitor actions, delay gratification and control impulses (Shonkoff, 2013). Brain science reveals that the most rapid growth of executive function skills occurs between the ages of three and five (ibid.).

CONTENT

The curriculum used is different in each country. The model indicates that an existing country's curriculum can be used. If none exists, one from another similar country can be used. The critical aspects are rather the approach and setup of the space that are outlined below.

DOSAGE: DURATION, FREQUENCY, INTENSITY

Early learning activities are meant to be for half a day, five days per week. This can be adjusted based on the realities in a country.

DELIVERY: SERVICE PROVIDER, MODE OF DELIVERY

The model envisions the use of pre-school teachers. These people can be existing teachers in the community or community members that require training. They can be certified or not, depending on the realities in the country and communities. Many of the individuals recruited can be primary trained teachers who are taught play-based approaches for younger children.

The CLAC model encourages simple, stable structures, community involvement and ownership in establishing the safe spaces. All spaces should be established, where possible, close to where children live and ideally close to primary schools as well.

There should be a daily routine in each early learning space. A general structure for the day should include: a morning welcome in a circle through music; play-based structured and unstructured activities that integrate fine and gross motor skills, pre-math, pre-literacy and communication skills; outdoor play and a closing done through music. Within this general structure, teachers hired and trained to implement CLAC can make modifications. The morning welcome can include more than greetings such as a discussion of the weather, news of the day, etc. The day then includes play-based structured and unstructured activities (free play and guided play), including songs and rhymes that teach concepts such as the importance of hygiene and washing their hands and body, brushing their teeth, combing their hair, counting to 10 or more, drawing, painting, moulding clay, etc. Songs are sung in both English and their mother tongue. There are usually four corners set up in the space that addresses different aspects of a child's development—dramatic play corner, sand/water play corner, math corner (with rocks, sticks, leaves, etc.) for children to practice emergent math skills such as counting, identifying patterns, sorting, etc. Another corner is usually a literacy corner that has books, paper, crayons and markers so children can look at books, draw and write (thereby developing their fine motor skills). Unstructured outdoor play is also an important aspect of the day to help children socialise with other children and develop gross motor skills. Children can develop many critical skills when they have to manage themselves in an environment with their peers. The day should end with a closing meeting, usually in a circle. The space should be print rich with words, alphabet, number charts, calendars, pictures, colours, etc. An early learning programme quality checklist should be used to monitor the quality of the early learning centre and its implementation of the curriculum.

Implemented in a development context: Lira, Uganda

Intended outcomes: The focus was on school readiness, which includes early literacy, numeracy and writing skills.

CONTENT

The Government of Uganda has a pre-school curriculum that they use in all early learning spaces. In Lira, children from four to six years participated in these activities. Plan staff mentioned that they did not have funding to have classrooms for three-year olds so they prioritised early learning for four- and five-year olds. While the general content remained the same, the teachers in Lira used some different approaches for teaching—particularly more active, play-based approaches. The teachers also contextualised the Ugandan curriculum for their specific local needs. For example, rural and urban children would find different things interesting and relevant to their lives.

DOSAGE: DURATION, FREQUENCY, INTENSITY

The duration of each cycle of learning was in line with the regular academic school year in Uganda. In essence, the implementation of early learning in Uganda was like a formal pre-school, pre-kindergarten or kindergarten in a government-run space. This is because the government wants to expand these pre-school services, but currently does not have the financing for it. So, the government relies heavily on NGOs to take the government mantle and implement high-quality services for Ugandan children on their behalf. As with other children in Uganda, the children in Lira spent a half day at the centres for five days per week, usually in the morning until lunchtime.

DELIVERY: SERVICE PROVIDER, MODE OF DELIVERY

Certified primary teachers or pre-school teachers were the preferred individuals hired for the early learning centres. However, in some locations, un-certified members of the community were hired. All teachers hired to support young children went through a training programme prior to starting their work with children.

Plan established early learning centres in the same communities where parenting groups were set up. As indicated earlier, targeting the same family with multiple inputs and services can strengthen the overall family and the child's environment, thereby increasing the likelihood for positive development and learning outcomes.

In Lira, Plan worked with community members and local leaders to find a safe space for the establishment of early learning centres. Plan then worked with the community to build these spaces with local materials and furnish the spaces with basic teaching and learning materials (i.e. chalkboards, mats for children to sit on, locally available developmentally appropriate toys, writing materials for children). While Plan contributed to this, the community did as well, supplying some local materials and labour. In addition to designing and building community early learning spaces, the community generally helps in establishing a safe outdoor play environment as well with local materials. Community involvement and contribution are important aspects of the establishment of the early learning centres so the community has a sense of ownership and is ready to maintain early learning activities for children once Plan phases out its support. In many of the community learning spaces, parents used local materials to set up a playground for children.

In some of the community early learning spaces, Plan included a classroom for three-, four- and five-year olds. However, as indicated earlier, in most places, there was only funding to support four- and five-year olds.

As mentioned earlier, classes were scheduled for half a day five days per week, with children attending in the morning and going home at lunchtime. Each classroom had about 30 children and 1 teacher. Early learning spaces had four distinct corners with developmentally appropriate play materials for children ranging from art and crafts to imaginative play to sand, water, rocks and other natural materials. This is in line with the original CLAC model and Vygotsky's approach to using the external environment to explore and learn about the world (Terzi, 2008). Play is central to this interaction with the outside world so children can learn and develop cognitively, socio-emotionally, physically and linguistically (ibid.). KII and FGDs indicated that the ECD staff and parents' groups made some of the toys and materials used in the classrooms. One father indicated that they made drums and other musical instruments from local materials for the children's classrooms. All of these local toys and materials were used to develop different learning for children, including counting, sorting and recognising patterns and numbers, cooperation, sharing and problem solving, developing fine and gross motor skills, communication and early literacy skills. The approach used in each classroom was slightly different based on the teacher, but included a mix of child-centred and teacher-centred approaches. Child-centred approaches are envisioned in the original model, but Plan staff mentioned that it was taking them time to help the teachers understand how to implement this. Most of the teachers had been primary school teachers beforehand so they struggled with making the shift to child-centred approaches. Children had a chance for free play, but also had to sit and listen to a teacher teaching sounds of letters on a blackboard. The approach used for teaching letters and sounds emphasised repetition where the teacher would say the sound and point to the letter and the children would repeat. This is normally the approach used to teach children in Uganda. Children were learning in their mother tongue in the early learning centres, but there was the introduction of English through songs and the teaching of letters and sounds. The environment in each classroom was rich with pictures, words, numbers and key messages about hygiene to reinforce literacy, numeracy skills and good hygiene practices.

First, children of different ages were separated so four-year olds (as reported by their parents) were separated from five-year olds. I observed teachers formally teaching the sounds corresponding to letters of the alphabet. Children in the four-year-old class had small slates and chalk where they practiced horizontal and vertical lines, circles as preparation for writing. Five-year olds were starting to write actual letters of the alphabet. Because of the varying level of capabilities of year's new group of entering students, each classroom teacher had to modify her/his lesson plans and expectations for children based on their starting point. I observed the teachers doing this with some students. The centres also used a combination of play-based learning (i.e. counting with rocks and toys, learning about key message through music) and more traditional rote-based learning. This combines theoretical underpinnings from the behaviourist approach to learning where children are passive recipients and constructivist approaches where children are actively a part of the learning process and can learn about the world through play and discovery (Gray and Mac Blain, 2015; Smidt, 2009). Based on my observation, the teaching of letters and corresponding sounds, the beginning of teaching reading, was delivered in a rote style. However, based on discussions with parents and Plan staff, they did not mind this approach because children in the early learning centres were ready for reading, writing and math. Parents and Plan staff mentioned that children in their centres were often ahead of other children who did not receive the same support.

Implemented in an emergency context: South Sudanese refugees in Uganda

INTENDED OUTCOMES

According to KIIs, because there were multiple grants, different donors and different durations of projects (from six months to one year), each one had a slightly different intended outcome. The shorter grants focused on children's protection and psychosocial well-being, while the longer grants focused on improved child development outcomes.

When I discussed this with Plan staff, they mentioned that the initial intended outcomes for this work were simply to provide a safe space for children to feel a sense of safety, normalcy, relieve stress and improve their psychosocial well-being. Now that the crisis has been ongoing for many years, the focus has shifted to longer term child development outcomes and school readiness as was intended with the original model.

CONTENT

For South Sudanese refugees, the Ugandan government's pre-approved pre-school curriculum was used as one from South Sudan did not exist. This provided an overarching structure for themes and learning outcomes. The team working on the refugee response used lessons learned from the Lira team and adjusted the curriculum similar to how it was done in Lira. Because of the stress children faced from the displacement, the Adjumani curriculum's adaptation had a greater focus on supporting children's psychosocial well-being so that it meant more opportunities to play, build friendships and focus on socio-emotional skills.

DOSAGE: DURATION, FREQUENCY, INTENSITY

The duration of each cycle of learning was in line with the regular academic school year in Uganda, so it was the same as with the centres in Lira. Children came for half a day, five days per week.

DELIVERY: SERVICE PROVIDER, MODE OF DELIVERY

People from the refugee community were hired and trained to lead early learning activities in the ECD centres. During KIIs, Plan staff mentioned that the starting capacity of the ECD caregivers/teachers was low as many had no formal qualifications and so they did not fully understand the why and how of ECD. Some of these people had been primary school teachers in South Sudan, but may not have had exposure to and training on how to work with younger children through play-based activities. Some of the people hired were community members who expressed interest and motivation in learning how to support the development of young children, but had no prior background in child development or early learning. Many of the hired individuals understood the importance of teaching children basic health/hygiene, singing songs, playing with children, teaching ABCs and counting through rote approaches. Most ECD staff did not understand how play—music, games, art—could be great opportunities for children to learn. Plan staff recognised that ECD caregivers/teachers needed more capacity development support.

Some of the Plan staff that hired and managed the refugee ECD teachers/caregivers and the grants had lots of experience with ECD activities while others had limited experience. This also affected the implementation of the early learning activities in the settlements. While all staff hired to manage the refugee teachers/caregivers were Ugandan, they did not all have expertise in ECD. Human resources during humanitarian contexts is often a challenge because positions are regularly offered for six months to one year for people to live in difficult areas and under challenging conditions. Within limited funding, salaries and benefits are set. Under these circumstances, compromises need to be made as it is not always easy to find people with the most experience in a particular technical area. Further, these staff are often new to the organisation and may not have the benefit of learning from lessons from other contexts or have connections with a national technical advisor. In Uganda, Plan had a strong ECD technical advisor, but she did not have expertise working in emergencies nor did she have the time the team in Adjumani needed for technical support. Strong technical support is essential for quality implementation, especially in humanitarian crises; however, this support is often not properly budgeted.

The early learning services were delivered through ECD centres. In refugee camps, the space for a centre may not be a formal space (Shah, 2013). It could be in a tent, semi-permanent space constructed with local materials, in a temporary shelter or outside under a tree. Early learning centres in refugee contexts are sometimes part of a humanitarian intervention known as child-friendly spaces. These are usually tents established in the aftermath of an emergency or crisis where children 0–18 years can first be physically safe and protected from harm. Activities that usually start in child-friendly spaces are different types of play and recreational activities that can help children relieve stress and therefore promote their psychosocial well-being. Messages and activities focused on safety (i.e. mine safety), hygiene and health concepts are also included. Depending on the type of emergency or refugee situation, a focus on pre-numeracy and pre-literacy might come a little later once children are settled (ibid.).

In Adjumani, Plan established early learning centres in areas designated by United Nations High Commissioner for Refugees (UNHCR), refugee leadership and other authorities. Based on my observations and KII, the designated area was fenced to help keep children safe and there were large signboards to indicate the purpose of the space. The early learning centres were temporary structures using tents supplied by UNICEF. According to KIIs, due to the emergency situation, the first priority was on getting some spaces up so there was not community contribution like there was in Lira to establish these spaces. This did affect the community's sense of ownership. During FGD with parents and KII with a few refugee leaders, it was clear that they had high expectations from international organisations and did not expect to contribute to getting services (not just early childhood learning) up and running. This can be seen as a negative aspect of emergencies where communities can become too dependent on other agencies to provide the services they need rather than being resourceful and setting things up themselves. In Adjumani, while community contribution overall was much lower than in Lira, slowly the community in some areas contributed to building playgrounds, volunteering as teacher assistants or cooking food for children. However, it took time for Plan staff to convince the community in some areas to contribute. At the time of data collection, community contribution across the settlements was low.

In the Adjumani refugee camps, three large tents were set up in each designated area, one for each age group of three-, four- and five-year olds.

Each tent had mats so children did not have to sit directly on the ground. Plan supplied teaching and learning materials that were stored in large tin containers. These were provided for by UNICEF and are UNICEF's ECD kits. These pre-prepared kits include basic play materials and games that are developmentally appropriate for early childhood. Teachers in the various centres decorated the spaces with children's art, pictures, numbers, letters, words, etc.

Some of the spaces had posters with key messages about washing hands and overall hygiene. Whereas each early learning classroom in Lira had four corners established with different developmentally appropriate play materials, this was not the case in the Adjumani centres. According to KIIs, the reason for this was that in Lira, the space served only one purpose so all materials could stay where they were. There was no risk of materials being taken from the space. For Adjumani, the space was used as an early learning centre in the morning and as a child-friendly space that had accelerated learning and sports/play activities for adolescents in the afternoon. The space was not locked. It was open to the refugee community. Plan staff mentioned that they had situations where materials were taken from the centres and they struggled to keep the play materials secure. We discussed adding a lock to the UNICEF ECD tin containers. However, these were not large enough to securely store all materials.

One similarity between the early learning centres in Lira and Adjumani were spontaneous production of local toys. In both situations, I saw toys and play materials made of local materials such as mud figurines, instruments made from local materials, etc. Plan staff mentioned that they did not actively encourage this in the settlements as was done in Lira; however, after seeing the spontaneity of the population to create their own toys, they understood the benefits of this and planned to actively encourage this in all of their early learning centres in the refugee settlements.

Children were learning in their mother tongue in the early learning centres in Adjumani just like in the centres in Lira, but there was the introduction of English through songs and the teaching of letters and sounds in both locations. Early learning services in both locations were for half of a day so children came in the morning and left around lunchtime (usually spending about three to four hours per day in the centres). Activities usually ran five days per week in both locations.

As mentioned previously, these same tents were used by adolescents and youth in the afternoon as "child-friendly spaces." Norwegian Refugee

Council conducted accelerated learning and catch up classes for adolescents in some of the spaces and the rest of the time, the spaces were available for youth groups and child clubs to meet and for recreation and sports.

In non-emergency contexts, there may not always be a need to use one space for multiple purposes, but during humanitarian situations, when space and resources may not be sufficient to meet all of the affected children's needs, compromises need to be made. While in Lira, it was possible to keep the ratio of teacher to child to 1:30, this was impossible to do in the refugee camp as the demand and need were significantly higher than the resources available. Based on my observation and KII, each classroom tent often had 100 or more children. There was at least one lead teacher for each classroom and then a few adult assistants. In some of the early learning centres in Adjumani, Plan saw that parents would bring their children in the morning and then stay to help as parent assistants. Such large classes and a ratio of 1 adult:100 children are not ideal so Plan was exploring ways to change that ratio and manage the large numbers.

As in Lira, the refugee children of different ages were separated into different tents so three-year olds (as reported by their parents) were separate from four- and five-year olds. I observed teachers formally teaching the sounds corresponding to letters of the alphabet. Children in the four-year-old class had small slates and chalk where they practiced horizontal and vertical lines, circles as preparation for writing. Five year olds were starting to write actual letters of the alphabet. Because not all children started when they were three- or four-year olds, each classroom teacher had to modify her lesson plans and expectations for children based on their starting point. The centres also used a combination of play-based learning (i.e. counting with rocks and toys, learning about key message through music) and more traditional rote-based learning. Based on my observation, the teaching of letters and corresponding sounds, the beginning of teaching reading, was delivered in a rote style. As was the case in Lira, parents and Plan staff in Adjumani were comfortable with the use of some traditional rote-based learning as they saw this as important for their school readiness.

Early learning, which is a second key component of the CLAC programme, had both similarities and differences in its implementation for humanitarian and non-humanitarian contexts. First, in the non-emergency context, where there can be more space, early learning spaces were not used for other types of activities. Their sole purpose was to provide early learning services for young children. This allowed the teachers to set up the space with four corners that had distinct types of activities that promoted different aspects of children's development. In the refugee camps the early learning spaces were shared where other children and youth could come to learn, socialise and play. This made it difficult to set up four corners as once the young children left, the teachers had to pack everything up for the next group of children to use. In the camp, most of the spaces were tents, whereas in Lira the spaces were built by the community with local bricks and other materials. These tents were not very durable and required replacement every few months. In contexts where the weather is variable—rain, strong winds—tents might need replacing much more frequently. KII revealed that in other refugee and emergency contexts, there are not constructed physical spaces so early learning happens outside or through mobile services during emergencies (i.e. Typhoon Haiyan in the Philippines, earthquake in Nepal, South Sudanese refugees in Ethiopia). So, space needs to be considered when starting early learning activities during emergencies. Spaces either have to be shared for other types of activities or where physical spaces are not available, mobile and learning outside can be alternatives.

In Lira, all of the materials were local materials that were culturally appropriate. In Adjumani, UNICEF ECD kits were initially used. While these provide ready to go teaching and learning materials, KII with Plan staff mentioned that they are often not culturally appropriate or sufficient for the larger number of children served in each space. While the kits have puzzles, balls, crayons, etc., they also have games like dominoes and dolls with blond hair and blue eyes. During KIIs with ECD teachers, they mentioned the inappropriateness of dominoes because in South Sudanese culture, youth and adults use them for gambling. They said parents approached them about their use of dominoes because they did not want their children to learn how to gamble. So these teachers had to explain to the parents that they were using the dominoes to teach emergent math concepts (i.e. counting the number of dots). Further, the dolls in the kits did not look like South Sudanese children. Many South Sudanese children have never seen someone with different hair and skin colour. According to KIIs with Plan staff, in the Philippines, Plan adapted the ECD kit to make their own culturally appropriate kits which they call the "Big Blue Bag." While the "Big Blue Bag" was used in the Philippines for emergency situations, the government and other ECD teachers wanted to use this for non-emergency situations and in particular for them to reach rural areas. The required adaptation needed for emergency contexts can lead to innovation.

Regarding ECD teachers, most in Lira had some qualification from the Ugandan government to teach early-years education whereas the majority of the ECD teachers in Adjumani had no formal qualification. Part of this reason is that the same type of system of professional development does not exist in South Sudan. Additionally, during an emergency, there is not enough time for extensive training of people before they begin to work. Therefore, in emergency contexts, unqualified people are often hired, and then trained to help them slowly improve their knowledge and practice. In Adjumani, there were more parents who stayed and supported ECD teachers than in Lira. This could be because they had the time to do this, and/or had an interest in learning and helping. Interviews with some parents, who stayed to help at the ECD centres out of interest, said they liked what their children were learning. This has actually increased the number of adults able to support children, thereby reducing the overall adult to child ratio. This spontaneous support from parents as volunteer teacher assistants is a positive outcome that must be promoted and replicated in other emergency programmes.

Approaches and methodology used in both Lira and Adjumani were similar. Both locations had a mix of child-centred and teacher-centred methods used. According to KIIs, Plan promotes more child-centred approaches and the use of play and manipulatives for children's learning. Further, Plan believes in using music and movement to teach about basic health and hygiene, teach language, etc. Neither locations had fully embraced this nor were using these approaches in the centres all the time. However, it is clear that whether it is an emergency or not, the use of child-centred and play-based activities is possible.

Component 3: transition to primary school

The third part of the CLAC model uses school- and community-based activities to help transition children to primary schools. A UNESCO study indicates that an estimated 60% of children do not begin school at the right age (UNESCO, 2005). Those children who do not enter school at the right age may remain out of school throughout their primary years (ibid.). This is particularly important for the most disadvantaged children whose parents may not know how to enrol their child or who may not see the value of educating their children. Transition support also aids primary schools be ready to take children who may have different capabilities entering primary school and those who did not go through an early learning programme. This component usually focuses on children six to eight years old.

Transition requires school readiness. While different definitions and conceptualisations of school readiness have been used in the past, in the last few years, science has helped shape a consensus on its definition (UNICEF, 2013; Woodhead, 2014). School readiness is defined by three interlinked dimensions: (1) ready children, (2) ready schools and (3) ready families (ibid.).

The dimension of "ready children" focuses on children's learning and development (UNICEF, 2013; Woodhead, 2014). This includes their ability to work with other children and executive function skills such as being able to follow rules, pay attention, control impulses, delay gratification, etc. (Shonkoff, 2013; UNICEF, 2013; Woodhead, 2014). "Ready schools" focuses on the school environment and primary school teachers' abilities to welcome and take on children who have been in an early learning environment (UNICEF, 2013; Woodhead, 2014). "Ready families" ensures families know when school starts, where and how to enrol, etc. (ibid.).

There are often huge differences between early learning and primary schools, including location of early learning classrooms and primary schools. In many refugee and emergency contexts, for example, it may not be possible to add a classroom to an existing primary school. Temporary spaces may need to be established and if the space is not available near or a part of a primary school, it will need to be established somewhere else. Second, language of instruction (mother tongue instruction vs. national language) and approach to learning (i.e. play-based and child-centred vs. rote-based learning and children sitting in rows behind desks) may also be different. Third, the content of the curriculum may also be different. Where early learning classrooms may focus on integrating subject areas with a goal of supporting various aspects of a child's development (cognitive, physical, socio-emotional, language), primary schools often do not and will teach reading, math, science, etc. Lastly, teachers in primary school and those in pre-schools may have only received training in a particular approach and so may not understand children's developmental and learning needs in pre-school and primary school. All of these differences can make it difficult for children to smoothly transition to primary schools. This can cause situations where parents prefer sending their older child to the early learning centre rather than primary school. In order to avoid these potential problems, the implementation of the CLAC model ensures a connection between early learning centre and primary school teachers and other education personnel.

Original model

Intended outcomes: Support children's smooth transition to primary school.

In the original model, this pillar does not have a clear approach or implementation strategy. So, this has to be developed within each context based on ground realities. According to KII, when implementing the CLAC programme, Plan usually works with early learning centres at the same time as they work with primary schools, making the transition of children from early learning to primary education smooth. According to Plans staff that were interviewed, the ideal situation is where early learning spaces can be established in primary schools themselves.

Implemented in a development context: Lira, Uganda

Intended outcomes: Support children's smooth transition to primary school.

As the CLAC model does not have a clear strategy or approach to transition children from early learning to primary school, each community had to determine this on their own. Overall, KII and FGDs conducted in Lira indicated that the majority of children who had gone through early learning centres continued to primary school. Once in school, they were more ahead and ready for continued academic learning and school than their age peers who did not have any early learning experience.

Supporting the smooth transition though was varied by realities in each community. In some villages early learning centres were part of primary school complexes or were separate complexes, but very close to primary schools. In these circumstances, transition was easier. However, in some villages primary schools were far from the ECD centres which made the transition much harder. When speaking with parents in the FGDs, they mentioned that they wanted their children to continue onto primary school, especially after they learned so much in the Plan early learning centres, but in some cases the nearest primary school was still too far for their young children to walk to. One father during a FGD said, "The primary school is really far and my son cannot go there from our house. Please can Plan International set up a primary school near the centre so my son can easily attend." There was a similar reaction and sentiment among other parents during the FGDs as well. When I asked Plan Uganda staff about this, the ECD Advisor mentioned that she understood this community concern and shared this view. However, she mentioned that their ability to fulfil this community request depended on financing and government permission. Despite this, she mentioned that they try really hard to support children's transition to primary school.

One common element with the approach to the transition of children was that the early learning teachers were trained in how to help students continue to primary school. Additionally, teachers hired in the Lira area for the early learning activities were also primary school trained, so they understood how to work with primary school teachers. They understood what would be expected from the children entering primary school and they understood how teachers teach in primary school and how prepared most students without early learning experiences would be. FGDs and KII indicated that early learning teachers did talk to primary school teachers in the area to support a smooth transition of children. However, in some villages, if the early learning centre was far from a primary school, this did not happen.

Implemented in an emergency context: South Sudanese refugees in Uganda

As mentioned earlier, the transition to primary school is about three areas: (1) children in early learning spaces being ready to begin primary school, (2) primary schools being ready to accept children and (3) parents being ready to transition their children to primary school (UNICEF, 2013). Unfortunately, in the adaptation of this model for the South Sudanese refugees in Uganda, this element was not fully implemented. As mentioned by FGD and KII participants, Plan Uganda made the decision not to implement the model in primary schools at the time of data collection as they were not able to focus on preparing schools to accept children from early learning centres. These participants also mentioned that UNHCR divided up the work in the camps between various agencies and Plan's focus was to provide ECD and child protection. In addition, Plan did not have authorisation to work with primary schools in the refugee settlements. Therefore, the Plan team in Adjumani mentioned that they could not implement this aspect of the CLAC model in its entirety. However, the early learning components did focus on preparing children and parents for the transition.

In other refugee and IDP contexts, the transition to primary school was easier when early learning spaces were established in existing schools or near them. Based on KII with Plan staff and project documents, Plan has had greater success in Ethiopia (with South Sudanese refugees), Niger (Malian refugees), Central African Republic (CAR) (internally displaced due to conflict), Nepal (internally displaced due to an earthquake) in implementing this aspect of the CLAC model. Further, KII revealed that when primary school teachers also support early learning centres, it allows for the smooth transition from early learning to primary school.

In most of the spaces in Lira, transition to primary school was done as there was a concerted effort to do so. In Adjumani, because Plan was not leading the implementation of primary education, there was not a strong focus to facilitate transition. This could also be because the Plan staff or ECD teachers were not aware of the full aspect of the CLAC model and in particular the importance of ensuring smooth transition from early learning to primary school.

Component 4: advocacy to influence policy

Original model

The fourth pillar of the CLAC model includes advocacy and partnerships with governments and other key stakeholders that could help change national policies and governmental budgets in support of young children. This part of the CLAC model looks at the other layers of protection in Bronfenbrenner's Ecological systems theory and at the broader environment and cultural influences of Vygotsky's Socio-cultural theory.

Intended outcomes: To influence ECD policy based on the context.

The CLAC model does not indicate what should be advocated or how. It does not state that advocacy should happen at a national, regional or local level. It does not mention whether it should be done by promoting multi-sectoral ECD response or that advocacy should be focused on a particular aspect of ECD (i.e. early learning, parenting). It does not specify what types of partnerships to develop. The model has advocacy and partnerships as a way to go beyond the individual child and family level, and impact the lives of more children.

Implemented in a development context: Lira, Uganda

Intended outcomes: To work with others to influence the Ugandan government to finalise a multi-sectoral ECD policy and implementation plan.

Advocacy and working to influence government policy is the fourth component of the CLAC model. According to KIIs, as the implementation of the CLAC model in Lira is a part of a larger project in multiple areas, the advocacy and influencing of policy is generally conducted at the national level in Kampala. This advocacy and influence to policy is a slow process of working with the government to improve their policies in favour of expanding early learning opportunities. In Uganda, as the government already has an early learning curriculum, the focus of the advocacy and policy work has been about helping them expand services throughout the country. The current Uganda ECD policy requests support from NGOs to expand early learning throughout the country. In some countries where there are little or no early learning services or where the concept is new (i.e. Central African Republic, South Sudan), the focus for the advocacy and influence of policy would be different. In addition to the national level advocacy, KII revealed that Plan engages in local level advocacy as well to help the local government to expand early learning services.

Implemented in an emergency context: South Sudanese refugees in Uganda

In refugee and other emergency situations, the first priority for programme implementation is ensuring services reach children. Advocacy and influencing policy is usually not a priority, especially as many emergency projects are short term of six months or so. However, depending on the situation in country (i.e. interest of government and key stakeholders in starting or expanding ECD or the chronic longer term nature of the crisis), advocacy and influence of policies can be integral.

Within the Adjumani context, as the humanitarian crisis has been going on for a few years, and because of Ugandan government's existing policy on early childhood development, Plan's focus on advocacy was more localised. Plan staff focused on advocacy among the South Sudanese refugee population and donors to raise awareness about early learning and its importance for children's development and well-being, especially for displaced children. The implementation of early learning services started first. Then, as it became clear to Plan staff that the refugees were not going to return soon to South Sudan, as the country remains fragile with continued fighting, they turned to advocacy and influencing policy.

As Plan had national advisors in Kampala that supported the operation in Adjumani, issues related to the crisis and early childhood education needs were also brought to the attention of the Ugandan government so they could make changes to their policies in order to help the South Sudanese refugee population.

Influencing policy through advocacy is a fourth component of the CLAC program and while possible to do in emergency situations, it is often not the first priority. Whereas in a non-emergency, each component of the CLAC model has equal weight and focus in terms of implementation, in an emergency context, as seen in Adjumani, there is greater weight and focus on early learning for children and parenting education than for helping children transition to primary school and to conduct advocacy to promote policy changes. In every context, these four components need to be reviewed and implemented slightly differently. According to KIIs with Plan staff, in CAR, which is also a refugee context, Plan CAR did do a lot on advocacy while at the same time focusing on the early learning and parenting piece because there was interest and an appetite from the government.

Conclusion

The CLAC model was developed and first piloted in Uganda specifically for resource-poor locations. Its four pillars approach does not tell parents and community members what to do, but aims to empower them so they can increase their capabilities and therefore provide the best environment, care and support for their children's development and well-being. The implementation of the model does not require fancy buildings or toys or high literacy levels among parents and community members. As it is implemented in each developing country, it uses locally available materials to make developmentally appropriate toys, local safe places (i.e. in homes, in local community centres, outside under trees). The language of instruction and discussion among parents is usually the local language. While Plan International staff help start early learning services and parenting groups, their ultimate goal is to slowly reduce and eventually withdraw their role completely so the community can fully take over the continuation of activities.

In conflict-affected emergency contexts such as that of the South Sudanese refugees in Uganda, a model developed in a stable context cannot always be used in the same way. Some reasons for this include the fact that funding for projects is usually short term, from six to 12 months. According to KII, Plan's grants in Adjumani were all between six months and one year and the total overall budget was limited. This meant that the full CLAC model could not be implemented, as was the case in a more stable context. Short duration projects also mean that expected outcomes for children's development, as indicated by evaluations, may be different. In a situation of displacement, the physical space for ECD activities may also be different—both in the setup and what is located inside the spaces. There may not be a building available and there may not be time to build something immediately after the crises. In emergency contexts, physical spaces may first be tents or under trees and then may develop into something permanent. In stable contexts, there may be physical buildings either donated by the community or built for the project.

Humanitarian and development practitioners have different knowledge, experiences and skill sets. Some people are hired for a short duration only for the immediate response. One cannot assume that transferring a development model for an emergency context simply requires adaptation. This example illustrates that capacity building is also critical for humanitarian practitioners before they are expected to implement a programme they have little experience with. While Plan led a short training for their emergency staff, they did not conduct the training in such a way that the whole CLAC model was clear to the staff. The staff simply started with establishing safe spaces and recreation activities, as per the grant agreements, that slowly developed into more targeted play-based child development interventions. There was not a clear strategy for implementing the full CLAC model, what adaptation should happen and how the activities could be sustained or scaled in advance. According to KII, this thinking was happening among the emergency staff while they were implementing the activities. This is not uncommon in humanitarian contexts, when they have to deliver in short periods of time, but it is something that needs consideration for future implementation of ECD models in emergencies.

While there has been some documentation of the impacts of this model (Aboud et al., 2013; Singla et al., 2015), there has not been an in-depth analysis of the model's design and implementation in both non-emergency and emergency contexts. The comparison of the design and implementation of an ECD model in a non-emergency vs. emergency context elucidates the changes that need to be considered in humanitarian situations and additional barriers that could arise in the implementation of the ECD model. Seeing how the model has been adapted and implemented in a refugee context fills an important gap in academic literature, but also a gap in knowledge for practitioners who are looking for useful models for ECD in emergency situations.

Guidance for ECD in emergency design and implementation

The case studies of Lira and Adjumani illuminate some challenges in adapting a development model for an emergency context. In this section, I draw upon lessons learned through the design and implementation of these models and my own professional experience as a humanitarian practitioner, to provide guidance and tips for future ECD in emergency programmes. The guidance is targeted to programme designers and implementers that work in both humanitarian and development contexts.

Lesson 1: do not try to implement all aspects of an integrated ECD model at once

The case studies of Lira and Adjumani illustrate the role of each pillar of the CLAC model. However, it may not be possible to implement all aspects at once or even fully. In humanitarian contexts, limited funding, short duration of projects and an initial focus on saving lives and protecting children from physical harm may require a prioritisation of the various elements of ECD.

Lesson 2: integrate elements of ECD where you can!

Due to limited funding for ECD in emergencies, it is important to be creative in the language used when trying to integrate the various aspects of ECD into sector proposals. Activities such as parenting, early learning, transition to primary school, policy and advocacy, maternal/newborn health, nutrition and protection from violence can be framed in different ways. It may require not using ECD terminology, but something that fits better with other contexts. For example, parenting support can be called life skills training and can easily fit into various sectors such as health and nutrition, food security, and livelihoods because capacity development is often a key element to many funded humanitarian projects. The approach taken will ultimately depend on the realities and opportunities on the ground.

Lesson 3: work with parent groups

Parenting groups can be set up in many ways. Based on analysis of the CLAC model and my own professional experience, here are steps to follow when setting up parent groups.

1. Hold a community meeting, with community leaders, to discuss the start-up of parenting groups.
2. Mobilise groups with a maximum of 30 people (ideally select parents whose children are in early learning or other activities so services can be layered and bundled for the family).
   a. Bring male and female couples together where culturally possible. Where this is not possible, there can be separate groups for females and males.
   b. If there are many adolescent mothers or pregnant women interested in the parenting sessions, consider separating them as their own group.
3. Identify one to two parent co-facilitators.
4. Finalise content for the core parenting sessions based on the context. Some critical content elements include: (a) health/nutrition; (b) play, stimulation and learning; (c) protection and positive discipline; (d) psychosocial support through play-based activities; and (e) communication within the family and in particular between couples. Other content area that should be considered in situations of conflict or where there is a lot of tension, fighting or domestic abuse is about conflict resolution and problem solving though non-violence approaches.
5. Train the parent co-facilitators in the parenting curriculum.
6. Decide, initially with the parent co-facilitators, location of the sessions, the frequency and length. This can then be modified at the first parent meeting based on others' perspectives.
7. Start parenting sessions.
   a. Invite parents to bring their children.
   b. Arrange for facilitators to care for children while parents are in the session, as needed.

   c Focus on practical skill building rather than simply giving information encouraging parents to practice activities with their children.

8 Provide homework for the parents to practice what they have learned at home with their children.

Lesson 4: go to parents!

In some circumstances, it may be easier to go to where parents are rather than set up new groups of parents specifically for ECD. For example, in humanitarian contexts, there may be child-protection or shelter committees, monthly food distribution, meeting of parents at water points. These could be opportunities to bring up issues around child development without organising new groups. In these situations, the parent curriculum may need to be shortened into bits of critical information rather than active skill building.

Lesson 5: conduct home visits for the most vulnerable only

Home visits can be important to check in on parents' progress with what they have learned in the session and to provide 1:1 psychosocial and other types of support. In emergency contexts, when the demand is huge and the funding is limited, a focus can be on those identified during group parenting sessions that may need additional support.

Lesson 6: establish early learning spaces

In an ideal situation, it is important to establish a space for young children, not just for early learning, but also so children in humanitarian emergencies feel safe and secure from harm. In emergency contexts, it could be a building, but it could also be a tent or simply a designated safe space outside under trees. Depending on which type of space is selected for early learning activities, it is important to consider the following:

1 Determine the space for the early learning activities.
2 Determine the number of days and the length of each day. In different emergency circumstances (also dependent on financing), there could be different options: five days/week full days, five days/week half days, three days/week full days and three days/week half days.
3 Determine the curriculum to use. If there is an ECD or early learning curriculum in the country of displacement, it would make sense to use that one. If one does not exist, one can be developed based on the duration of the project.
4 In a situation where a curriculum has to be developed, start with identifying a theme for every month of the project. Select games/activities that would promote all aspects of children's development that is connected to

that theme. If the theme is about animals, select activities that promote gross motor, fine motor, reading, speaking, writing, drawing and early math activities that are connected to the theme of animals.

5 Determine the feasibility of having four corners set up in the space. Often in emergency situations, space may be limited and if space for young children's activities needs to be shared, establishing four corners may not be possible.
6 If there are large numbers of children and insufficient spaces or teachers, make some decisions on how to manage the large classes. This could be to get parent volunteers on a rotational basis to assist the classes. It could also mean that the ECD caregivers will need to conduct activities outside and inside or that they will have to lead play-based activities that would work better for a large number of students.
7 Consider how to mobilise and engage the community to support with a meal (i.e. parents volunteering to make porridge for the children).
8 Establish an ECD centre management committee in order to increase the community's active participation and create ownership.

Lesson 7: go mobile

In humanitarian contexts, there may not be physical spaces where ECD activities can be initiated. This was the case after Typhoon Haiyan where there was so much rubble that a tent could not even be erected. Mobile approaches, where groups of people go to where displaced children and families are, can increase access to ECD in emergency services. Different types of mobile ECD in emergency interventions have been used in the Philippines after Typhoon Haiyan, Nepal after the earthquake and in Jordan for Syrian refugees. Further, mobile approaches require mostly human resources so it can cost less than establishing a space and can reach more people.

Lesson 8: consider adolescents and youth as ECD caregivers

While services for the youngest children often fall through the cracks, so do activities for adolescents and youth. Many adolescents and youth end up idle with little to do in the aftermath of an emergency. Adolescents and youth can therefore be used to be ECD caregivers or assistants that support young children in their survival, development and well-being. Where they cannot be caregivers or assistants, adolescents and youth could, for example, learn carpentry and build toys for ECD centres.

Lesson 9: build relationships for transition to primary school

Transition between early learning spaces and primary schools requires a relationship between teachers and key stakeholders managing both types of activities. Once a relationship is established between both sets of actors, they can together develop the most appropriate plan for transitioning children. Some ways to support transition can be by establishing early learning spaces in the same location as primary schools or nearby. Exchanges between teachers in the primary school and ECD centre can be facilitated so each can see what children are learning and doing at different levels. Primary school teachers can be trained in some early childhood approaches so they can better understand how younger children have learned and so they can help them transition to primary school better.

Lesson 10: conduct bottom up advocacy

Often advocacy focuses on simply changes at a national level. During humanitarian contexts, this will not be the priority nor will humanitarian staff have the time or experience to engage the national level government, who often would be in a capital far from refugee and displaced persons camps and settlements. Therefore, advocacy in crisis contexts can have greater success if it focuses on local change and goes from the bottom up. Humanitarian staff such as local refugee leaders or local UN staff can determine entry points for advocacy and change. They can consider small changes at the camp level that would have a positive impact on children and families such as sufficient space for children, ensuring allocation of space to children near primary schools and advocating to health/nutrition colleagues to integrate counselling training for front line health workers on child development. Some local level advocacy I have seen in other humanitarian emergencies is around teacher certification and acceptance of children's learning in refugee camps. Emergency programmes may train community members to be teachers and help children learn, but these experiences are not always recognised widely.

Lesson 11: disseminate child development information widely

In addition to organising spaces and going to parents for in-depth learning about child development, critical messages, such as breastfeeding, the importance of play and role of fathers, can also be disseminated using various methods (i.e. posters, radio spots, community performances) throughout a camp or settlement. Saturating a particular location with critical child development messages is not the same as in-depth active skills building, but it can raise awareness among the wider population about children's development.

Lesson 12: build relationships with clusters

Participation in multiple sector clusters—education, child protection, health/nutrition, could result in financing for ECD. Strategies for sectors are designed during cluster meetings and so active participation could provide opportunities to integrate aspects of ECD into sectoral strategies and plans, which ultimately could result in funds.

References

Aboud, F. (2007). "Evaluation of an early childhood parenting programme in rural Bangladesh", *Journal of Health, Population and Nutrition*, 25 (1), 3–13.

Aboud, F. et al. (2013). "Effectiveness of a parenting program in Bangladesh to address early childhood health, growth and development", *Social Science and Medicine*, 97, 250–258.

Black, M. et al. (2016). "Early childhood development coming of age: Science through the life course", *The Lancet*, Series: Advancing Early Childhood Development: from Science to Scale, 389, 77–90, London.

Britto, P. et al. (2016). "Nurturing care: Promoting early childhood development", *The Lancet*, Series: Advancing Early Childhood Development: from Science to Scale, 389, 91–102, London.

Britto, P. et al. (2018). "What implementation evidence matters: Scaling up nurturing interventions that promote early childhood development", In Yousafzai, A., Aboud, F., Nores, M. and Britto, P. (Eds.) *Special Issue: Implementation Research and Practice for Early Childhood Development*. New York: Annals of the NY Academy of Sciences, Vol. 1419, 5–16.

Bronfenbrenner, U. (1979). *The Ecology of Human Development: Experiments by Nature and Design*. Cambridge, MA: Harvard University Press.

Center on the Developing Child (2013). *Building Adult Capabilities to Improve Child Outcomes: A Theory of Change*. Cambridge, MA: Harvard University.

Center on the Developing Child (2016). *Building Core Capabilities for Life: The Science Behind the Skills Adults Need to Succeed in Parenting and in the Workplace*. Cambridge, MA: Harvard University.

Gray, C. and Mac Blain, S. (2015). *Learning Theories in Childhood*. London: Sage Publications.

Gustafsson-Wright, E. and Boggild-Jones, I. (2018). "Measuring the cost of investing in early childhood interventions and applications of a standardized costing tool", In Yousafzai, A., Aboud, F., Nores, M. and Britto, P. (Eds.), *Special Issue: Implementation Research and Practice for Early Childhood Development*. New York: Annals of the NY Academy of Sciences, Vol. 1419, 74–89.

Murphy K. et al. (2018). "Implementation research for early childhood development programming in humanitarian contexts", In Yousafzai, A., Aboud, F., Nores, M. and Britto, P. (Eds.), *Special Issue: Implementation Research and Practice for Early Childhood Development*. New York: Annals of the NY Academy of Sciences, Vol. 1419, 90–101.

Plan International (ND), https://plan-international.org/health-start/caring-mothers-so-they-can-care-their-children, last accessed 12 June 2016.

Plan International (2013). *What Is CLAC?*, youtube video: www.youtube.com/watch?v=i7Dua4hfH1c

Shah, S. (2013). *Investing in the Youngest: Early Childhood Care and Development in Emergencies*. Woking, UK: Plan International.

Shonkoff, J. (2013). "Strengthening adult capabilities to improve child outcomes: A new strategy for reducing intergenerational poverty", *Spotlight on Poverty and Opportunity*, http://spotlightonpoverty.org/spotlight-exclusives/strengthening-adult-capacities-to-improve-child-outcomes-a-new-startegy-for-reducing-intergenerational-poverty, last accessed 17 February 2018.

Singla, D., Kumbakumba, E. and Aboud, F. (2015). "Effects of parenting intervention to address maternal psychological well-being and child development and growth in rural Uganda: A community-based, cluster-randomised trial", *The Lancet*, 3, 458–469, London.

Smidt, S. (2009). *Introducing Vygotsky: A Guide for Practitioners and Students in Early Years Education*. New York: Routledge.

Terzi, L. (2008). *Justice and Equality in Education: A Capability Perspective on Disability and Special Educational Needs*. New York: Continuum Publishing.

UNESCO (2005), *Children out of School: Measuring Exclusion From Primary Education*, Montreal: UNESCO.

UNICEF (2013). *School Readiness and Transition*. New York: UNICEF, www.unicef.org/publications/files/CFS_School_Readiness_E_web.pdf, last accessed 8 August 2018.

Vygotsky, L.S. (1978). *Mind in Society: The Development of Higher Psychological Processes*. Cambridge: Harvard University Press.

WHO, UNICEF and World Bank (2018). *Nurturing Care for Early Childhood Development: A Framework for Helping Children Survive and Thrive to Transform Health and Human Potential*. Geneva: WHO.

Woodhead, M. (2014). *Early Childhood Development: Delivering Inter-sectoral Policies, Programmes and Services in Low Resource Settings*. Oxford: HEART, Dfid.

Yousafzai, A. K. and Aboud, F. (2014). "Review of implementation processes for integrated nutrition and psychosocial stimulation interventions", *Annals of the New York Academy of Sciences*, 1308(1), 33–45.

Part III

Evidence for Early Childhood Development in emergencies

Part III of this book delves into the evidence for Early Childhood Development (ECD) in emergencies. Mixed methods were used to investigate the nexus between ECD and humanitarian contexts. Chapter 7 outlines the methodology used to uncover evidence for ECD in emergency programmes. Chapter 8 presents the process of developing a culturally relevant tool to assess child development. Chapter 9 uses that child development tool and others to compare South Sudanese children aged three to five years from the Dinka tribe who received ECD in emergency services and those that did not receive services (control). The data illustrate how quickly children learn and develop when provided with opportunities.

7 Research methodology

Scope of the research

While ECD includes the full range of children from prenatal to 8 years and their protective environment, including parents and community members, this research focused on children from three to five years that have and do not have access to ECD in emergency interventions (focused on early learning and development) and their parents. Children that accessed ECD services were enrolled in the international non-governmental organisation (NGO) Plan International's ECD model known as Community-Led Action for Children (CLAC). Plan International provided partial funding and related logistics for the research and approval to conduct this research on children and parents involved in its programme.

The research looked at the South Sudanese refugee situation in Uganda. The research's main location was in two South Sudanese refugee camps in Uganda, namely Ayillo 2 and Ayillo 1 refugee camps, in the Adjumani catchment area. Other locations included a conflict-affected village called Lira in Uganda, which is near the South Sudanese refugee camps, and the town of Mingkaman in South Sudan which has internally displaced persons (IDPs). The reason for the multiple data collection sites are elucidated below.

Research design

The overall research design was *mixed methods multi-strand* which includes sequential mixed design and fully integrated mixed design (Teddlie and Tashakkori, 2009). There were two strands of this research (part 1—results in Chapter 8 and part 2—results in Chapter 9). The first part started with qualitative data. Part 2 used qualitative and quantitative data. Part 1 (Chapter 8) was conducted first and was an important step before starting part 2 (Chapter 9). The purpose of using a mixed methods design was due to the merit and value that each type of data brings to illuminating different aspects of the phenomena being researched. Mixed methods emerged over the last 20 years as an alternative to quantitative and qualitative traditions (ibid.). It advocates for using whatever methodological tools will help answer the research questions (ibid.). Tashakkori and Creswell defined mixed methods

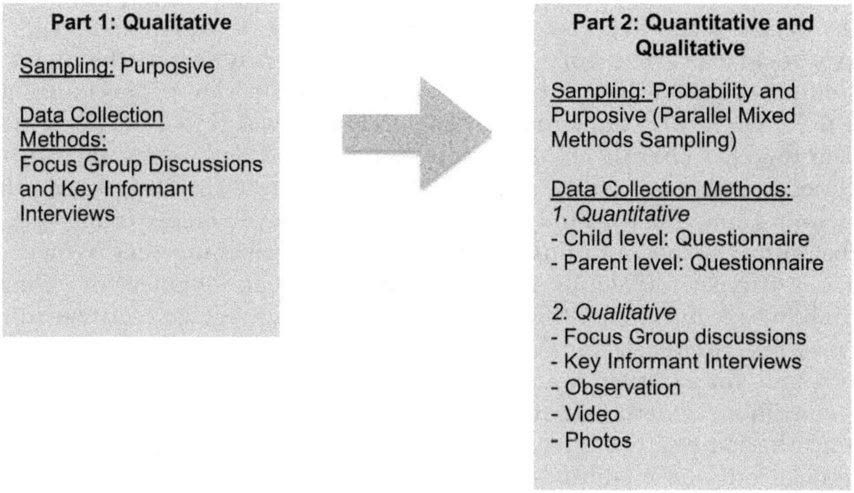

Figure 7.1 Mixed methods research design.

as "research in which the investigator collects and analy(s)es data, integrates the findings, and draws inferences using both qualitative and quantitative approaches or methods in a single study or program(me) of inquiry" (Tashakkori and Creswell, 2007). There are different ways of using mixed methods research where the study at every stage uses mixed methods, i.e. if one part uses qualitative, another part uses quantitative and another mixed methods approach (Teddlie and Tashakkori, 2009). Many different combinations of using qualitative and quantitative methods are possible within mixed methods research based on the research questions being investigated (ibid.).

Figure 7.1 illustrates the overall research design.

Part 1 of the research

Key Research Question 1: What is ECD in emergencies from the South Sudanese cultural perspective?

a What are the capabilities and child development outcomes young children can and should achieve with ECD in emergency programming from the South Sudanese cultural perspective?

The result of this part of the research produced a set of capabilities and child development outcomes for South Sudan children. This was the basis of adapting a quantitative tool measuring children's development outcomes. The adapted tool was then used (Chapter 9) to assess child development outcomes of South Sudanese refugee children that enrolled in ECD services and those that had not.

Design and data collection methods

The design is the first place where the Capability Approach and Vygotsky's Socio-cultural theory were brought together to deepen the understanding of the mediation between culture and theories of development in the context of a humanitarian emergency. It was important to bring them together because child development does not outline specific capabilities like the Capability Approach does and the Capability Approach does not frame the capabilities based on a child development framework. The critical purpose of bringing these two perspectives together is to provide a stronger foundation for understanding the development of young children's capabilities by filling in gaps of both perspectives. Further, the Capability Approach and Vygotsky's Socio-cultural theory have never been brought together and applied in a refugee context and allowed me to contribute something new to academic literature, early childhood and humanitarian practices. Based on Amartya Sen's assertion that capabilities can only be established and clarified based on the cultural context and should not be imposed from outside (Terzi, 2007), the first part of this research used qualitative methods to develop a set of capabilities and outcomes for South Sudanese young children based on child development theories. In particular, Vygotsky's Socio-cultural theory, which also places an emphasis on the child's external environment including his/her cultural context, along with the capabilities approach frames the first research question (Vygotsky, 1978, 1981).

The first part of the research therefore looked at cultural sensitivities and then also adapted quantitative research tools to the South Sudanese context and a refugee situation. Data were collected in both South Sudan with IDPs and South Sudanese refugees in camps in Uganda. Both of these groups were included in the research to get more data looking at the cultural sensitivities of the South Sudanese population, thereby allowing us to determine culturally appropriate capabilities and child development outcomes to include in the quantitative questionnaire. In both locations, the Dinka ethnic group, one of the largest groups in South Sudan, was the main focus for data collection. While the conflict that erupted after 2013 was mainly between the Dinka and Nuer ethnic groups and while there are many similarities between the two groups, including only those from the Dinka tribe allowed the research to look deeply into this sub-group's perspectives on child development and what they want for their children. Once the first part of the research was completed and capabilities and child development outcomes that are sensitive to the South Sudanese context and specifically the Dinka ethnic group were determined, the quantitative data collection tool was adapted and refined for the second part of the research.

Through a review of literature, no child development questionnaire or data collection tool that comes from South Sudan or even Africa was found. Most recently, Save the Children, another international NGO, has developed a child development tool that looks specifically at three- to five-year-old children. It uses continuous data and is known as The International Development and Early Learning Assessment (IDELA) (Pisani et al., 2015). Through a series of tests, Save the Children has begun to validate this tool for global use. While it is a promising tool for developing contexts because it is thought to be easier to use than current existing tools, considers practical aspects of collecting data in developing countries and considers the cultural context of developing countries, it is still a new tool that I was not familiar with. Further, the tool has not been adapted for the South Sudan context. I chose a reliable and valid tool from the Western context and adapted it to the South Sudanese cultural context. While there are many data collection tools available from the Western context such as the Bayley Child Development Scale, the "Ages and Stages Questionnaire-3" (ASQ-3) was selected for a number of reasons. First, the ASQ-3 has been found to be reliable and valid based on rigorous research with a sample of over 15,000 diverse children. It has been adapted in other developing countries as well, resulting in a version in Spanish, French, Portuguese, Norwegian and Korean, to name a few (D'Aprano et al., 2014; Filgueiras et al., 2013; Heo et al., 2008; Schonhaut et al., 2013; Tsai et al., 2006). Second, the ASQ-3 questionnaire focuses on children aged between 1 month and 5 ½ years, which is the age range for this research. Third, I had access and approval to use this tool. The Bayley Child Development Scale in comparison only includes children aged from 1 month to 42 months, which would have left out 4- and 5-year olds, who were key participants of this research (Schonhaut et al., 2013). Fourth, the ASQ-3 is a questionnaire that can be completed by parents and requires less training and fewer research assistants than other child development tools such as the Bayley Child Development Scale. However, it does require parents to be at a fourth or fifth grade reading level. Luisa Schonhaut et al. (2013) found that the Bayley Child Development Scale had a high cost, required more time and required the test be administered by trained professionals (Schonhaut et al., 2013). Additionally, the ASQ-3 looks at five domains of child development: communication, gross and fine motor skills, problem solving and personal-social skills, which is in line with the domains of child development presented earlier (Schonhaut et al., 2013; Tsai et al., 2006). While the Bayley Child Development Scale and the ASQ-3 look at child development a little differently, Schonhaut found that there was overall agreement between the two tests, especially as the child's age increased (ibid.). Lastly, the ASQ-3 was easier and less expensive to access than tools such as the Bayley Child Development Scale. I also have experience with the ASQ-3 and felt more comfortable with it than with the Bayley Child Development Scale which is new to me. As this research included a quantitative element that required a larger sample, having an easy to follow questionnaire that did not require a huge amount of training was more feasible.

In this research, the ASQ-3 was adapted to ensure the inclusion of both capabilities and outcomes (or functionings) as described previously and a consideration of the South Sudanese cultural context. I used qualitative methods to achieve this. Specifically, I developed a Focus Group Discussion (FGD) guide and a Key Informant Interview (KII) guide with semi-structured questions as the basis of the qualitative data collection. Some of the questions included in the semi-structured interviews involved aspects of the ASQ-3 so views on it could be obtained and it could be properly adapted. Aspects of child development and early learning that may be valued in the South Sudanese culture that were not included in the original ASQ-3 were then added for the second part of the research in Chapter 9.

Sample and data analysis

I used purposive sampling for this part of the research in order to get diverse perspectives from different stakeholders including parents, government staff, local leaders, local NGO partners and Plan International staff.

Specifically, the sample included:

1 *Two FGDs* (each focus group had 12 males and 8 females—20 parents in total). Most of the male participants spoke English so I did not require as much translation support. For the female FGD, a number of female participants spoke very little English so I relied on translators provided by Plan International. I used homogenous sampling, as mentioned earlier, to make sure each focus group had similar people. All people included in the FGDs were from the Dinka tribe, from the same part of South Sudan and had similar literacy levels (Teddlie and Tashakkori, 2009). All of the FGD participants were from Jonglei where sporadic fighting and violence continue. All of the FGD participants were displaced people, driven from their homes due to the violence. One group included only women, while a second included only men. The reason for separating the sexes in FGDs was to make sure that women felt comfortable speaking. In my experience, in many cultures, women may not feel as free to express themselves when they are in a mixed group with men. Further their perspectives and desires for their children may be different from those of men.

I initially planned on doing a third FGD with children aged six to ten years (50% girls and 50% boys) as Biggeri and Mehrotra (2011) mentioned that few research focused on understanding capabilities from a cultural context included children's voices (Biggeri and Mehrotra, 2011). However, once I got to Mingkaman, South Sudan I found this difficult to organise due to logistical challenges and my limited time in Mingkaman.

In future research I would use participatory techniques such as the use of photography and video to understand what was important for children and obtain their perspectives.

In total 20 people were included in two FGDs. All of these people were from the Dinka tribe and from the state of Jonglei which is where the majority of South Sudanese refugees in the Adjumani catchment areas of Uganda reside.

2 *Five KIIs* (i.e. government, local leader, NGO partner, Plan International staff—total of five people). I used typical case and reputational purposive sampling for the KII.

In both the FGD and KII, I used semi-structured questions because I wanted to provide a general framework based on child development domains, the ASQ-3 and literature on the subject, but I also wanted to allow for things to come up that I was not expecting.

As there were only 2 FGDs and 5 KII, I decided to code and analyse the data manually. I used editing approaches which included a few a priori codes including gross motor, fine motor, cognitive, language and communication and socio-emotional areas (Robson, 2002). I collected the various responses on flip chart paper so the FGD participants could also interact and disagree with each other's responses if they wanted. Through the process people could tell me if they agreed with a particular point, which I duly noted in my notes, and if they had additional things to add. I then took all of the raw data, looked for patterns and areas where the majority of people said the same thing or agreed with the same points and then put them into key categories based on child development domains: physical development, cognitive development, language and communication and social and emotional development. This process allowed me to develop a capability framework structured around child development for young children in emergencies in the South Sudanese context. The presentation of this will follow in the next section.

Part 2 of the research

Key Research Question 2: What are the outcomes and capabilities for children and parents through the implementation of the ECD model (Community-Led Action for Children—CLAC) in a refugee context? Are these outcomes better, the same or worse than when ECD services are not provided at all?

Child level

Hypothesis: Children in the CLAC programme during emergencies will have the better child development outcomes and capabilities than children in another South Sudanese refugee camp that did not receive the CLAC programme.

Parent level

Hypothesis: Parents with higher knowledge of child development have children with higher child development outcomes.

Design and data collection methods

In order to answer the second key research question, a quasi-experimental design using quantitative and qualitative data was used to compare two groups: an intervention and a wait list control group. The intervention group was already receiving early learning opportunities based on Plan International Uganda's CLAC model while the control group, at the time of the data collection, was not. All children and families who participated in the research are from the Dinka ethnic group. Further, they are all from the same parts of South Sudan, where there has been intense fighting. The intervention group is from Ayillo 2 refugee camp while the wait list control group is from Ayillo 1 refugee camp. Plan and other agencies had been providing education and early learning support for more than eight months at the time of the data collection in Ayillo 2. While Ayillo 1 had been open for more than a year, it had more new arrivals from South Sudan at the time of data collection. Some services were being provided in Ayillo1, but at the time of the data collection, the block of Ayillo 1 where I collected data for this research did not have early learning or education services. Given how far each block is from the other in the camps, it is safe to say that there should have been minimal spill over to the control group in Ayillo 1. Further, the group of refugees used as the wait list control group arrived in Adjumani, Uganda only a few weeks to a month prior to the data collection. It therefore provided the perfect control group comparison. In refugee situations, information about services provided spreads quickly, so while, at the time of collecting data, there was no early learning services in Ayillo 1 refugee camp, Plan International had plans to start services. The selection of the two sites for the research was done very carefully to ensure an appropriate intervention and control group. Variables that I looked at include: ethnic group, where in South Sudan the refugees were from, their socio-economic background and age (as reported by parents). Majority of the refugees in both sites and actually overall in all of the South Sudanese camps in Uganda were single parent households as most fathers remained in South Sudan either to work or support the war effort. Doing this background investigation took a lot of time, which Plan Uganda and Plan South Sudan's staff supported prior to my going to Uganda to collect data. In the end, the only difference I could see among the two populations where I collected data was that one group had been in Uganda longer and had a chance to begin early learning services, while the other group was new to Uganda and so did not receive early learning services. Additional areas where the research could have further compared the groups include physical characteristics such as height, weight and whether the child was malnourished or not. In the data presentation section below, I further elaborate the implications and potential effects of the research not looking at physical characteristics when determining the comparison groups.

1 Quantitative data

Quantitative data were collected focusing on two target groups: children and parents. There was one data point where I compared children who received the programme in Ayillo 2 and children who were the wait list control in Ayillo 1. Data were further collected with parents of children in Ayillo 2, but was not collected with parents of Ayillo 1 mostly due to logistical challenges in the camps. A limitation of this approach is that the research includes only one data point rather than a pre and post. A pre and post would have allowed for deeper understanding of the changes over time for children in the programme and control groups. This approach can help identify the gains due to the intervention (Wiersma and Jurs, 2005). Due to various logistical, time and financial reasons, this was not possible. A challenge I would have faced had I collected data among the groups at two points in time is lost to follow up and this was another reason why I decided to only collect data at one point. I saw first-hand in the refugee camps that the movement of the refugees across the border to South Sudan was occurring regularly. I realised that it would be extremely difficult to find the same children again to collect a second data point and I would likely have a much lower post sample.

The first part of collecting quantitative data was the adaption of the ASQ-3 as explained in the first part of the research. After the adaptation of the ASQ-3, it was used in both Ayillo 2 and Ayillo 1 to investigate children's capabilities and functioning. This allowed me to compare children who received some early learning services vs. those that did not receive any. This helped answer the question of whether early learning (based on Plan International's CLAC model) aided children continue on their normal development path and if it made a difference when compared with children who received no services. The approach to collecting data changed multiple times during the pilot and research collection process as we tried different approaches in the field. The initial plan was to create three play groups of children aged three years, four years and five years, two times per day, with 20 children per group, reaching 120 children per day per refugee camp. The boxes below illustrate the initial plan. I realised that due to the heat, families and ECD caregivers (who were research assistants) did not want to participate in the afternoon. So, we were not able to collect data in the afternoon (Figure 7.2).

The idea was that I would have one ECD caregiver and Plan International Uganda staff (paired together) to support parents to do the activities

Day 1 (Programme group)

morning- Ayillo 2 - 3 year old (20 children) afternoon - Ayillo 2 - 3 year old (20 children)	morning- Ayillo 2 - 4 year old (20 children) afternoon - Ayillo 2 - 4 year old (20 children)	morning- Ayillo 2 - 5 year old (20 children) afternoon - Ayillo 2 - 5 year old (20 children)

Day 2 (Control group)

morning- Ayillo 1 - 3 year old (20 children) afternoon - Ayillo 1 - 3 year old (20 children)	morning- Ayillo 1 - 4 year old (20 children) afternoon - Ayillo 1 - 4 year old (20 children)	morning- Ayillo 1 - 5 year old (20 children) afternoon - Ayillo 1 - 5 year old (20 children)

Figure 7.2 Programme and control groups.

with their children and fill out the ASQ-3. Even before I started the data collection, the research team and I realised that the majority of the mothers (mothers were more likely to come than fathers) did not have basic literacy skills in English nor any experience doing the activities with their kids. So, I decided that the activities needed to be led by the ECD caregivers and Plan staff. I decided that it was important to invite mothers and fathers to remain with their children, both so the children felt comfortable and also as a chance for parents to learn how to do the activities with their kids. I also initially thought that one ECD caregiver/ Plan staff leading activities for 20 children at once would work, but in reality I quickly realised that I needed smaller groups of children and more ECD caregivers.

The final design of the data collection on the first day of collecting data was as illustrated in the boxes below. I relied on the parents and the ECD caregivers to confirm the age of the children. In the situation of South Sudanese refugees, however, there are many illiterate parents, so I used refugee research assistants to fill out the questionnaire (Figure 7.3).

First, I oriented and trained Plan Uganda towards the purpose of the research and how to collect data using the adapted ASQ-3 and the parents' survey. As the Plan Uganda staff are ECD Officers and are accustomed to doing the types of activities required in the ASQ-3, it was

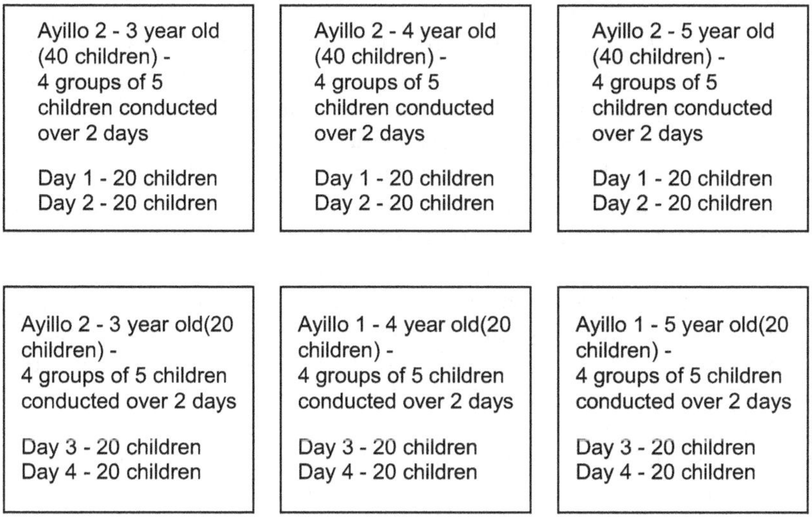

Figure 7.3 Samples for Ayillo 2 and Ayillo 1.

not hard for them to understand it and collect data. I also recruited and trained 15 ECD caregivers from the South Sudanese refugee population to be research assistants. The ECD caregivers had been oriented as to the purpose of the research and their role before the actual training was conducted and Plan Uganda selected the best performing and most active ECD caregivers to be research assistants. Since all of the selected research assistants were ECD caregivers they have had previous professional development and orientation on child development and how to work with children. They were all South Sudanese refugees from the Dinka tribe with the skill set needed for the research. All research assistants could speak, read and write in English and translate between English and Dinka. Some of the selected research assistants were primary school teachers in South Sudan. The training was conducted in three hours due to the limited time we had in the camps for data collection. While ideally the research assistants could have benefitted from more practice and training in using the tools, a Plan Uganda staff member stayed with each small group that worked with the children and parents. This allowed for on-the-job training and support to continue. As an additional motivator, I provided a stipend to all research assistants as this work went beyond their normal jobs as ECD caregivers for the Plan Uganda programme. I also purchased snacks (bananas and biscuits) for the participating children, parents and research assistants.

For the first day of the data collection, I planned on collecting data from the intervention group in Ayillo 2. I decided to collect data in a safe location that the refugee children and families know: two ECD centres in Ayillo 2. I randomly chose two centres in the camp. More details about the sampling are given in the next section. Plan Uganda colleagues and I also talked to community leaders about this research prior to starting to get their buy-in. Parents brought their children to the ECD centre as they normally do in the mornings, but I invited them to stay so they could take part in the parent questionnaire. Each dyad (parent-child pair) that was randomly selected for the research was given the consent forms; each had an equal chance to be selected for the research. As many dyads parents selected for the research could not read or write in English, the forms were explained by the research assistants. Rather than obtain signatures, we accepted people's thumb prints as part of the consent process. In total, I collected data from 90 dyads. As some children saw that those children who came with their parents could do a different activity, they ran home and came back with their parents. Once everyone had a chance to understand the purpose of the research and fill in the informed consent forms, I took the various groups into different locations. I asked the research assistants to take all three year olds and their parents in one ECD centre/tent, four year olds and their parents in another ECD centre/tent and the five year olds and their parents into another ECD centre/tent. This was important as the ASQ-3 for each age group has some different activities. Once inside each tent/ECD centre, the research assistants and Plan Uganda staff made small groups of five children so they could start the activities with the children and assess them. Plan provided developmentally appropriate toys to use for the various activities where we assessed them. In the small groups, the South Sudanese research assistants along with a Plan Uganda staff asked children to do the various activities. During this process, parents were invited to stay and participate. Normally the questionnaire could take between 10 and 15 minutes for parents to fill out. I thought that since this is a new exercise for research assistants and Plan Uganda staff we may need 45 minutes to collect data from each small group. In reality, it ended up taking more than 1 hour. This was because there were a lot of disturbances such as other children and parents who came once the small groups were established who wanted to participate and people who simply were interested and wanted to watch. It made the spaces crowded and chaotic. During this process, I walked around to support the research assistants and Plan Uganda staff as they did the activities with the children and as they slowly filled out the questionnaire. When I found that the research assistant was not doing the activity fully or correctly, I had to show them. This could have had some effect on the data collection if someone did something incorrectly when I was not there.

Quantitative data were also collected to understand parents' knowledge about child development in order to investigate the hypothesis that parents with higher knowledge of child development have children with higher child development outcomes. The parenting component of the CLAC programme had not yet fully started at the time of data collection. Groups had been set up and some groups had gone through one to two sessions and some had not gone through any. So these data were collected and used as a baseline for the overall parenting programme and also used to compare parents' starting level knowledge about child development, health and nutrition and how that corresponded with how their child scored on the ASQ-3. A parent questionnaire was based on a parent questionnaire developed by Plan International's East African country offices. The original questionnaire, which considered the CLAC model and the culture of East Africa, was developed for non-emergency contexts. While reviewing it with Plan Uganda colleagues, I realised that there were too many questions and it was too long, not all of the content included in the questionnaire were being included in the parenting education that was planned for Ayillo 2 and Ayillo 1 refugee camps. Further, the language in the questionnaire was not simple enough for the refugee research assistants to read and help parents answer. Through a process of revising, testing (with the refugee and Plan Uganda research assistants), we shortened, simplified and adapted this questionnaire. Initially we started off talking to parents while their children were simultaneously doing the various activities. Parents-child dyads were selected so any child that was assessed through the ASQ-3's parent was targeted with the parent questionnaire). However, I quickly realised that we did not have enough staff to do this as each parent needed one-to-one attention. Further, I realised that this needed to be done on a one-to-one basis; otherwise, parents would answer the question in the same way as a person who might be sitting near them. So, I tasked the research assistants to go house to house to talk to the parents in a more relaxed setting. Some of the parent questionnaires were completed before I left Uganda and the rest came after I left Uganda.

2 *Qualitative data*

Qualitative data were collected using FGDs and KIIs targeting teachers and early learning facilitators, parents and community members. Each FGD or KII was guided with semi-structured questions so the interviewees could provide more information than what was specifically asked. Each FGD and KII took about one hour; some discussions took two or more hours. I also supplemented this data with unstructured observation, videos and photos of activities in both Ayillo 1 and Ayillo 2.

Sample and data analysis

I used Parallel Mixed Methods sampling for this part of the study (Teddlie and Tashakkori, 2009). For the qualitative data, I used purposive sampling while for the quantitative aspect, I used multi-stage cluster sampling (ibid.).

1 *Quantitative methods:* I used multi-stage cluster sampling of children and their parents for this aspect of the data collection (Teddlie and Tashakkori, 2009).

   The first step in the multi-stage cluster sampling process was to randomly select the intervention ECD centre to include in the research. Plan International has multiple centres in Ayillo 2 and it randomly picked the two spaces where the research would be conducted. Each ECD centre in Ayillo 2 had an equal chance of being selected for the study as the intervention group.

   During the next step, Plan colleagues and I randomly selected child-parent dyads. Each child-parent dyad had an equal chance of being selected for the study. Plan Uganda had generally provided a message to the refugee community in Ayillo 2 that this research was taking place for child-parent dyads that were already participating in the ECD centres.

   In Ayillo 1, because Plan Uganda was in the preparatory stage of starting early learning activities, they told the whole community that this research was taking place and that some people could participate. Each child from three to five years had an equal chance of being selected.

   a ASQ-3 adapted questionnaire for children three to five years. Total: 60 parent/children per location. Total questionnaires: 120 for the first data point in Ayillo 2 and 120 in Ayillo 1.
   b Parents' survey—60 parents from the same parent/child pairings for Ayillo 2. Total: 60 parents for Ayillo 2.

2 *Qualitative methods:* I used purposeful sampling of the teachers and parents in order to get a representative sample.

   Total: 30 ECD teachers/caregivers, 30 parents, three Key Informants, two NGO staff implementing the project.

   a Teachers: FGDs (1 location × 3 locations × 10 people/location). Total: 30 people.
   b Community leaders KIIs—one per location. Total: 3 KII
   c NGO staff implementing the project: two KIIs during the first data point.
   d Observation, video and photos—I conducted observation (unstructured) and took videos and photos of the ECD activities in Ayillo 2. This additional primary data helped triangulate the other qualitative and quantitative data collected.

The computer programmes SPSS and R assisted me in analysing the data from the quantitative elements of the research. I manually analysed the qualitative data that were collected through KIIs, FGDs, pictures, video and my own observation notes as the overall sample was not too large. I conducted the qualitative data analysis using a combination of editing and template approaches which included some a priori codes based on the CLAC model and child development domains included in the ASQ-3 (Robson, 2002). There were also points brought up that did not fit into these categories and that was kept in a separate category of Other. I collected the various responses from the FGD and the KII on paper. Because the FGD was done in a circle with the group, participants had the opportunity to listen to others' points and agree or disagree with them and add points that were not previously mentioned. I then read the notes multiple times, highlighting key patterns from the discussions and categorising key patterns.

I also used unstructured observation, videos I took while visiting the sites and photos to supplement some the FGDs, KIIs and quantitative data collected through the adapted ASQ-3 and the parenting questionnaire. For the observation, videos and photos, I similarly looked for patterns and coded what I saw in the videos and photos.

This process allowed me to use the various types of data to triangulate what I saw in the quantitative data collection.

Limitations of the research

There were many limitations of this research.

1 *Regular movement of the South Sudanese refugees*

First, the conflict and humanitarian situation of the South Sudanese population were a major limitation. While people had fled South Sudan to be in refugee camps in Uganda, they were going back and forth between Uganda and South Sudan due to the porous and close border. This meant that some of the initial South Sudanese refugee caregivers Plan International recruited to be research assistants were not in the camps when I went to begin collecting data. So others had to be recruited at the last minute to replace them. The constant movement of people also meant that if we were able to collect data from children one day, we could not find the parents to take the parent survey a day or few days later.

Regular movements also meant that not all of the programme children had the same amount of time with the programme activities. The activities run similarly to a school year with a specific curriculum and themes for the lesson plans and activities. However, if a child arrived to the camp a few months after the programme's year started,

Plan still accepted the child. This means that children did not all get the same amount of input from the programme at the time of data collection. This could impact on the overall child development score and results.

2 *Food distribution and other activities in the camps*

While many of the refugees are seen idle, there are many activities in the camp that made it difficult to keep all participants and research assistants focused on the research. During the middle of our data collection, there was a distribution of food. Food distributions in refugee camps can last for days and require refugees to wait in line for full days. This caused problems because the first set of South Sudanese refugee research assistants I trained and prepared needed to go to food distribution on the third day of the data collection. We dealt with this problem by recruiting other refugees; however they had not gone through the first training. So, Plan Uganda colleagues and I worked with these new research assistants to orient them to what they needed to do. I paired them with other refugees so they were not alone doing the activities, which provided an opportunity for them to learn.

3 *Limited experience*

While all of the research assistants, both South Sudanese refugees and Plan Uganda staff, have been working on the ECD programme in the camps for a number of months, this area of work and the CLAC model are new to them. So, while they could generally understand how to lead the activities with children some of the activities were new to them. They also did not necessarily understand how the activities we did with the children looked at different aspects of child development. So, it required a lot of mentoring and a lot of on-the-job training. The positive aspect of this was that the Plan Uganda staff and South Sudanese refugee research assistants expressed how much they learned by going through this process. They each wanted copies of the ASQ-3 for multiple years so they could then do the activities with their own children at home and help them where they found their child needed support.

4 *Low literacy levels*

Very low literacy levels among the South Sudanese refugee population created a lot of challenges. While the South Sudanese research assistants could read and write, not all of them had high level literacy skills in English. This was evident because they struggled with reading and understanding the questions and activities they needed to do with the children. This was remedied because I walked around and supported each of them. Plan Uganda staff who have higher literacy and education levels also walked around and often worked with certain research assistants to help them. Many of the parents who participated in the research (majority were women) were illiterate. This is not surprising to me and I expected low literacy levels; however, this did cause challenges in filling out the parent survey and the consent forms. The research team had to often work one-on-one with mothers to ensure they fully understood the purpose of the research and could fully consent to it.

5 *Limited time for training*

I had limited time to conduct training with the research assistants. As this was still a new concept and approach to collecting data (most had never collected data), they needed a lot of support. While I made efforts to provide training and then on the job support, this may have affected the research assistants' ability to do the activities with the children and conduct interviews with parents, thereby affecting the data. The research assistants did not always fill in the forms correctly and ones that were not filled in correctly had to be discarded during the data cleaning process.

6 *Age of children and children's normal development*

Children grow and develop all of the time. While tests such as the ASQ-3 have certain milestones, children's development has a range with some children learning things faster than others. Most children are in the normal range and the ASQ-3 tests for outliers and those children who are far below their peers in the various child development domains. Small children can also change quite a bit in as little as one to three months and especially a lot in one year. The ASQ-3 test that was adapted and ultimately used for this research only looks at three milestone periods of a child's life—age 3 (or around 36 months), age 4 (around 48 months) and age 5 (around 60 months). However, the original ASQ-3 has a different test for children who are 42 months or 3½ years or 54 months or 4½ years. Children can develop a lot in six months. However, in this research we did not further separate children in this way because birth registration is not common in South Sudan so parents may not always remember their child's exact birthday. The research age groupings were done based on parents telling us how old the child was. So within the children that took the three-year old test, there may have been those that were 36–47 months. Similarly, for the four-year old and five-year old, children could have been closer to 48 or 60 months or within the range. All of this could affect their test score.

7 *Challenge of using tests for small children*

This research has used a quantitative child development test on South Sudanese children. Using a quantitative test is not uncommon; it has been done myriad times by researchers and early childhood practitioners to get a sense of a child's development levels and in particular if there might be some developmental delays that require further attention (Aboud, 2007; Nahar et al., 2009, 2012; Singla et al., 2015; Yousafzai and Aboud, 2014; Yousafzai et al., 2014). However, it has its own limitations. Early-years researchers Gray and MacBlain (2015) mention the challenges of gathering data from children aged five years and below (Gray and MacBlain, 2015). In the first five years of a child's life, there is a great deal of brain development, including learning how to communicate, organise thoughts, etc., but that development is not complete (ibid.). When using a quantitative child development tool, one is assuming that the child understands the questions that are being asked and the tasks that he/she needs to do, can organise his/her thoughts and then communicate them back to an adult (Gray and MacBlain, 2015). Early years researchers mention the importance of observing children over a period of time and using other measures to supplement the quantitative test (ibid.). Further, using a quantitative test assumes that children have been asked by adults to perform certain tasks for them or answer certain questions for them. In the South Sudanese population, children may have never had this experience so this needs to be considered while looking at the results of the quantitative data. In order to mitigate potential risks, the research design used mixed methods, a quantitative test along with qualitative data. The qualitative data, in the form of FGDs, targeted parents and caregivers the children see regularly, along with observations made by the research team to triangulate data on children's development.

8 *Definition of parent*

When speaking with the South Sudanese refugee community, we asked for children to come with their parents so we could set up child-parent dyads. The definition of a parent in Western countries could be different from that in South Sudan. So, it is not clear if the child-parent dyads are biologically related or just adults who have informally "adopted" a child and considers him/her their child. This could be important because a biological parent might care for a child differently than a non-biological child.

9 *Translation*

Translation is another limitation of this research. While the South Sudanese research assistants all spoke English and Dinka, their levels of English varied so there could have been error in their translation when conducting the activities with the children, when asking parents questions, how they filled in the forms for the parents or children's questionnaires and how they translated the content of the FGDs and KIIs. Most of the data collection process was conducted in Dinka.

In Chapters 8 and 9, the evidence and analysis for the data collected from this research are presented.

References

Aboud, F. (2007). "Evaluation of an early childhood parenting programme in rural Bangladesh", *Journal of Health, Population and Nutrition*, 25(1), 3–13.

Biggeri, M. and Mehrotra, S. (2011). "Child poverty as capability deprivation: How to choose domains of child well-being and poverty, Ch. 3. In Mario, B., Jerome, B. and Flavio, C. (Eds.) *Children and the Capability Approach*. New York: Palgrave, 46–75.

D'Aprano, A. et al. (2014). "Adaptation of the Ages and Stages Questionnaire for remote aboriginal Australia", *Qualitative Health Research*. doi:10.1177/1049732314562891.

Filgueiras, A., Pires, P., Maissonette, S. and Landeira-Fernandez, J. (2013). "Psychometric properties of the Brazilian-adapted version of the Ages and Stages Questionnaire in public child daycare centers". *Early Human Development*, 89(8), 561–576.

Gray, C. and MacBlain, S. (2015). *Learning Theories in Childhood*. London: Sage Publications.

Heo, K. H., Squires, J. and Yovanoff, P. (2008). "Cross cultural adaptation of a pre–school screening instrument: Comparison of Korean and US populations", *Journal of Intellectual Disability Research*, 52(3), 195–206.

Nahar, B. et al. (2009). "Effects of psychosocial stimulation on growth and development of severely malnourished children in a nutrition unit in Bangladesh", *European Journal of Clinical Nutrition*, 63, 725–731.

Nahar, B. et al. (2012). "Effects of a community-based approach of food and psychosocial stimulation on growth and development of severely malnourished children in Bangladesh: A randomised trial", *European Journal of Clinical Nutrition*, 6(6), 701–709.

Pisani, L., Borisova, I. and Dowd, A.J. (2015). *International Development and Early Learning Assessment Technical Working Paper*, Save the Children.

Robson, C. (2002). *Real World Research* (2nd edition). Oxford: Blackwell Publishing.

Schonhaut, L., Armijo, I., Schonstedt, M., Alvarez, J. and Cordero, M. (2013). "Validity of the ages and stages questionnaires in term and preterm infants", *Pediatrics*, 131, e1468.

Singla, D., Kumbakumba, E. and Aboud, F. (2015). "Effects of parenting intervention to address maternal psychological wellbeing and child development and growth in rural Uganda: A community-based, cluster-randomised trial", *The Lancet*, 3, 458–469, London.

Tashakkori, A. and Creswell, J.W. (2007). "The new era of mixed methods", *Journal of Mixed Methods Research*, 1, 3–7.

Teddlie, C. and Tashakkori, A. (2009). *Foundations of Mixed Methods Research*. Thousand Oaks: Sage Publications.

Terzi, L. (2007). "The capability to be educated", in Walker, M. and Unterhalter, E. (Eds.) *Amartya Sen's Capability Approach and Social Justice in Education*. New York: Palgrave Macmillan.

Tsai, H. L. A., McClelland, M. M., Pratt, C. and Squires, J. (2006). "Adaptation of the 36-month ages and stages questionnaire in Taiwan: Results from a preliminary study", *Journal of Early Intervention*, 28(3), 213–225.

Wiersma, W. and Jurs, S. (2005). *Research methods in education: An introduction*. New York: Pearson Education.

Vygotsky, L.S. (1978). *Mind in Society: The Development of Higher Psychological Processes*. Cambridge: Harvard University Press.

Vygotsky, L. (1981). *Thought and Language*. Cambridge, MA: MIT Press.

Yousafzai, A. K. and Aboud, F. (2014). "Review of implementation processes for integrated nutrition and psychosocial stimulation interventions", *Annals of the New York Academy of Sciences*, 1308(1), 33–45.

Yousafzai, A.K., Rasheed, M. A., Rizvi, A., Armstrong, R. and Bhutto, Z. (2014). "Effect of integrated responsive stimulation and nutrition interventions in the Lady Health Worker program in Pakistan on child development, growth and health outcomes: A cluster randomised factorial effectiveness trial", *The Lancet*, 384(9950), 1282–1293, London.

8 Developing a culturally appropriate child development tool

While there are many tools assessing child development from Western contexts, few tools are available that are adapted to African countries' cultural contexts. No child development tool has been adapted considering humanitarian situations. As there are more than 60 tribes in South Sudan, all of whom have differing values and expectations for their children, this research delved into the cultural perspectives of the Dinka tribe. The Dinka tribe is one of the largest in South Sudan and the group of refugees that went to the Adjumani catchment area of Uganda where the research was conducted. This chapter addresses the first research question presented in this book about the definition of Early Childhood Development (ECD) from a South Sudanese cultural perspective. It outlines the process for developing a child development tool that is both culturally appropriate for the Dinka tribe in South Sudan and considers a refugee situation. This process can be used to adapt either the Ages and Stages Questionnaire version 3 (ASQ-3) or other child development assessment tools for other tribes, ethnic groups or countries. The tool itself can be used both in the refugee camps where the Dinka tribe reside and also in South Sudan.

Prior to adapting the ASQ-3, a Capabilities Framework for young Dinka children was developed. Since Sen spearheaded the Capabilities Approach, much work has been done by various researchers looking at the applicability of this model (Nussbaum, 2011; Saito, 2003; Sen, 1999; Terzi, 2007; Unterhalter, 2009; Walker and Unterhalter, 2007). Biggeri highlighted that there is little work that has been done looking at children's capabilities (Biggeri, 2007; Biggeri and Mehrotra, 2011). This research therefore takes a step forward and contributes to the discourses on the Capability Approach by doing a few new things: (1) looking at capabilities from an early childhood lens, (2) looking at capabilities from a South Sudanese perspective and (3) applying culturally relevant capabilities to a refugee context.

Through Focus Group Discussions (FGDs) and Key Informant Interviews (KIIs) with South Sudanese from the Dinka tribe, I developed a set of capabilities for young children framed around general child development domains and Vygotsky's Socio-cultural theory. Based on the process that Sen (1999), Nussbaum (2011), Biggeri (2007) and others followed to develop a set of capabilities for adults, I used a similar process for young children. As a Capability framework for young children has not been developed before, I used the key child development domains based on Vygotsky's Socio-cultural theory to frame the capabilities that South Sudanese Dinka valued. Once the Capability framework was developed, considering the Dinka values and culture, this provided the basis to adapt the ASQ-3. The adapted ASQ-3 was then used to collect quantitative data on ECD in emergency services.

Qualitative methods allowed for in-depth discussion and understanding of the values in the Dinka tribe which shape their understanding and expectations for child development. I used purposive sampling to conduct two in-depth FGDs (one with 12 males and the other with 8 females) in Mingkaman (Lakes state) South Sudan along with five KIIs with South Sudanese and Ugandans (ECD experts who have been working with the Dinka tribe for many years) in order to understand the capabilities and child development outcomes young children should achieve with ECD in emergency programming. The FGD took about three hours as I wanted to provide enough time for participants to reflect and for us to delve deeper to uncover cultural values and expectations for Dinka children's development. Each group of males and females had a mixed age range from people in their twenties to those in their sixties or above. The mixed age group was important because culture and perspectives can also change through generations and time. It was important to capture perspectives that might be different for the varying generations. Further, culture is an interactive process where generations can influence each other. Mixing the generations into one FGD allowed participants to interact with each other, agree, disagree and come to a consensus on the values and expectations they had for their youngest generation.

After conducting the FGDs and KIIs, an analysis of the responses allowed for the development of the Capability framework for young Dinka South Sudanese children. I analysed patterns from the FGDs and KIIs. I updated the ASQ-3 based on these patterns, had ECD experts review the tool and then piloted the tool before finalising it. Some of these patterns are based on codes I included for categorising information based on child development domains, but others such as tolerance and peace, as mentioned below, were new issues that I had not considered and do not currently fit into the original ASQ-3. It must be noted that there was a low understanding of child development as it is defined in many Western countries. So rather than using the terminology of child development as I realised quickly that this term was new to them, I posed the question *"What are your hopes and dreams for your children? What do you think they should be able to do at age 1, 2, 3, 4, 5 and before entering primary school?"* While I collected data from the FGDs and KIIs about children from 0 to 5 years, I present the data on children three to five years as they were the main focus of this study.

Capabilities framework for young South Sudanese children

Based on the qualitative data collected and using Nussbaum and others' approach to presenting capabilities, here are key capabilities identified through the FGDs and KIIs that are relevant and important in the South Sudanese context. I used the four child development domains, illustrated below, that include (1) physical development, (2) cognitive development, (3) linguistic development and (4) social and emotional development to frame the capabilities identified (Figure 8.1).

Physical development

1 Ability to run, jump, hop.
2 Ability to write.

Cognitive development

1 Reading.
2 Knowledge of numbers.
3 Knowledge of letters.
4 Knowledge of colours.

Linguistic development

1 Ability to speak English.
2 Able to understand and follow directions from elders.

Socio-emotional development

1 Cleanliness.
2 Ability to go to toilet and wash hands with soap.
3 Having friends.
4 Ability to resolve conflicts peacefully.

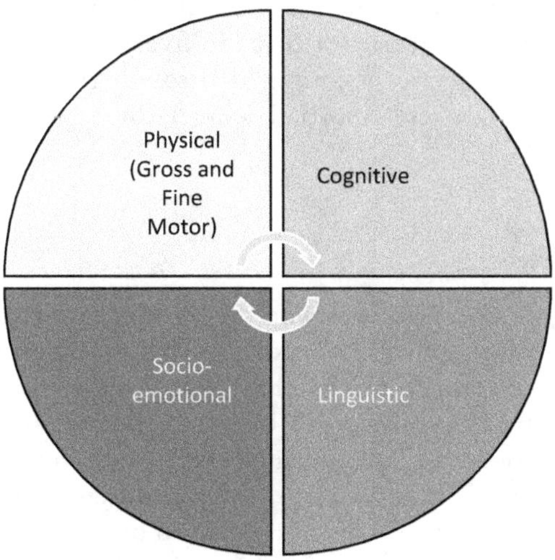

Figure 8.1 Domains of child development.

Physical development

Physical development includes gross and fine motor skills and all aspects of physical health, nutrition, etc. The key points brought up by focus groups and KIIs included the importance of the following capabilities for children three to five years.

The majority of the FGD participants and KII included some important physical development capabilities for children three to five years. These include the ability to walk, run, skip and jump as important for gross motor skills. Many of the aspects of gross motor skills mentioned by participants are already measured in the ASQ-3 for children three to five years such as the ability to walk, run, skip and jump. The original ASQ-3 includes questions to see if children can button and unbutton clothes, zip and unzip clothes, and climb stairs. These three capabilities were taken out of the adapted ASQ-3 because the majority of refugee children do not have clothes with buttons or zippers and there are few stairs for children to climb in villages in South Sudan and also in the refugee camps in Uganda. Participants did not mention much in terms of fine motor skills and actually were not clear on what that meant. Learning how to write was cited as important for participants as one mother said, "I want my children to learn to write," but they did not specifically mention holding a pencil using the pincer grasp like the original ASQ-3 mentions. As holding a pencil correctly and practicing writing is something Plan International includes in their Community-Led Action for Children (CLAC) model according to a KII conducted with a Plan International staff, this question was kept in the adapted ASQ-3. The Plan International staff said during the same KII, "We practice writing with the children in the ECCD centre so they are ready for school. With the youngest children we help them learn how to make lines and then circles and then we slowly practice writing letters." The original ASQ-3 includes questions about drawing horizontal and vertical lines, drawling circles and shapes, and writing one's names (capabilities for three to five years). Due to the fact that these are all aspects that are encouraged through the CLAC programme (even if not prioritised by research participants), these questions were kept in the adapted ASQ-3.

Cognitive development

Learning and cognitive capabilities were very important to the research participants, but they were not clear on exactly what that meant beyond knowing how to read, write and do math. They all felt that education and learning would help their children succeed in life. Both fathers and mothers in the FGD and KII mentioned that they wanted their children to get jobs and earn money. Some parents said they wanted their children to be doctors, teachers. One KII participant said, "I want my son to be educated so he can leave South Sudan and get a good paying job." Based on KIIs and FGDs, cognitive development was brought up as one of the most important things for children. Women, many of whom are illiterate, especially wanted their children to learn how to read, write and succeed in school. One mother said "I do not know how to read, but I want my children to read so they can succeed in life." Parents overwhelmingly felt that it was the teachers' jobs to teach children and fill them with knowledge which is very much in line with the perspective of a child as a "tabula rasa" or a vessel to be filled. This is not in agreement with Vygotsky's Socio-cultural theory, but is in line with long held beliefs in their culture. They never experienced children being part of the process for their own cognitive or overall development so this was not mentioned.

Another aspect the parents did not mention is related to executive functioning such as critical thinking or problem solving. However, some of these aspects were already integral to activities in the original ASQ-3.

Linguistic development

Research participants mentioned the importance of language and the ability to communicate with others as very important, but this was not seen as too important when children are very young and during the infancy and toddler years (0–2 years). This is because community members felt that children are unable to talk and communicate at this age. Many mother and fathers mentioned that when children are small, they cannot talk so they did not need to talk to them. Virtually all research participants wanted their children to learn English. "All children should learn English so they can get good paying jobs and be successful," one father said. Mothers had a similar perspective. One mother said, "I want my child to go to school and learn English, not Dinka. English is more useful for their life." They saw success as having a good paying job and knowing English was a key way for their children to achieve that. It is an important language of the South Sudanese government, but people recognised very well that an ability to speak, read and write in English would help their children later in life. The Plan International CLAC programme uses a bi-lingual model when working with children. While most of the activities are conducted in their mother tongue (especially for the younger years), there is an increasing use of English (especially for the older ages). English is not taught as a formal subject in the CLAC programme as that usually starts in grade 1 of primary school. However, CLAC teachers and teaching assistants used music, games and poems in English to help children learn basic conversation skills.

The original ASQ-3 did not have specific questions related to a child's ability to speak English as the original is already in English. As part of the adaptation, I added a simple question to test for all three age groups—three-year olds, four-year olds, five-year olds—to see if they could communicate basic greetings in English.

Following directions and respecting elders came up in many of the FGDs and KIIs. "Children should respect their elders and do as they say," a father and community leader said. This sentiment was echoed by many others, men and women, through the FGDs and KIIs. A mother in the FGD said, "My children need to listen to me and follow directions. That is important." The original ASQ-3 did have specific questions related to children following directions so I simplified them, but kept them in the tool.

Social and emotional development

a Cleanliness and personal hygiene

This was seen as extremely important in South Sudanese culture. Not only did research participants mention this as a priority, I observed that this was the case as well. Each morning I was in the ECD centres in the camps, I saw children participating in a morning welcome circle. Before this, the children lined up and teachers checked their nails, faces and shoes to make sure they were clean. If they were not, children were taught to go to the water point and use soap to clean themselves. A mother and ECD teacher said, "Every morning the children need to be checked to make sure they are clean. That is the first thing we check every morning."

b Having relationships with family members and other children

An overwhelming majority of participants, both men and women, said that children needed other children in their lives as friends and support. They were happy to report when their own children had friends. The notion of family is also larger and broader than in many Western contexts that just include the biological nuclear family and the words brother, sister, auntie, uncle, mother were brought up a lot during the FGDs and KII, even when research participants were not talking about blood relatives. I was sometimes confused about whether the participants were talking about blood relatives or part of their broader notion of family, particularly when a few participants mentioned auntie and uncle.

c Children doing household chores (i.e. cleaning, cooking, collecting firewood) and helping care for younger siblings.

The ability to support the family with household chores and help care for younger siblings was mentioned multiple times during the FGDs and KIIs by both women and men. These capabilities were particularly important for girls in the family. This was cited as important preparation for girls when they are older and mothers themselves. "My daughter helps me collect firewood. She takes care of her younger siblings. This is important for when she gets married," one mother said. A father from a FGD agreed and said, "Girls need to do household chores. This is important for when they get married." One father, who was also an ECD teacher, did not disagree with the fact that girls need to help with household chores, but he did say, "I want my daughter to be educated. I am glad Plan has set up this school because she has the chance to learn. Girls should have the chance to learn like boys."

d Tolerance, cooperation and learning to live together peacefully

These themes came out very strongly in the FGDs and KIIs. All adults that spoke, both men and women, were aware of the violence that has plagued their country for generations and they want to see a better future for their children. A father, who is also an ECD teacher said, "We want our children to learn about peace and not fight anymore." A mother in one of the FGDs said, "Our children fight a lot. Our community fights a lot. This is not good." A KII with Plan International staff said, "Many people in our community fight. They do not know anything else. We grew up seeing this all of the time." Unfortunately, the Plan International's CLAC programme does not currently include activities that specifically promote tolerance, cooperation and learning to live together peacefully so this was not included in the ASQ-3. However, this perspective from families provides good feedback for the modification of the CLAC model for its future implementation among the South Sudanese community.

Adapted Ages and Stages Questionnaire-3

While tools such as the ASQ-3 and Bayley Scales of Infant and Toddler Development have been adapted in various cultural contexts, no tool has been adapted considering the South Sudanese cultural context and no tool has been adapted to use in a humanitarian context (Bornstein and Lansford, 2013). Further, while there is broad consensus that tools assessing ECD should look at certain key areas such as physical development (gross and fine motor skills), socio-emotional development, language development and cognitive development, there is no agreement on what some of the key indicators or capabilities should be for different cultural contexts (ibid.). Further, while some cultures may not prioritise things such as executive functioning or twenty-first-century skills, there is now global consensus in the ECD field that these areas are important. In the adaptation of child development assessment tools, there can be a balance between cultural and global perspectives.

Adapting the ASQ-3 was an important step to embark upon because despite broad consensus that it is important to develop culturally grounded capabilities and child development assessment tools, the process takes time and resources, which are often not available (Engle et al., 2013). In humanitarian contexts, where speed can save lives, it is less likely that this process would be followed. However, this process can be followed in high risk areas as preparatory measures. If a particular tool is developed for an emergency context and there is no acute emergency, it can also be used for a non-emergency context because it will be culturally relevant to the target population.

Some researchers and practitioners such as Engle et al. (2013) and UNICEF call for a global tool to measure children's development across countries for larger scale macro data that could be used for policy change (Engle et al., 2013). However, many other academics and practitioners working on child development disagree with having a global tool and set of capabilities. Modern academics including Sen (1999), Biggeri and Mehrotra (2011), Harkness et al. (2013) and others along with Vygotsky would all disagree with this notion because developing a global tool, while it could provide some benefits, especially for data comparisons across countries, could never include all the various external environments and cultures of the world (Biggeri and Mehrotra, 2011; Harkness et al., 2013; Sen, 1999; Vygotsky, 1981). As mentioned earlier, Vygotsky's Sociocultural theory emphasises the role of the external environment of the child on his or her development (Vygotsky, 1978). Bronfenbrenner (1979) and Rogoff (2003) extend that perspective to indicate the importance of culture in children's development (Bronfenbrenner, 1979; Rogoff, 2003). While the various cultures around the world have similarities, they also have differences and this affects parents' and society's expectations for children and therefore their capabilities at certain ages (Harkness et al., 2013). Harkness et al. cite a wide range of capabilities of children based on the cultural context they live in and the expectations or perceptions of the child that their parents and society have of them (ibid.). In some countries, cultural agendas may focus on motor skills and obedience while in others it may focus on independence and verbal skills (ibid.). During a meeting with colleagues from the Middle East, they mentioned that they do not promote their children's independence. In their culture, they want their children to remain close to them. These nuances and cultural values would be lost with a global tool.

Western academic literature and research on brain development indicate that children are prime for language development and need regular input and practice with people speaking to them (Fox et al., 2010; Grantham-McGregor et al., 2007; Shonkoff and Richter 2013). In some cultures, this is difficult for parents to understand and they do not feel it is important to talk to children until they can respond back as is the case with the South Sudanese research participants (Harkness et al., 2013). Other research found that motor skills in some African infants were reached earlier than in some Euro-American infants (Harkness et al., 2013). In Indonesia, for example, it was important that children learned their daily prayers rather than certain types of verbal communication (Plan International, 2011). Further, in much of sub-Saharan Africa, including South Sudan, I learned from FGDs and KIIs that girls as young as five years were expected to help their mothers care for younger siblings. This is something you would rarely see in Western societies (Harkness et al., 2013). This capability is seen as developmentally important to prepare girls for socially responsible roles (ibid.). The use of standardised child development tests such as the Bayley Scales of Infant and Toddler Development in developing context without a process of cultural adaptation found that, for example, African children scored poorly in comparison to European or American children because certain aspects of the test are not prioritised or seen as important in those African cultures (ibid.).

Further, these two theoretical perspectives have a lot in common, but have never been considered jointly in the process of developing culturally appropriate capabilities and a quantitative data collection tool (Harkness et al., 2013). When capabilities have been developed, it has not focused on young children and has not considered child development frameworks.

While the process undertaken in this research was able to uncover some very important capabilities for children based on South Sudanese cultural context, there are avenues for greater investigation in this area. First, this process could be done again using a larger sample of people to understand in greater depth the expectations of community members with regard to their children's development and generally society's perceptions of children.

Second, South Sudanese community members mentioned the importance of their children being able to solve problems and potential conflicts rather than using violence. This was not included in the adapted ASQ-3 because while it is a capability identified by community members, it is not something that Plan International is currently focusing on. So including an indicator or two looking at this particular capability did not make sense in this research. The issue of ECD programmes' ability to influence and help children develop these crucial soft skills that promote peace, tolerance, diversity, acceptance of the other, empathy, using non-violent ways to resolve conflict is really important and can be investigated in future research.

Third, future research can also look at the involvement of children in shaping cultural perceptions of child development and expectations on children's capabilities. Participatory research methods could be used to help children fully express themselves in a way that is developmentally appropriate. As mentioned previously, due to limited time in South Sudan and Uganda, this research was unable to set up FGDs with different groups of children of varying ages to understand the expectations they feel from community members and elders for their own development. Vygotsky, Biggeri and others believe in the role of children in their own development and this could be further investigated in future research (Vygotsky, 1978; Vygotsky, 1981; Biggeri, 2007; Biggeri and Mehrotra, 2011).

Lastly, uncovering and developing indicators and tests to measure physical development and gross and fine motor skills were easier to do than developing indicators and tests to measure social and emotional development. While the adapted ASQ-3 had questions focused on social and emotional development such as whether children had friends, more can be done in this area to really make it more rooted in South Sudanese culture.

References

Biggeri, M. (2007). "Children's valued capabilities", In Walker, M. and Unterhalter, E. (Eds.) *Amartya Sen's Capability Approach and Social Justice in Education*. New York: Palgrave Macmillan, 197–214.

Biggeri, M. and Mehrotra, S. (2011). "Child poverty as capability deprivation: How to choose domains of child well-being and poverty", Ch. 3. In Biggeri, M., Ballet, J. and Comin, F. (Eds.) *Children and the Capability Approach*. New York: Palgrave Macmillan, 46–75.

Bornstein, M. and Lansford, J. (2013). "Assessing Early Childhood Development", Ch. 18. In Britto, P., Engle, P. and Super, C. (Eds.) *Handbook of Early Childhood Development Research and Its Impact on Global Policy*. New York: Oxford University Press, 351–370.

Bronfenbrenner, U. (1979). *The Ecology of Human Development: Experiments by Nature and Design*. Cambridge, MA: Harvard University Press.

Engle, P., Rao, N. and Petrovic, O. (2013). "Situational analysis of young children in a changing world", Ch. 3. In Britto, P., Engle, P. and Super, C. (Eds.) *Handbook of Early Childhood Development Research and Its Impact on Global Policy*. New York: Oxford University Press, 35–64.

Fox, S., Levitt, P. and Nelson, C. (2010). "How the timing and quality of early experiences influence the development of brain architecture", *Child Development*, 81(1), 28–40.

Grantham-McGregor, S. et al. (2007). "Developmental potential in the first five years for children in developing countries", *The Lancet*, 369, 60–70, London.

Harkness, S. et al. (2013). "Culture and early childhood development: Implications for policy and programs", Ch. 7. In Britto, P., Engle, P. and Super, C. (Eds.) *Handbook of Early Childhood Development Research and Its Impact on Global Policy*. New York: Oxford University Press, 142–160.

Nussbaum, M. (2011). *Creating Capabilities: The Human Development Approach*. Cambridge: Belknap Press of Harvard University.

Plan International (2011). *Benefits of Early Childhood Care and Development in Emergencies: Indonesia, Pakistan, Bangladesh*. Unpublished report.

Rogoff, B. (2003). *The Cultural Nature of Human Development*. Oxford: Oxford University Press.

Saito, M. (2003). "Amartya Sen's capability approach to education: A critical exploration", *Journal of Philosophy of Education*, 37(1), 17–33.

Sen, A.K. (1999). "Investing in early childhood: Its role in development", Conference on Breaking the Poverty Cycle. Washington, DC: Investing in Early Childhood, Inter-American Development Bank.

Shonkoff, J. and Richter, L. (2013). "The powerful reach of Early Childhood Development: A science based foundation for sound investment", Ch. 2. In Britto, P., Engle, P. and Super, C. (Eds.) *Handbook of Early Childhood Development Research and its Impact on Global Policy*, New York: Oxford University Press, 24–34.

Terzi, K. (2007). "The capability to be educated", In Walker, M. and Unterhalter, E. (Eds.) *Amartya Sen's Capability Approach and Social Justice in Education*. New York: Palgrave Macmillan, 25–43.

Unterhalter, E. (2009). "Education", Ch. 9. In Deneulin, S. and Shahini, L. (Eds.) *An Introduction to Human Development and Capability Approach*. London: Earthscan, Taylor and Francis, 207–227.

Vygotsky, L.V. (1981). *Thought and Language.* Cambridge, MA: MIT Press.
Vygotsky, L.V. (1978). *Mind in Society: The Development of Higher Psychological Processes.* Cambridge, MA: Harvard University Press.
Walker, M. and Unterhalter, E. (2007). "The capability approach: Its potential for work in education", In Walker, M. and Unterhalter, E. (Eds.) *Amartya Sen's Capability Approach and Social Justice in Education.* New York: Palgrave Macmillan, 1–18.

9 Mixed methods evidence for Early Childhood Development in emergencies

This chapter presents and analyses data collected using the adapted Ages and Stages Questionnaire version 3 (ASQ-3) child development assessment tool. The research questions include: What are the outcomes and capabilities for children and parents through the implementation of the Community-Led Action for Children (CLAC) model in a refugee context? Are these outcomes better, the same or worse than when the CLAC model has not been implemented at all? This chapter presents the findings from the testing of the adapted CLAC model. The testing of the model investigates changes in children and parents. At the start of the research, the two hypotheses for the testing of this model included:

Child level

Children in the CLAC programme during emergencies will have the better child development outcomes than children in another South Sudanese refugee camp that did not receive the CLAC programme.

Parent level

Parents with higher knowledge of child development have children with higher child development outcomes.

In order to answer these research questions, I used mixed methods including a quantitative child development survey for children (adapted ASQ-3), a questionnaire for parents, Focus Group Discussions (FGDs) and Key Informant Interviews (KIIs). While the intention was not to put together an observation checklist, I was also able to triangulate data through my own observation of children playing and being involved in the various play group activities where we collected data and these children's interactions with parents and caregivers. Additionally, I also took videos and photos in both Ayillo 2 and Ayillo 1 refugee camps to provide additional qualitative data.

Characteristics of the refugee children and parent research participants: homogeneity of groups

In an emergency situation with refugees in camp settings, it was very difficult to do an experimental research with complete random sampling of the whole South Sudanese refugee population. The child and parent participants of this research all are from the Dinka tribe, which is one of the largest tribes in South Sudan (BBC, 2016). It is also the current South Sudanese President's tribe (ibid.). The majority of the refugees in the Adjumani area of Uganda come from Jonglei state, which was one of the most heavily hit areas during intense fighting between the government (led by a Dinka President) and the opposition group (led by the newly re-instated Vice President who is from the Nuer tribe) after South Sudan's independence. The majority of South Sudan is rural and there are few primary schools and even fewer secondary schools, especially in Jonglei state (Plan International, 2015; Save the Children, 2015). According to FGDs and KIIs, the concept of early learning and development is new for many Dinka people, but it is a concept that they have been very supportive of, after they have seen the benefits of early learning and development activities for their children. Among the research participants, most of the children live with their mothers and have fathers who have either died or are currently in South Sudan trying to earn a living for the family. Many South Sudanese men sent their families across the borders into Uganda, Ethiopia and Kenya in order to keep them safe. So, a smaller percentage of men are in the Uganda refugee camps. Most of the children and their siblings live with their mothers. The children and parents speak Dinka; few of them speak English. The only English speakers are those that were teachers in South Sudan or are from Juba. The refugees did not come with much money or possessions. Due to the homogeneity of the child and parent research participants in both the programme group in Ayillo 2 and the wait list control group in Ayillo 1, a comparison between the two could more easily be made.

I considered using Propensity Score Matching (PSM) to reduce the likelihood of observable bias of the research participants. I collected the following data from each child participant and his/her family: (1) ethnic group, (2) mother tongue, (3) parent literate or not, (4) location in South Sudan where they came from, (5) parent completed primary school or not, (6) parent completed secondary school or not and (7) whether the child lived in a single-headed household. However, looking at the raw data, which is summarised in Table 9.1, there was not much variability in the participants which

Table 9.1 Characteristics of research participants: frequencies

Location	*Ethnic group*	*Mother tongue*	*Parent literate?*	*Location from South Sudan*	*Parent completed primary school?*	*Parent completed secondary school?*	*Single-headed household?*
Ayillo 2 (programme)	Dinka: 176 Non-Dinka: 0	Dinka: 176 Other: 0	Yes: 8 No: 168	Jonglei: 176 Other: 0	Yes: 9 No: 167	Yes: 3 No: 173	Yes: 159 No: 17
Ayillo 1 (wait list control)	Dinka: 74 Non-Dinka: 0	Dinka: 74 Other: 0	Yes: 5 No: 69	Jonglei: 74 Other: 0	Yes: 6 No: 68	Yes: 1 No: 73	Yes: 62 No: 12

would mean that doing PSM would not help us much. Further, doing PSM would have further reduced the overall sample, weakening the ability to do comparisons between the programme and wait list control groups. The raw data shows very homogenous group of participants from the programme children and the wait list control.

Some conditions that the research did not account for when establishing the comparison groups, which could have affected the results, are physical factors such as height, weight based on the child's reported age. Children should be growing and if a child is reported to be 36 months vs. 46 months, there should be a range in height and weight that correlates with that. Further, if a child was malnourished (as determined through a mid-upper arm circumference measurement (MUAC) that looks at the width of the upper arm) and has a very low body mass index and very low weight (where Paediatricians would determine the child's failure to thrive), this could have effects on his/her overall development. Physical factors such as the ones mentioned are important determinants of a child's development and a child who is not reaching his/her potential physically might have lower child development scores. However, measuring this as part of the comparison group determination was logistically difficult due to the size of the sample. Plan Uganda did not have the appropriate materials needed to do these types of measurements and I did not have experience measuring these things in children. If the research had been able to measure these in addition to the factors mentioned earlier, I could have looked at these as explanatory factors. It would have helped me more accurately compare the two groups of children.

There could also be non-observable factors such as motivation and interest that could affect the comparability of the two groups; however, getting this information and analysing this statistically are not easy. A regression analysis can help with this, but the overall sample is small. Therefore, I used the *t*-test to compare the means of the two groups of children and triangulate that data with qualitative data.

Description of the children's data set

The children's survey was first coded. It has three possible answers, yes, sometimes and no. These were coded as 3, 2 and 1, respectively. The code "sometimes" also meant "partial" completion of the task. I then added the scores for each sub-section: communication, gross motor skills, fine motor skills, cognitive skills, socio-emotional/personal-social skills, which is in line with the main domains of child development presented earlier. After cleaning and entering all of the completed or mostly completed questionnaires, the total sample of all children for analysis was $N = 200$. This section presents the data by the total score, sub-groups, etc. The breakdown of the sample by gender, age and location is given below.

This is fewer than planned total sample of 240 (120 for Ayillo 2 and 120 for Ayillo 1). I planned on having equal number of children in both camps. However, in Ayillo 2, the presence of children and parents was more than what we expected at the centre. They were ready to participate in the research to the point where we sometimes used the same questionnaire to record scores for two children as we did not had enough forms with us. It was interesting that as we started registering parents/children for the research in Ayillo 2, other children whose parent was not at the centre ran home to bring their parents. They then wanted to participate in the research and we tried our best to include them. This revealed to me the keen interest among children and parents in the early learning activities in Ayillo 2. This is a potential confounding factor; however, the same issue was present among the wait list control group in Ayillo 1. During FGDs with parents in Ayillo 2, many of them mentioned how happy they were that their child got the chance to participate in the activities that Plan was running. Those with older children sometimes preferred their older child participated in the early learning centres rather than the formal schools in the camps because they thought they were more interesting, engaging and because parents said their older children did not have the chance to go through this type of programme. This increased the overall number of children that we obtained data from; however, after cleaning and taking out questionnaires that had many missing questions, we came to a total of 126 as shown in Table 9.2.

In contrast, the refugees in Ayillo 1 had arrived two weeks prior to data collection. We ended up reaching a smaller number of children in Ayillo 1 than the anticipated 120. There are many reasons for this. First, many parents and children had not seen early childhood development (ECD) activities in practice. While many parents were interested in learning more, which is the main reason why they brought their children to participate in the research, they did not understand the purpose of the ECD centres and the potential benefits for their children. So, while families in Ayillo 1 also had an interest in participating, this was the same as those in Ayillo 2. Additionally, the data were collected by running games and activities for children. Many of these new children were unfamiliar with doing these types of activities, being asked questions by adults they did not know. So, many children, especially three-year olds, started crying during the games and during data collection. In these cases, I told the research assistants to let the parent take the child home. I did not want to do harm to children by forcing them to do activities they were uncomfortable doing. Based on KIIs, FGDs and my own observation, socialisation and simply being accustomed to doing activities and

Table 9.2 Gender by location

	Gender		
	Male	Female	Total
Ayillo 1 (wait list control)	41	33	74
Ayillo 2 (programme)	67	59	126
	108	92	200

answering questions with adults children did not know were new to many children in Ayillo 1. While I did not go to the camps with an observation checklist, I could clearly see the difference in the comfort levels of children doing the activities in Ayillo 2 vs. Ayillo 1. This was especially the case with the younger children of the group—those around age 3.

I tried as much as possible to have gender balance. It became difficult to manage this in practice as it got a bit chaotic and crowded when registering children and parents for the research. So, in the end as Charts 9.1 and 9.2 illustrate, we ended up with more boys than girls in the research. However, the difference was not too great. It was actually interesting to see that parents brought their daughters to participate almost as much as their sons (Tables 9.3 and 9.4).

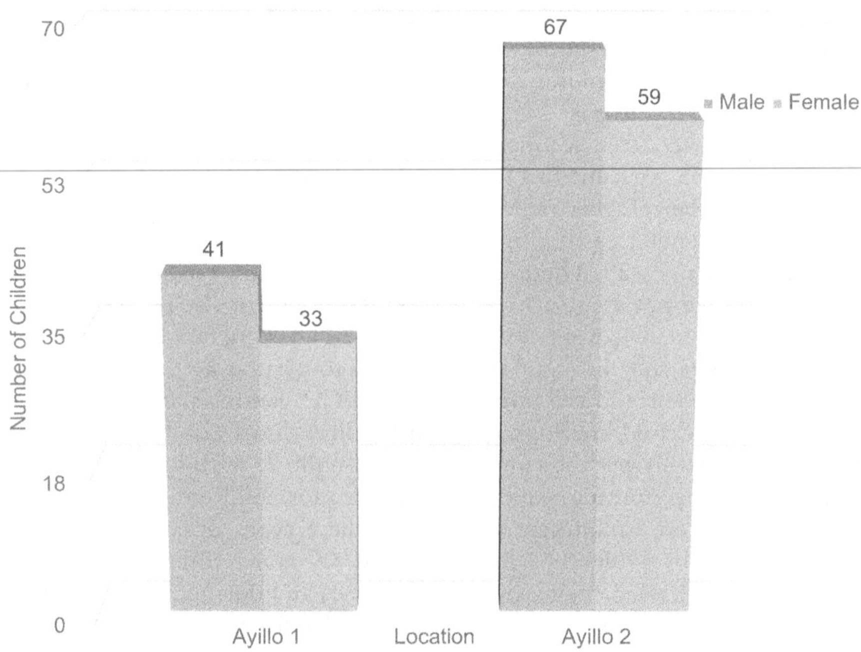

Chart 9.1 Gender among child participants per location.

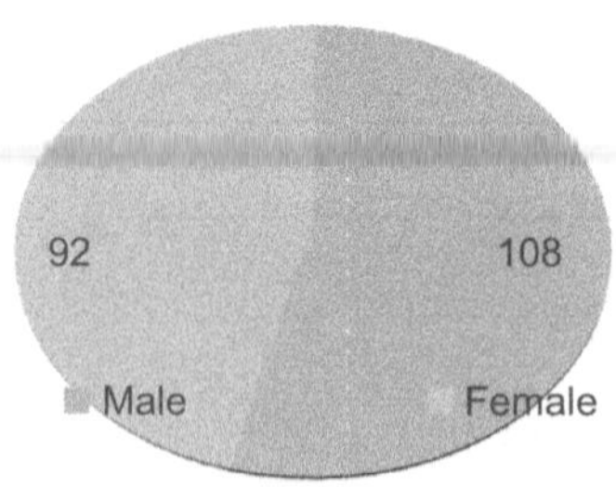

Chart 9.2 Gender among child participants.

Table 9.3 Age of total child participants

	Number of children	*Percentage*
Three-year old	63	31.5
Four-year old	65	32.5
Five-year old	72	36
Total	200	100

Table 9.4 Age by location

	Age			
	Three-year old	*Four-year old*	*Five-year old*	*Total*
Ayillo 1 (wait list control)	21	26	27	74
Ayillo 2 (programme)	42	39	45	126
Total	63	65	72	200

Inferential statistics: child development scores for children in the programme and wait list control groups

In order to compare the programme (children from Ayillo 2) and wait list control groups (children from Ayillo 1) based on their overall child development score, the independent samples one-sided *t*-test was used. A one-sided *t*-test was used because my hypothesis indicates a direction for the effect of the programme. I used two statistical programmes to do the inferential statistics analyses: SPSS and R. The analysis further includes key information collected through FGDs, KIIs, observation, photos and videos to triangulate the data.

Independent samples t-test (one-sided)

This test looked at the total child development scores from the child questionnaire for all children. It compared the children by location: Ayillo 1 is the wait list control group and Ayillo 2 the programme group (Chart 9.3, Tables 9.5 and 9.6).

Through this test, the *t*-value was −11.604 and our degree of freedom (df) was 198. Using the *t*-test for independent samples (one-sided), I found a significant difference between the programme group in Ayillo 2 and the wait list control group in Ayillo 1 ($t = -11.604$, df = 198, $p < 0.0001$; 95% confidence interval. Chart 9.4 illustrates the difference in the child development scores by camp. It shows that children in Ayillo 2 had significantly higher scores than those in Ayillo 1. There was a greater range of scores present in the Ayillo 1 group, whereas the children in Ayillo 2 group had less variability

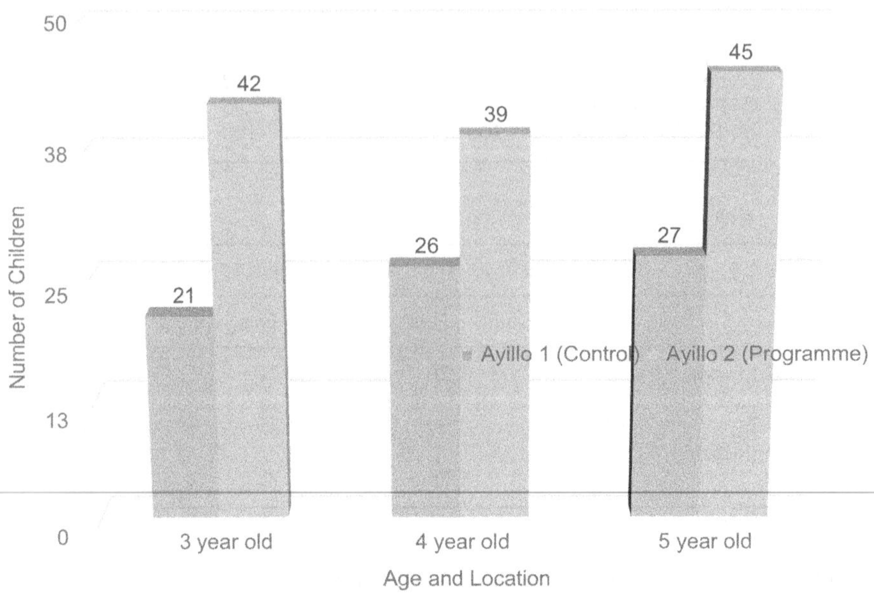

Chart 9.3 Age of child participants by location.

Table 9.5 Total means for child development score by group

Ayillo 1 (wait list control)	$N = 74$	$M = 40.66$	Std. deviation—10.24	Std. error mean—1.19
Ayillo 2 (programme)	$N = 126$	$M = 55.10$	Std. deviation—7.28	Std. error mean—0.65

Table 9.6 Total child development score by group

T-test for equality of means				
T score	*Degree of freedom*	*P value—sig (one-tailed)*	*Means difference*	*95% Confidence interval of the difference*
−11.604	198	$p < 0.0001$	14.433	−12.378

in their development scores. Chart 9.4 does indicate some overlap on child development scores between children in Ayillo 1 and Ayillo 2. This could be as a result of a number of factors such as the interaction and learning that the child has with his/her family outside of any services that could have helped the child do better on the test. The Ayillo 2 scores show some outlier scores.

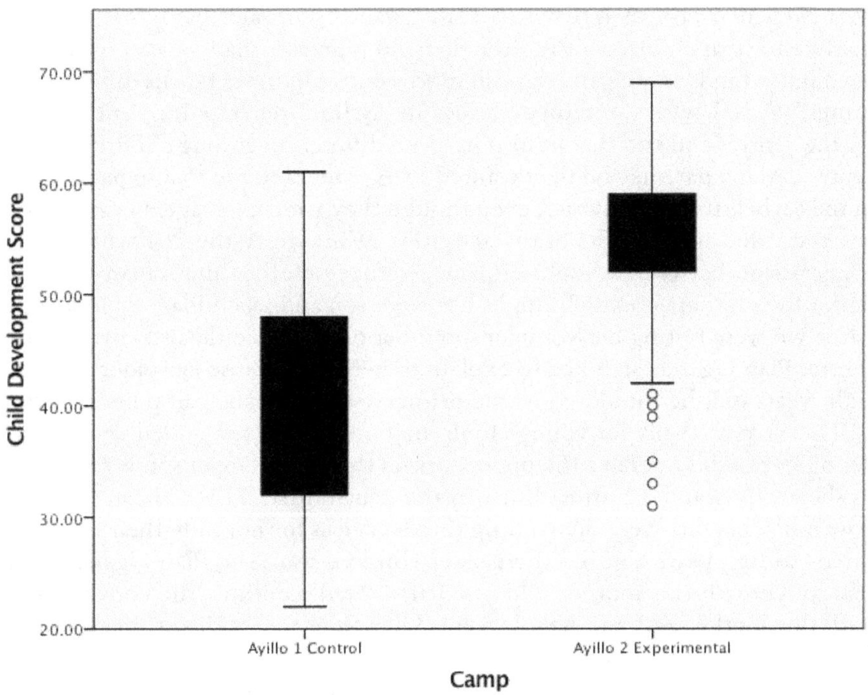

Chart 9.4 Child development score distribution by camp.

While all of the children in Ayillo 2 were enrolled in the programme, it is not clear how long each child had been enrolled at the time of the data collection. As mentioned previously in the methodology section, one challenge in this research was the constant movement of people back and forth across the South Sudan border and the constant flow of new South Sudanese to Uganda. According to a KII I conducted with a Plan Uganda staff, they did not turn away children that came to enrol in the programme even after the programme started. So, some of the low scores from Ayillo 2 could be children who recently arrived to the camp, but have not been participating in the program the same length of time as other children.

These results are supported by KIIs, FGDs, my own observation of the children when they were completing the tasks on the adapted ASQ-3, photos I took and videos I took. During FGDs, many parents said that they saw big differences between children that have gone through ECD activities. One mother said, "My child has learned some English. He expresses himself more now. He teaches me the songs in English that he learned." Another mother said of her son, "He has learned so much here. I am happy. I want him to succeed. There are more opportunities here than back home in South Sudan." I observed that this same mother stayed with her son when the test was being given and at some points even got angry with him when he could not fully do a particular task. A KII with a Plan Uganda staff said that while they do not like to turn children away, "the demand is greater than we can fulfil. We need more funds so we can establish more centres in other blocks in the other camps." A KII with the refugee leader in Ayillo 2 reiterated his enthusiasm for the centres and said that he also has seen differences among children in the centres. Many parents said they wanted their older children to also participate in the early learning activities, even though they were over-age, because they saw the value and benefits of the activities. While in Ayillo 2, I witnessed a conversation between a South Sudanese refugee mother and a Plan Uganda staff. One mother actually brought her older son and asked Plan Uganda staff while we were testing her younger son if her older son could also enrol in the centre. Plan Uganda staff had to explain to her that because her older son was eight years old, he should go to the primary school in the camp because the ECD centre was only for young children. This mother responded saying that her older son did not have the opportunities that her younger son is receiving so she really wanted him to learn in the centre first. This indicated to me how much parents were demanding these services for not only their children three- to five-years old, but their older children too. The Plan Uganda staff that spoke with this mother told me that she will continue the conversation with this mother and will help her enrol her older son in the primary school which is near the ECD centre. She also mentioned to me that this was not an unusual request as they receive those types of requests regularly. As few early childhood services exist in South Sudan, many children had no opportunities and now they have the opportunity to go to primary school, but they saw the ECD centre as a more attractive option. KIIs also indicated that children that go through early childhood activities in the camp are much better prepared for primary school than those who have not been in the programme. One KII with an ECD caregiver said, "Sometimes our kids are so ahead of other kids that the teachers in the primary school do not know what to do."

According to KIIs with Plan staff, normally they have six ECD caregivers to cover the three age groups of children—three, four, and five years old. This is two caregivers per group. However, the sheer number of children who come and enrol is large. Plan mentioned that they do not have the budget to reduce the adult to child ratio in the centres. Videos I took and observations I made in Ayillo 2 showed that parents were spontaneously staying at the centre with their children and helping out the caregivers. I first noticed this because there were some people who were not actively doing activities with the kids, but were in the background or helping manage the sheer numbers. When speaking with Plan staff through a KII, they told me that these people were not staff; they were parent volunteers who on their own wanted to be there and help. Without any sort of payment, these parents decided to help. I interviewed a father who was a parent volunteer and asked him why he was there. He said, "My kids are learning something good and I am free. I don't mind that I don't get paid. I want to help." A Plan Uganda staff later told me in a KII that she wants to capitalise on the spontaneous volunteer support from some parents as they need more adults to manage the large number of children.

In contrast in Ayillo 1, which was the wait list control group, parents brought their children to participate due to their own curiosity and interest in learning more about the services Plan could offer. During a KII with a Plan Uganda staff and my own observation during the testing of children in Ayillo 1, some children, especially three-year olds, started to cry. When I saw this happening, I would intervene and tell the research assistant to stop the activities and tell them to let the child go home with his/her mother/caregiver. On some occasions, parents did not want to take their children home even if they were crying. Plan Uganda staff had to convince them to take their children home and explain that the research team did not want a child to cry during the process because it was not good for the child. This behaviour of the children and parents indicated to me that the parents were very interested in the potential services that were to come to their block in Ayillo 1 and that children did not have experience interacting with many adults outside of their families or doing the kinds of activities included in the test. They were uncomfortable and I could observe this very clearly. Children in Ayillo 2 were very comfortable with the activities in the test because they had already done them before through the ECD centres.

The child development score includes five key areas that are connected with the child development domains mentioned earlier: (1) communication skills that are connected to the communication and language domain (i.e. communicating in their mother tongue and basic greetings in English), (2) gross motor skills that are connected to the physical health and well-being domain (i.e. running, jumping; balancing on one foot), (3) fine motor skills that are also connected to the physical health and well-being domain (i.e. drawing a straight line, drawing a circle, writing one's names), (4) cognitive skills connected to the cognitive domain (i.e. knowledge of colours, numbers, large/small concepts, problem solving) and (5) personal-social skills that are connected to the socio-emotional domain (i.e. ability to wash hands, go to toilet independently). In order to better understand where the programme had the greatest impact on children's development, below is an analysis of the two groups in Ayillo 1 (wait list control group) and Ayillo 2 (programme group) by each child development sub-set. This was done in order to determine which aspects of the programme made the largest difference in children's lives.

COMMUNICATION SKILLS

The sub-group of questions focused on communication included developmentally appropriate activities such as following directions, saying who their friends are, saying what they would do when they are hungry or sleepy, speaking a full sentence in their language and being able to say basic greetings in English. Normally the question about English is not on the ASQ-3 test when it is administered in the United States as this is the normal language of most children. Among South Sudanese refugee children, and in particular the children in this research, Dinka is their mother tongue. As mentioned previously during the process of adapting the test to the South Sudanese cultural context and determining the capabilities parents wanted their children to have, speaking English was at the top of the list. Parents clearly see the importance of their children speaking English and so this was included in the ASQ-3. The questions included the following answers: Yes (which received a score of 3), Sometimes (which received a score of 2) and Not Yet (which received a score of 1). The highest score a child could get in this section for his/her age group is 15, whereas the lowest score could be 5 (Table 9.7).

As indicated in Table 9.7, majority of the children had some communication skills and were speaking in their language. None of the children got a score of 5, but many more had scores closer to 15. This was an overall positive indication. The overall mean score for the children in Ayillo 1 (wait list control) was 10.93 with a standard deviation of 3.2 while for the Ayillo 2 (programme) the overall mean score was 14.54 with a standard deviation of 2.7. So even with standard deviations, not many of the children in Ayillo 1 and Ayillo 2 had the same mean scores in the area of communication. When looking at the specific data set and scores, the ability or inability to speak English and use basic greetings in English seems to have made a huge difference in the mean scores as virtually none of the children from Ayillo 1 could greet people in English. Chart 9.5 illustrates the distribution of the communication scores among children in Ayillo 2 and Ayillo 1 and does indicate some overlap in communication scores among children in Ayillo 1 and Ayillo 2. However, the chart still shows a difference between the majority of the communication scores in Ayillo 1 and Ayillo 2.

As Table 9.8 shows, there was a significant difference among the programme and wait list control groups at 95% confidence interval ($t = -5.8646$; $p < 0.0001$; df = 198). These results were further supported and triangulated

Table 9.7 Total means for children's communication score by group

Ayillo 1 (wait list control)	*N* = 74	*M* = 10.93	Std. deviation 3.23	Std. error mean 0.38
Ayillo 2 (programme)	*N* = 126	*M* = 14.52	Std. deviation—2.75	Std. error mean—0.25

Table 9.8 Total communication skills score by group

T-test for equality of means				
T score	*Degree of freedom*	*P value—Sig (one-tailed)*	*Means difference*	*95% Confidence interval of the difference*
−5.8746	198	$p < 0.0001$	3.053	−2.194

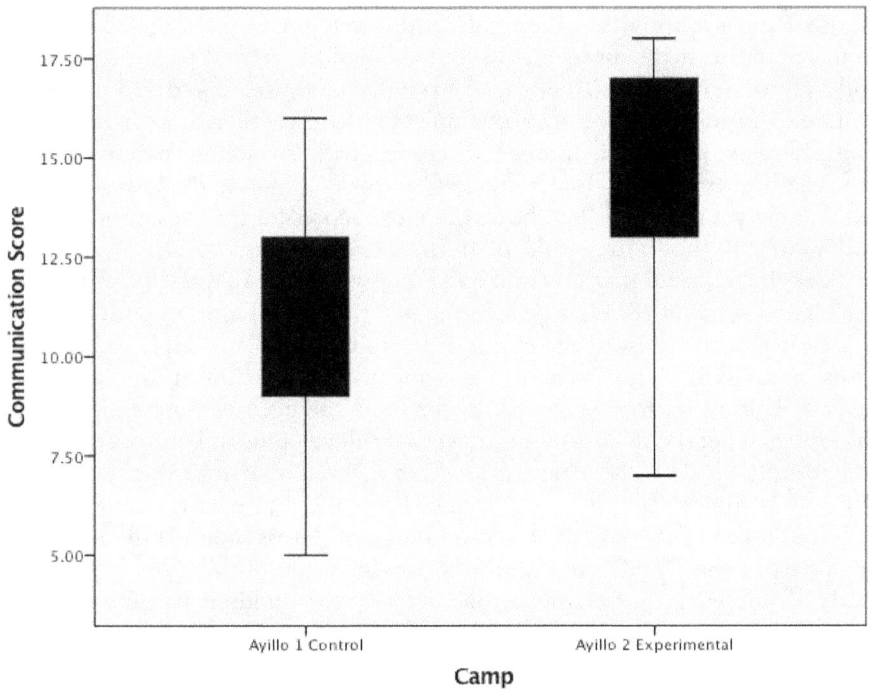

Chart 9.5 Communication score distribution by camp.

through KIIs with community leaders, FGDs with parents and my own observation of the children in the two groups. During KIIs, research participants mentioned that the children could speak English through their involvement in the programme, and that they were confident speakers. In my observation, I could very clearly see a difference in children's communication abilities, both in Dinka and in English. Children's ability to speak English in Ayillo 2 was further supported by videos I took of children participating in ECD activities. There were multiple songs in English which taught children the English language, but also concepts such as how to brush their teeth, wash their face, how to count to 10 and different colours. Virtually no children in the wait list control group in Ayillo 1 spoke English, while many in the programme group had basic conversational skills in English. I could see this not only during the testing but also during their free play and the way they greeted me and Plan Uganda staff. I observed that children were learning how to express themselves more both in their language and in English through the CLAC programme. They interacted with other children and adults on a daily basis and seemed to feel comfortable answering questions, doing different sorts of activities and expressing themselves. In contrast, the children from Ayillo 1 sometimes did not answer questions or were quiet because they were shy and not used to answering questions even if they could do it.

GROSS MOTOR SKILLS

Another sub-group within the total child development score includes questions related to gross motor skills. These are skills related to large muscles and a child's physical well-being. The types of questions asked and activities children did include running from one side to the other, hopping on one foot, skipping, jumping a distance, catching a ball, throwing a ball overhand, etc. The highest score a child could get on this is 18, while the lowest score a child could get is 6. Table 9.9 shows the mean scores for the gross motor skills and Table 9.10 shows the results of an independent samples *t*-test.

Table 9.9 indicates that no child had the lowest score of 6 and no child had the highest score of 18. However, looking at the mean scores of both groups, it is clear that the most of the children are in the middle to higher range for gross motor skills. This is positive as it means that no child in the sample is severely behind in gross motor skills for their age even if some children on the lower end of the spectrum may have some developmental delays or are not able to fully do all of the activities asked of them. This can be due to the fact that some children simply may not have been asked to ever try some of the activities asked of them such as hop on one foot. Gross motor skills activities are a part of the CLAC programme so the inclusion of them seems to have made a difference. For example, one activity the children participate in is singing a song and hopping on one foot and then another. They do activities where they jump up and jump forward. These are all part of the test questions.

Further, through *t*-test for independent samples, the *t*-value comparison of children in Ayillo 1 with those in Ayillo 2 was −7.3814. As the data indicate, there was a significant difference between the programme group in Ayillo 2 and the wait list control group in Ayillo 1 (p <0.0001) at 95% confidence interval. However, looking at the actual mean scores, the standard deviation and the distribution of the scores as illustrated in Chart 9.6,

Table 9.9 Total means for children's gross motor skills score by group

Ayillo 1 (wait list control)	$N = 74$	$M = 11.89$	Std. deviation—3.85	Std. error mean—0.45
Ayillo 2 (programme)	$N = 126$	$M = 15.32$	Std. deviation—2.65	Std. error mean—0.24

Table 9.10 Gross motor skills by group

T-test for equality of means				
T score	*Degree of freedom*	*P value—sig (one-tailed)*	*Means difference*	*95% Confidence interval of the difference*
−7.3814	198	p <0.0001	3.410	−2.646

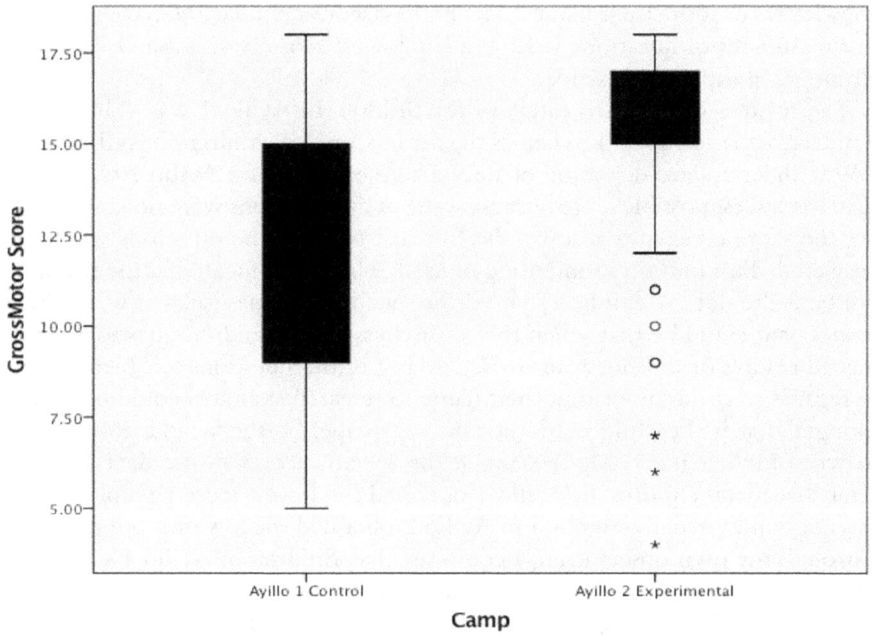

Chart 9.6 Gross motor score distribution by camp.

there is overlap in gross motor skills scores among the sample in both groups. The mean score for children in Ayillo 1 was 11.89 with a standard deviation of 3.85, whereas the mean score for children in Ayillo 2 was 15.32 with a standard deviation of 2.65. This means that some children in Ayillo 1 (those with the highest scores among the group) had the same gross motor skills scores as children in Ayillo 2 (those with the lowest scores among the group). My own observation, videos and photos I took and KII with Plan Uganda staff did not seem to indicate statistical significance. In my own observation, children in both camps seemed to be doing well on gross motor skills. Based on my observation and a KII, a difference in the scores could have been because children in Ayillo 1 were shy to try the activities even if they could do them.

FINE MOTOR SKILLS

Another sub-group of questions in the adapted ASQ questionnaire is related to fine motor skills. The types of questions asked were related to a child's ability to hold a pencil using the pincer grasp, drawing a straight horizontal and vertical line, being able to draw circles and other shapes and being able to copy letters or write their names. The highest score a child could have received in this sub-set of questions is 12 and the lowest score is 4. Table 9.11 shows children's abilities in this area.

The mean score for this category for children in Ayillo 1 was 4.34 with a standard deviation of 0.71, whereas the mean score for children in Ayillo 2 was 7.69 with a standard deviation of 1.83. The mean score for Ayillo 1 was lower than the lowest possible score because some of the questions were not answered. So, the score takes into account the fact that some of the questions were not answered. This indicates something in itself. This could mean that the research assistants did not ask children to do those specific activities (such as write their name) or it could be that when the researchers asked children questions, they started crying or did not want to try. Many of the questions left blank were in regards to children writing their name so research assistants could have also thought that if the child could not draw a shape, he/she would not be able to write his/her name. By looking at the specific scores in the data set, it is clear that many children in Ayillo 1 obtained the lowest score possible in this category and virtually no child in Ayillo 2 obtained the lowest score possible. Through my own observation, I could see that children in Ayillo 1 struggled in this area and were unable to do the activities requested of them. The CLAC programme, like the majority of early childhood education programmes, has a strong emphasis on fine motor skills. In the CLAC programme, the teachers practice holding a pencil, drawing straight, curved and other lines that are pre-writing skills. For older children that are four- or five-year olds, there is an emphasis on teaching children how to write letters and their names. The t-test for independent samples further confirms that in the data there was a significant difference. The t-value, as seen in Table 9.12, is −14.763 with $p < 0.0001$ at 95% confidence interval. Fine motor skills are key school readiness skills and based on the data, it seems that the effect of the programme intervention very strongly supports the development of these skills (Chart 9.7).

Table 9.11 Total means for children's fine motor skills score by group

Ayillo 1 (wait list control)	$N = 74$	$M = 4.34$	Std. deviation—0.71	Std. error mean—0.08
Ayillo 2 (programme)	$N = 126$	$M = 7.69$	Std. deviation—1.83	Std. error mean—0.16

Table 9.12 Fine motor skills by group and age

T-test for equality of means				
T score	*Degree of freedom*	*P value—sig (one-tailed)*	*Means difference*	*95% Confidence interval of the difference*
−14.763	198	$p < 0.0001$	3.630	−3.22306

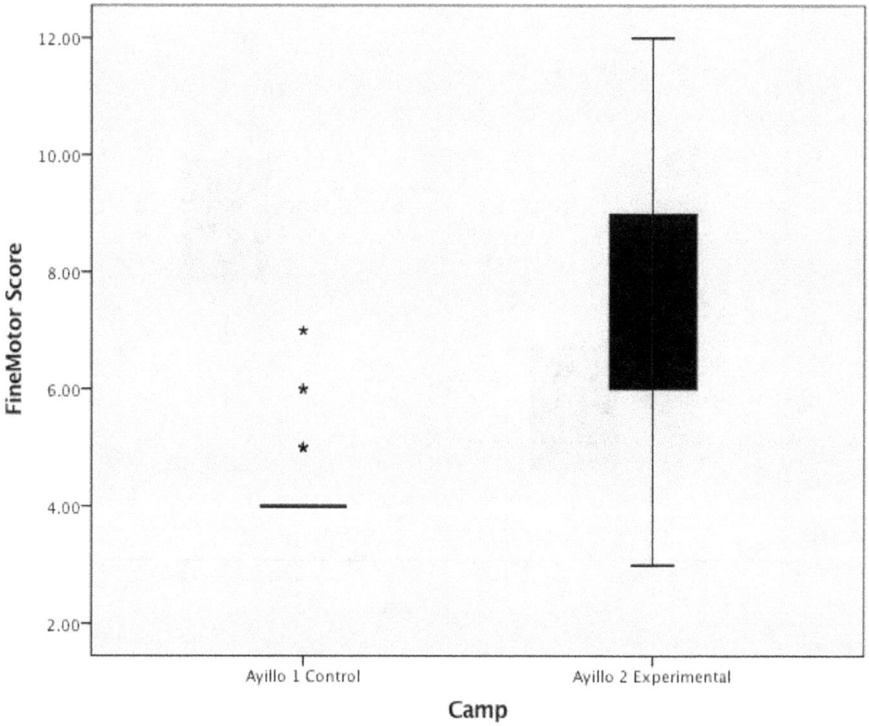

Chart 9.7 Fine motor score distribution by camp.

COGNITIVE SKILLS

Children's cognitive development is the next sub-set of questions included in the child development questionnaire. These questions included problem solving, understanding concepts of opposites such as above and below, small, larger and largest. Questions also included recognition of numbers (1, 2, 3) and letters in English (as Dinka is not a written language) and ability to count to 10. The highest score possible in this sub-set of question is 12 and the lowest score is 4 (Chart 9.8).

As Table 9.13 indicates, the mean score for the children in Ayillo 1 was 6.47 with a standard deviation of 1.45, whereas the mean score for children in Ayillo 2 was 8.89 with a standard deviation of 1.89. This indicates that some children in Ayillo 1 and Ayillo 2 had the same score in this sub-category. The mean score for Ayillo 1 was also quite low at 6.47, the lowest possible score being 4. This indicates that some children had very low scores in this category. In contrast, children in Ayillo 2 had a mean score of 8.85, which is in the middle of the range (4–12). The *t*-test for independent samples (as shown in Table 9.14) illustrates a significant difference between the two groups with a t score of −8.7176, df of 198 and p <0.0001. While the difference in the

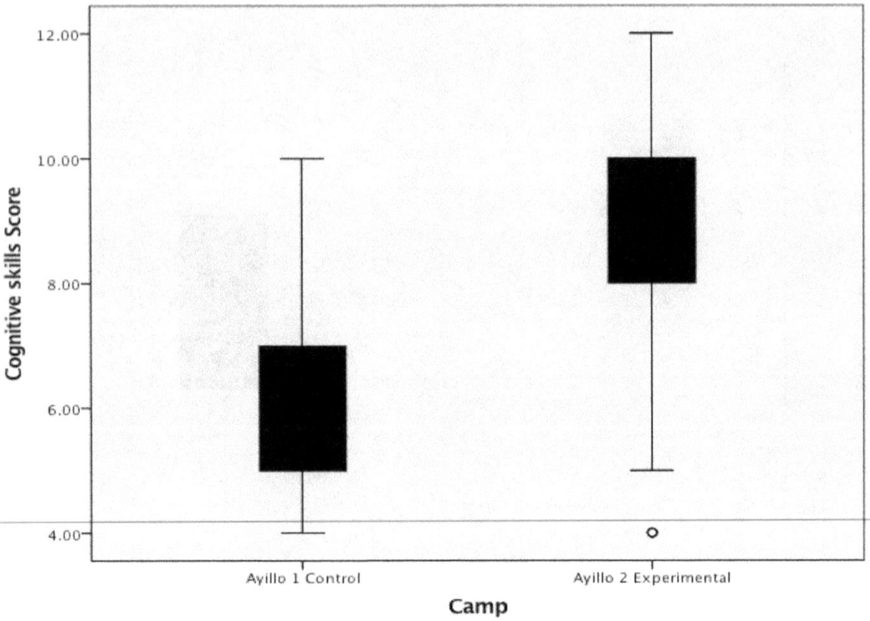

Chart 9.8 Cognitive skills score distribution by camp.

Table 9.13 Total means for children's cognitive skills score by group

Ayillo 1 (wait list control)	$N = 74$	$M = 6.47$	Std. deviation—1.45	Std. error mean—0.17
Ayillo 2 (programme)	$N = 126$	$M = 8.89$	Std. deviation—1.89	Std. error mean—0.17

Table 9.14 Cognitive skills by group and age

T-test for equality of means				
T score	*Degree of freedom*	*P value—sig (one-tailed)*	*Means difference*	*95% Confidence interval of the difference*
−8.7176	198	$p < 0.0001$	2.368	−1.919

scores is significant in the sample, the fact that the scores for the children in Ayillo 2 are in the middle of the range indicates that they are learning something through the programme, but it is not enough to bring the majority of scores closer to the highest score of 12. During my observations of children of both groups doing the activities, I could see the difference in abilities in both groups, but the difference was not as acute as what I observed with children regarding fine motor skills. Further, part of this could be as indicated as one of the limitations earlier in the research methodology that we had no clear indication of how long each research participant had been in the programme—whether for eight months or one month as it was chaotic at the time of registering children for the research.

PERSONAL-SOCIAL SKILLS

The last sub-group within the test includes questions related to children's personal and social skills—especially related to whether they could independently go to the toilet, wash their hands, have friends and know the names of their friends, etc. Within the CLAC programme, there is a strong emphasis on this sub-group where children sing songs daily related to handwashing and keeping themselves clean. ECD caregivers and parents reiterated the importance of personal hygiene and how they promoted it with their children every day. The highest score a child could get in this sub-group is 16 (Chart 9.9, Table 9.15).

The means for the two groups did show a difference (8.66 for children in Ayillo 1 and 10.63 for children in Ayillo 2); however, the standard deviation is 2.64 for Ayillo 1 and 1.90 for Ayillo 2. This again indicates that there are children from both Ayillo 1 and Ayillo 2 with the same score in this area. It

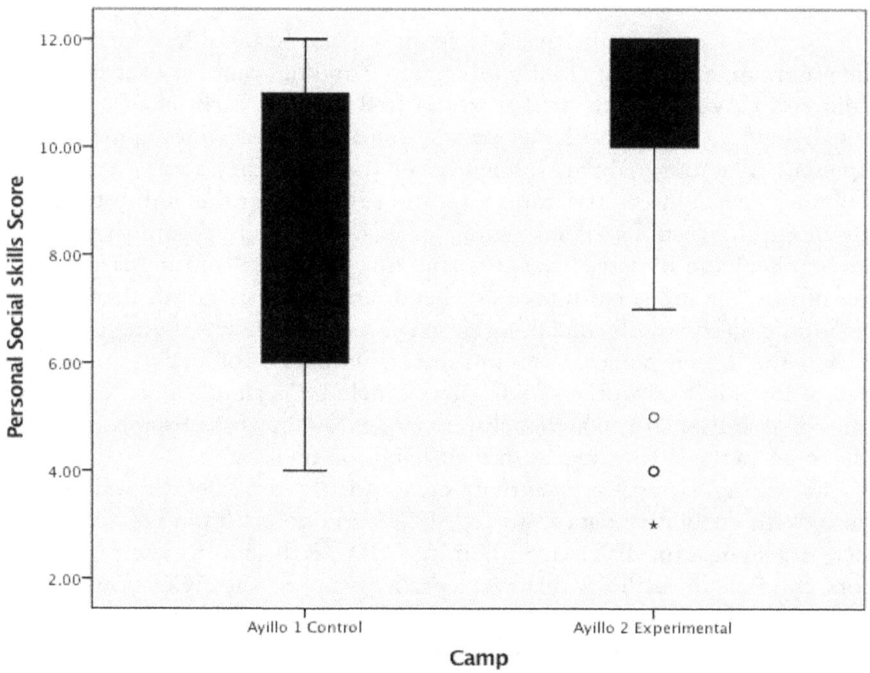

Chart 9.9 Personal-social skills score distribution by camp.

Table 9.15 Total means for children's personal-social skills score by group

Ayillo 1 (wait list control)	$N = 74$	$M = 8.66$	Std. deviation 2.64	Std. error mean 0.31
Ayillo 2 (programme)	$N = 126$	$M = 10.63$	Std. deviation 1.90	Std. error mean 0.18

Table 9.16 Socio-emotional/personal-social skills by group and age

T-test for equality of means				
T score	*Degree of freedom*	*P value—sig (1-tailed)*	*Means difference*	*95% Confidence interval of the difference*
−6.0125	198	$p < 0.0001$	1.973	−1.3257

also means that both groups generally did pretty good on this sub-group of tests. It makes sense as parents during FGDs and ECD teachers both mentioned the importance of these skills. The *t*-test for independent samples in Table 9.16 did show a statistical significance at 95% confidence interval ($t = -6.0125$; df = 198; $p < 0.0001$).

Child data

The quantitative and qualitative data do show a significant difference between the programme group of children in Ayillo 2 and the wait list control group children in Ayillo 1 with total scores as well as when each set of questions was divided and analysed based on the domain of child development they represent. The four main areas investigated in the children's survey included linguistic development and communication—including the ability to speak basic English greetings. The second area of focus is with regard to physical development and in particular, gross and fine motor skills (using large muscles of the legs and small muscles of hands and fingers). Third, there was a focus on cognitive skills including problem solving; understanding concepts such as small, big, bigger; over and under; numbers; colours; etc. The last area of investigation in the child's survey includes personal-social or socio-emotional skills such as whether children share, do they have friends, are they able to go to the latrine and wash their hands on their own.

After triangulating the quantitative data for the total child development scores with qualitative data from KII, FGDs and observation, it is clear that there are significant differences. During FGDs, KIIs and my own observation, children in Ayillo 2 that were participating in the ECD programme could do more and had greater capabilities than those in the wait list control group. This could be because of the programme, but the difference could also be accounted for because the children in Ayillo 2 were used to doing activities like the ones presented in the survey, whereas the Ayillo 1 children found these activities new and did not feel totally comfortable doing them with people they did not know. In addition to the measures mentioned in the survey, FGDs, KII and my own observation also indicate that the children were happy, confident and excited to participate in the ECD activities. During FGDs with parents, many mentioned they saw huge changes in their children's development. Some parents, who were not part of the FGDs or KIIs, also told Plan centre staff that they wanted their older children to participate in the activities rather than go to primary school because they saw the value of what children were learning and because their older child had not gone through ECD and so had not learned what the younger children were learning. Children in Ayillo 2 were so excited that those who did not have their parents with them at the time of registering research participants but wanted to participate went home to get their parents so they could sign up and do the activities.

In terms of linguistic development, the quantitative survey showed significant differences and this is supported by the qualitative data collected. When I entered the question about whether the child could speak basic greetings in English, almost no children from the Ayillo 1 wait list control group could speak English, while significantly more children in Ayillo 2 could. This is because the teaching of English is integrated into the children's play and activities. In particular, the ECD teachers use songs to teach children English language and language in general. The children in Ayillo 2 were more confident to speak and when they spoke, they spoke more clearly (usually in their mother tongue). The CLAC programme, during the morning circle time, has an activity known as "news news" where a few children every day can share with their peers some news in their lives. This gives children the opportunity to express themselves and do it in front of others. Many children in Ayillo 1 were shy so they scored low on particular tests even if they actually could speak and would do so more clearly at home.

Physical development (gross and fine motor) skills were another area where the data showed significant differences. Based on my observation, I could see that while the CLAC programme is encouraging the use and development of gross motor skills, it is not as intentional and focused as its attention to other aspects. While the *t*-test showed significant differences in gross motor skills, through observation, I did not see such stark differences in the two groups. In the areas of fine motor skills, the survey, KIIs and my own observation all support the large and significant differences between the two groups. Fine motor skills are intentionally practised in the Plan ECD centres with children practicing writing, drawing, doing puzzles, lacing, etc. Many parents during the FGDs and in the parent surveys mentioned that they were not able to carry a lot when they left their homes in South Sudan; they had to leave many things. In the parent surveys and FGDs, parents explicitly mentioned toys as things of their children's they could not bring with them. While the research team did not explicitly ask about items such as pencils and pens, it is very likely that if the families had these items in their houses to begin with in South Sudan, they did not carry them to the camps which helps account for the difference between the two groups. The Ayillo 2 children have access to writing materials in the ECD centres, while the Ayillo 1 wait list control groups do not have access to such items where they could practice developing their fine motor skills.

Cognitive development was another area where qualitative data support the statistical significance found in the quantitative data. Areas such as recognition of numbers, colours, and shapes are intentionally taught in ECD centres and children in Ayillo 2 scored higher on these tests than the children in Ayillo 1. Concepts of over and under, small, big and bigger are also integrated into the various play, songs and games that the children experience in the centres. The results could also be because parents may understand the importance of children learning these things, but they may not know how to teach their children. Their interest and motivation might encourage children in Ayillo 2 to learn well. Helping children understand these concepts through play, songs and games is one of the skills that would be practised in the parenting groups. As the parenting programme and the early learning centres had not started in this particular block of Ayillo 1, the difference makes sense.

The last area that was explored in the adapted ASQ-3 survey was personal-social/socio-emotional skills. This area also showed quantitatively a significant difference, but through FGDs, KIIs and my own observation, this was another area where the stark difference between the two groups was not as strong as the other sub-areas. During the adaptation process for the ASQ-3, parents mentioned the importance of cleanliness and hygiene which could account for the fact that the differences between the two groups were not stark. The other aspect of the personal-social/socio-emotional questions was about sharing, whether children had friends, etc. Through my own observation, it was clear that one of the key contributions of the ECD centres and the CLAC model was how it brings children together and helps them develop their social skills. While there are teaching and learning materials in the centres, there are not enough materials for the number of children. This is a reality of working in humanitarian settings where the needs and demands for services usually are greater than the resources available. So the idea of sharing and working together in groups is integral to the curriculum and a way to teach and develop children's capabilities.

Description of the parents' data set

I followed a similar process for cleaning, coding and then adding up the scores for the parents' data set. The parents' survey was developed based on a Plan regional survey for parenting programmes. It is based on the content of the CLAC parenting manual that is used in many countries in East Africa. The content assesses knowledge, attitudes and practice, but they are all self-reported. One limitation of this approach is that this research did not use an observation method such as the Home Observation for the Measurement of the Environment (HOME) to triangulate the data on practices, but other methods such as KIIs and FGDs do help to provide greater depth to the data. The parents' survey has both multiple-choice questions and open-ended questions. Each answer was coded with a score of 3, 2 and 1, indicating whether the answer was correct (3), partially correct (2) and not correct (1). I then totalled the full score of the parents' data. The possible total could be 87 (with the highest score of 3 for each question and 29 questions in total). The initial plan was to collect two data points using the survey from Ayillo 2 and Ayillo 1, but due to the lack of time and sufficient human and financial resources, I made the decision while in Uganda to change the design of this research to something simpler—one data point and only one group of parents.

Out of the total of 126 children whose data we collected from Ayillo 2, we were able to match 90 parent surveys. The majority of the 90 parent surveys were conducted with mothers, but there were some fathers that responded to the questions. The characteristics of the parents surveyed that are included in the first table show that they were all from the Dinka tribe, all spoke Dinka as their mother tongue, most were illiterate and did not complete primary or secondary school. Further, most of the parents were in single-headed households. More parent surveys were collected than analysed because about one-fourth had many missing answers. Additionally, there were some parent surveys that could not be matched with their child's ASQ-3 because the handwriting on the parent survey was too difficult to decipher. The total score for the parent survey could be 87. The mean and median for the parents' data for this research were both 61. The total scores ranged from 40 to 76. For a majority of the parents, they got a 70% score on the parents' survey (61/87 × 100) meaning that they got this percentage of right answers (in terms of knowledge, attitudes and practice) (Table 9.17).

While reviewing the scoring of each parent survey, I saw a very clear pattern with the responses. Parents generally had better knowledge of issues related to basic nutrition, health and hygiene. For example, with regard to basic health, many parents mentioned the use of Oral Rehydration Salts for use if a child has diarrhoea, the importance of taking their sick child to the health centre in the camp. During FGDs and KIIs, parents and community members generally knew where key services, including health centres, were located in their camps. Almost all parents mentioned the importance of using soap and frequently washing hands before and after meals and after using the latrine. This was also a pattern with the child surveys where a majority of children knew about the importance of using soap, washing hands frequently.

Table 9.17 Parents' survey scores

Total cases	*Mean score*	*Median score*	*Total possible score*	*Minimum score*	*Maximum score*
N = 90	61	61	87	40	76

With nutrition, many parents understood the importance of breastfeeding, having variety in a child's diet such as protein. Many parents said that they provided two meals a day to their child, but that was because there was not enough food in the camp. This was reiterated through the FGDs and KIIs. Some parents during FGDs said that they would work with other community members to make porridge for all children at the centres by volunteering to cook, provide cooking and eating utensils and firewood. They asked Plan, however, to support in getting the key ingredients for the food such as sugar, oil and flour. As mentioned previously, food distribution in the camp meant that we lost people, including research assistants, who needed to wait in line for their family's food ration. So the issue of food is very important to the refugees and acutely on their minds. Parents' greater knowledge in relation to health, hygiene and nutrition could also be because of other services focused on these areas in the camp which increased their knowledge.

The areas that parents seemed to need more support in understanding and practicing were issues related to positive discipline, child development, child stimulation and early learning. No other agency in Ayillo 1 and Ayillo 2 was focusing on these areas at the time of the data collection and Plan was in the early stages of its parenting programme so it makes sense that their knowledge, attitudes and practices in this area were not strong. Child stimulation and early learning are major parts of the CLAC parenting curriculum, but positive discipline is not. While there are modules about family relationships and in particular the relationship between the mother and father, the curriculum does not focus on alternative ways to discipline a child. In the surveys, many parents said that if their child was being naughty or not behaving, they would hit him/her with a cane, would not give him/her food. Very few respondents said they would use alternative nonviolent means to discipline their child.

Based on the responses to the questions, many parents did not understand general developmental stages in relation to nutrition, learning, etc. For example, some parents thought it was ok to give juice to a four-month old or thought that semi-solid foods should start at one year. Juice is not recommended for four-month old babies because exclusive breastfeeding is promoted. Further, starting semi-solid foods at around six months can provide additional vitamins for children that breast milk does not provide. In terms of ways for children to learn, many parents did not understand how simple household items can be used for learning, especially in contexts where the availability of toys is difficult. Further, most parents did not think about making toys for children from local materials. Some parents did understand that books were important for learning and preparing children for school, but many did not read themselves and many did not have books with them in the camps. Most parents did not play enough with their children. Based on their responses, they did not understand that normal home activities could be fun and rich learning experiences for children. Lastly, most parents did not understand children's abilities, particularly during infancy, first year of life. There is a question about when a child can benefit from colourful moving objects and pictures. Infancy is the time when there is rapid eye growth and development so providing contrasting colours and patterns for children to look at is good for eye development. All of the aspects mentioned here that parents generally did not understand or practice are included in the CLAC parenting programme.

Correlation between parent knowledge, attitudes and practice and child's development

A lot of early years and education literature in non-emergency contexts states that when parental knowledge and capabilities are high, including their education and socio-economic status, this will provide a more stimulating and supportive environment for children to develop in, thereby positively affecting their development (Center on the Developing Child, 2016; Hoover-Dempsey and Sander, 1995; McLoyd, 1998; Senechal and Le Fevre, 2002). Parents with larger vocabularies and those that interact more with their children can have children with a larger set of words that can prepare them for later reading and writing in school (Hart and Risley, 1999; Roberts et al., 1999).

This evidence in literature was tested in a refugee camp situation where the population was displaced from their homes so the majority brought few belongings with them (i.e. toys, books for children). This population also generally had low education levels, low socio-economic status and low knowledge about child development and what they could do to support their children's learning and development. The concept of ECCD, while now a part of the South Sudan national education policy, is still relatively new and services have not reached all parts of the country (UNESCO, 2015).

Unfortunately, data found in this research do not provide further evidence to support existing literature in non-emergency contexts where parental education and socio-economic status correlate with children's higher development and educational learning outcomes.

Table 9.18 shows the correlation coefficients of all of the children and their parents and then the correlation coefficients of children and parent by age.

As none of these correlation coefficients are close to 1 or −1 and all are very close to 0, it indicates that no relationship, positive or negative, was found between the two groups' scores. When looking at the raw data (as illustrated in Chart 9.10), it was also clear that the scores of the parents and children had no pattern; they were all very scattered.

Table 9.18 Correlation between parent knowledge, attitudes and practice and children's development

	Correlation coefficient	*T score*	*P value*	*Degree of freedom*
Total	−0.2875	−2.8158	0.997	88
Three-year old	−0.0942	0.51801	0.6959	30
Four-year old	0.1004	0.5432	0.2956	29
Five-year old	−0.1053	0.5230	0.6995	25

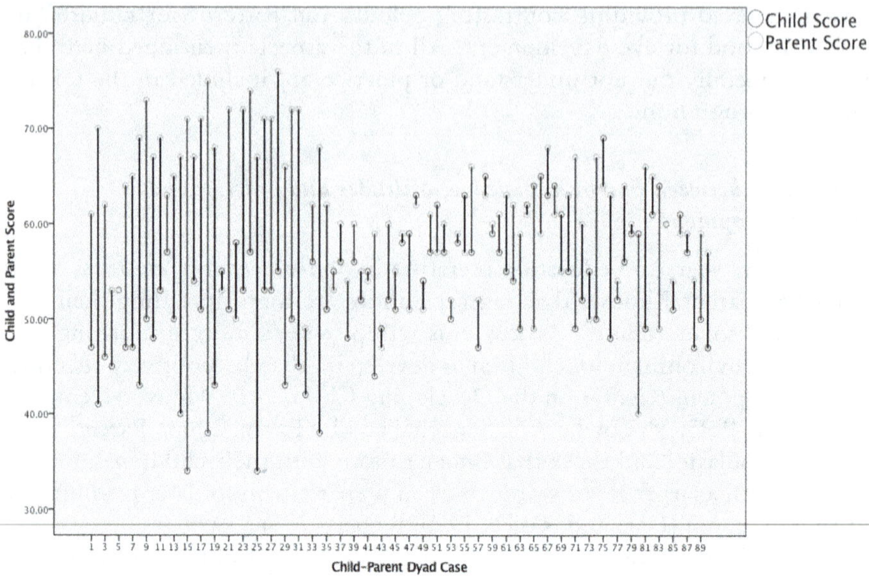

Chart 9.10 Child-parent dyad scores.

Correlations are just one type of analysis to look at the relationship between variables. I considered using Chi Square as well, but the variable of the scores are continuous while Chi Square analyses require categorical variables. I could have gone back to the data to categorise each set of scores, but I would then have had to make a decision as to the cut off for what scores would be categorised where. The decision itself of where the cut off for the scores could be argued to be biased so I decided not to do this. This does illustrate a methodological limitation. Future research could build on and deepen the analysis for this type of data.

There could be a number of reasons for this. It could be simply that this research was conducted in a more homogeneous population than other research which would show a broader range of education, socio-economic status, etc. This population generally all have low education levels, low socio-economic status and few things from home that could be used for children's cognitive stimulation. There was also a small sample ($N = 90$) which could account for the inability to conduct proper correlation analysis. While the parenting programme had started, it was still in the early stages so it may be that many of the concepts included in the parents' surveys had not been reviewed in parenting sessions. There is a lot of movement between Adjumani, Uganda and South Sudan, as the border between the two countries is close and easy for South Sudanese to cross without visas. I found that many people were going back and forth across the border so it could be that some parents participated in more sessions than others or that some of the parents surveyed had not yet participated in any parenting sessions. There could have also been a miscommunication of the question and a difference in the way research assistants led the interview process for filling out the parent surveys. Yet another possibility is that emergency situations are different as they add additional stressors to parents' lives where they need to search for food and focus on daily survival, that this may have affected how they answered the questions on the surveys, especially in terms of practices. Literature statues that the stress of emergencies affects people differently than daily stressors of life in developing countries and this stress affects parents' ability to care for their children as they did before (Center on the Developing Child, 2016). As the practice aspect of the survey is approximately one-third, scoring lower on this section vs. the knowledge section could have affected the overall parent score.

This quantitative data were triangulated with qualitative data presented in the parent survey questions that were not multiple choice, but where parents could, in their own words, answer the questions. Further, FGDs with refugee parents and KIIs with Plan staff, refugee leadership and others also helped to triangulate the quantitative data. Through qualitative data and by looking at the specific scores and answers on the parents' surveys, there is a clear pattern that parents have higher knowledge about basic health, nutrition and hygiene than about child development and in particular activities that could promote children's cognitive, communication, socio-emotional, gross and fine motor development. As the parenting programme was in the early stages of implementation at the time of the data collection, this could be the reason for this. It could also be that parents are getting some of these key messages about health, nutrition and hygiene from other sectors and service providers in the camp in which case the Plan parenting programme at this point is not having a huge effect. The parents' data are in line with research and evaluations done on parenting programmes where simply having sessions about knowledge were not enough to have a significant impact, but the use of practice, problem solving and peer to peer learning were crucial to having impact on parents' capabilities (Aboud et al., 2013; Singla et al., 2015). As Plan moves forward with the parenting element of this programme, they will need to look more closely at this component and ensure it aligns with evaluations and lessons learned from other parenting programmes and in particular with evaluations conducted on the CLAC programme in non-emergency situations (Aboud et al., 2013; Singla et al., 2015).

Unintended benefits of the research

While this research focused on refugee children, three to five years, and their parents, there were some unintended benefits of this research. First, the process of doing the research was a learning and professional development experience for Plan Uganda staff and the South Sudanese refugees that were ECD staff and research assistants. Through the process, the Plan Uganda staff indicated that it was a nice learning experience for them and it helped them improve their existing skills and capacities as ECD Officers. They felt more confident about child development, parenting education, asking questions, collecting data and conducting research (which is important for their ongoing data collection for programme monitoring purposes). They learned new games to play with children in the ECD spaces. Similar responses were reported from the South Sudanese ECD staff/research assistants. Many ECD staff/research assistants and Plan Uganda staff (including the driver) requested additional child surveys so they could test their own children at home and monitor their development.

References

Aboud, F. et al. (2013). "Effectiveness of a parenting program in Bangladesh to address early childhood health, growth and development". *Social Science and Medicine*, 97, 250–258.

BBC (2016). *South Sudan Country Profile*, www.bbc.com/news/world-africa-14069082, last accessed 28 May 2016.

Center on the Developing Child (2016). *Building Core Capabilities for Life: The Science Behind the Skills Adults Need to Succeed in Parenting and in the Workplace.* Cambridge, MA: Harvard University.

Hart, B. and Risley, T.R. (1999). *The Social World of Children: Learning to Talk.* Baltimore: Paul H. Brookes Publishing.

Hoover-Dempsey, K. and Sander, H. (1995), "Parental involvement in children's education: Why does it make a difference?" *The Teacher's College Record*, 97(2), 310–331.

McLoyd, V. (1998). "Socio-economic disadvantage and child development", *American Psychologist*, 53(2), 185–204.

Plan International Assessment (2015). Unpublished document.

Roberts, J. E., Burchinal, M. and Durham, M. (1999). "Parents' report of vocabulary and grammatical development of African American preschoolers: Child and environmental associations", *Child Development*, 70(1), 92–106.

Save the Children (2015). *Hear It from the Children*, South Sudan, Juba.

Senechal, M. and Le Fevre, J.A. (2002). "Parental involvement in the development of children's reading skill: A five-year longitudinal study", *Child Development*, 73(2), 445–460.

Singla, D., Kumbakumba, E. and Aboud, F. (2015). "Effects of parenting intervention to address maternal psychological well-being and child development and growth in rural Uganda: A community-based, cluster-randomised trial", *The Lancet*, 3, 458–469, London.

UNESCO and Ministry of Education and Training (2015). *Education for All 2015 National Review Report: South Sudan*, http://unesdoc.unesco.org/images/0023/002316/231645e.pdf, last accessed 16 February 2016.

Conclusion

The way forward

Globally, there has been an increase in humanitarian emergencies that are affecting more people, are lasting longer and are costing more money. Generations of young children are growing up as refugees and internally displaced persons with little prospect for their futures. This book illuminated the critical role that Early Childhood Development (ECD) services in emergencies can play in shaping children's brains and lives so that even in humanitarian situations, they can develop to their full potential and become tomorrow's workers and leaders. The nexus between ECD and emergencies is an emerging area of work.

While international attention is growing for ECD with (1) its integration into the Sustainable Development Goals, (2) increase in donor interest, (3) increase in ECD national policies, (4) establishment of the ECD Nurturing Care Framework and (5) more research, myriad challenges remain, especially in humanitarian contexts. The definition of ECD is not clear and there is no agreement on what activities fall within ECD, especially among humanitarians and governments. This creates confusion with government departments as it is unclear who should lead the development and implementation of ECD policies. The science of ECD is not well understood, especially for non-ECD and humanitarian workers. While not insignificant and unimportant, emergencies change the dynamics of people's lives—children, parents and communities. Therefore, a stronger evidence base for understanding this is important for implementation of programmes. While the evidence base for ECD generally is growing, huge gaps remain for emergency contexts. Humanitarian work is still underpinned by Maslow's Hierarchy of Needs, which has ECD and especially early learning services, as a low priority. Few evidence-based programmatic models exist for emergencies, especially that bundle various aspects of the Nurturing Care Framework. Lastly, there is limited financial and political investment for this area of work.

We are at a unique juncture where the interest in ECD in emergencies is growing exponentially. This book strives to contribute to the international dialogue, practice and evidence base. Using mixed methods research and analysis, along with my professional experience in this field, I investigated the nexus of ECD and emergencies. The research of South Sudanese refugees in northern Uganda brought forward a new theoretical lens for understanding

ECD in emergencies by overlaying Vygotsky's Socio-cultural theory with Sen's Capability Approach. By working on a context that had no culturally relevant tools for measuring child development, I created a new tool for measuring children's development in refugee situations. Through investigation of the implementation of the Community-Led Action for Children (CLAC) ECD model in non-emergency and emergency locations, I established an evidence-based programmatic model. This research revealed that a model like CLAC cannot be implemented in the exact same way in non-emergencies and emergencies. Basing emergency programmes on theoretical foundations developed in non-emergencies alone is not enough to explain the myriad phenomena occurring. Further, they do not fully help develop programming models that are the most relevant and effective for children. Lastly, the research found evidence for the importance of ECD services in emergencies. Refugee children in the programme group scored across the board significantly better than those who did not receive the ECD support.

As Helen Keller said, "Alone we can do so little; Together we can do so much." Donors, governments and policy makers, practitioners and academia have a lot to contribute to the growth of this area of work and shape future programming and government policy.

Recommendations for donors

1. *Increase financing for ECD*

   While more evidence is needed for ECD in emergencies, this research illustrated the benefits of providing ECD services vs. not providing them. As children in an environment of relationships, direct support to children should be coupled with support for parents/primary caregivers. Donors can look at both humanitarian and other sources of funding. They can pool funds or create coalitions to bring smaller donors on board. As ECD is multi-sectoral, support can be provided not only through education but also through health, nutrition, child protection and other sectors. The Education Cannot Wait global fund and other existing mechanisms can be used to support ECD in emergencies.
2. *Support rigorous research and evaluations for ECD in emergencies*

   While the evidence base for ECD in emergencies is growing, donors will need to continue supporting rigorous research evaluations in order to strengthen the evidence base and shape future programming.

Recommendations for government and policy makers

1. *Establish an inter-ministerial group focused on ECD*

   The confusion of what ECD is, the lack of understanding of its importance and lack of coordinated efforts to support the multi-sectoral needs of children can be remedied through an inter-ministerial group focused on ECD. This is starting to happen in some countries including the Central African Republic and Ivory Coast. It is critical that an inter-ministerial group has some budgetary and planning control and some decision-making authority or connection to a decision maker in order to have an impact on ECD at a national level.

2 *Integrate ECD into existing national-level sector plans to help reach multiple government goals*

   As ECD is multi-sectoral and can impact multiple goals for governments such as goals on stunting, malnutrition and learning, integrating ECD and parenting services can bolster a government's ability to reach multiple national-level goals.

Recommendations for practitioners

1 *Adapt and use ECD models that have worked in a non-emergency context:* The case studies presented in this research illustrated that ECD models developed for development contexts can be adapted for a humanitarian context.
2 *Adapt data collection tools to the cultural and emergency context:* The research also illustrated that measures for child development and early learning can be developed based on local cultural context and the situation of the emergency.
3 *Integrate ECD into various sectors:* As financing is siloed by sectors, integrate elements of ECD into various sector projects in the same location so children can receive all of the necessary inputs for their positive development.

Recommendations for academia

Through review of literature it was clear that little evidence has been collected in emergency situations and so huge gaps remain in understanding the various models that can be used in these contexts and their effectiveness for positive child outcomes and stronger parents' capabilities (Yousafzai and Aboud, 2014).

1 *Research the effectiveness of different models in various emergency contexts:* This research provided evidence of one model—CLAC—that worked in the South Sudanese refugee context in Uganda. Other models can also be researched and assessed for child and adult outcomes. Future research can include mixed methods research, qualitative or quantitative (i.e. collecting two data points in a difference in difference methodology).
2 *Develop a set of capabilities for the South Sudanese context and develop a set of capabilities for other contexts:* A set of capabilities were developed in this research for the South Sudanese context. This could be further developed to capture broader consensus and perspectives of South Sudanese, including the voices of children themselves. Limitations of this research prevented me from actively engaging young people themselves in developing these sets of capabilities.

3 *Conduct cost-effectiveness studies*: As funding is never sufficient to meet all needs of everyone, choices need to be made. Cost-effectiveness studies could help shed light on approaches that are promising given the costs related to providing them. Yousafzai and Aboud (2014) mention the limited number of cost-effectiveness and cost-benefit studies in early childhood and there have been none focused on ECD in emergencies (Yousafzai and Aboud, 2014). The CLAC model is weaker in the areas of health and nutrition, conflict resolution, positive discipline and peace building, so future research could look at other ECD models that have a stronger integration of these elements and compare the results with a model having a stronger learning and cognitive stimulation component like the CLAC model. There is also evidence that more holistic programming that has inputs from multiple sectors provides for better results in children and is more cost effective (Heckman, 2006). In particular, the integration of early learning and stimulation with nutrition has been cited as having positive results (Yousafzai and Aboud, 2014). Therefore, research that looks at interventions that have a multi-sectoral approach (including early learning and nutrition, but also beyond to include health and protection) vs. one sector in an emergency situation would make a contribution.

4 *Investigate early childhood, peace and gender equality:* The potential for ECD to shape a child's identity and promote gender equality and peace (i.e. tolerance, empathy, ability to see the other) is another area of potential future research. Research investigating ECD and peace is already conducted, but many of these studies have not yet looked at conflict countries in Africa.

5 *Study parenting programmes in emergencies:* Parenting programmes in emergencies is another burgeoning area that can be investigated further, both from the qualitative and quantitative perspective. It is unclear what dosage (duration, frequency and intensity), mode of delivery (group, individual or a combination) and content in emergencies and non-emergencies have the best outcomes and are cost effective. The model of nurturing care, which has responsive parenting at its centre, needs testing in crisis situations.

ECD services are critical and may help children survive today, and become productive adults and leaders that contribute to peace and prosperity of societies. Our world's safe and peaceful future needs people who are educated and have reached their full potential. It all starts in early childhood.

References

Heckman, J. (2006). *Return on Investments: Cost vs. Benefits*. Chicago: University of Chicago.

Yousafzai, A. K. and Aboud, F. (2014). "Review of implementation processes for integrated nutrition and psychosocial stimulation interventions", *Annals of the New York Academy of Sciences*, 1308(1), 33–45.

Index

www.ingramcontent.com/pod-product-compliance
Lightning Source LLC
LaVergne TN
LVHW011125300926
849160LV00008B/516
* 9 7 8 0 3 6 7 7 7 7 5 9 3 *